The Unplanned Obstacle

From Injury to Triumph: A Canine Recovery Story

JENNIFER ANN CARTER

Disclaimer

I want to make it clear that I have not received any financial compensation or incentives for mentioning or endorsing specific products, brands, or companies within this book. Any references included are there solely for clarity—to identify the types, sources, and ingredients I personally chose to use during Luce's recovery.

Please note that I am not a veterinarian. I do not diagnose, treat, or offer medical advice as a veterinary professional. Everything shared here is based on personal experience with Luce—knowledge gained through ongoing learning, consultation with professionals, and significant trial and error. These insights were meaningful to us, but they may not apply universally.

My goal in writing this book is to offer guidance and reassurance to others navigating similar challenges. However, the information provided here should never replace individualized advice from a licensed veterinary professional. Always consult with your vet before making any health-related decisions for your dog.

Contents

Dedication

To Robby Ann Carter...

For your unwavering support, your faith in me, and your constant reminder that I could shape meaning from the blank page. This book exists because you believed in the one writing it.

And to Luce...

My light. You have been my guide, my companion, my teacher, and the quiet strength behind every insight these pages hold. Without you, I would not have found the path to write this book—nor the clarity to help others find theirs.

Forward

S o often science, and indeed history in general, moves forward because someone wondered what other circumstances might be possible, what might exist beyond existing established boundaries. *The Unplanned Obstacle* is the story of one person's journey through the difficult veterinary choices presented when her beloved dog Luce severely damaged her knee, tearing her cranial cruciate ligament and meniscus. Dogs being dogs, the injury didn't even occur in some dramatic circumstance during sports or hiking in some exotic locale, but just running in the yard. But of course... dogs being dogs.

For me, and for many of us, there is nothing more devastating or unsettling then when a cherished pet injures itself. We want their pain to stop now. We want solutions now. We want it to go away, for the movie to rewind, for this all to be over, to make the best decisions, the right decisions, the perfect decisions to make it all better. And, if we are professionals in the dog world, we can deal calmly and elegantly with anyone else's emergency, but not when it is our own beloved Muffin that sleeps in the crook of our body at night, has this, that or the other cute mannerism, twinkle in the eye, flip of the tail. Oh no, when it happens to our own, we get 'er done, but we are as much of a basket case as anyone else while doing so.

It is all the more telling that in this case, my colleague Jennifer hit the pause button on the immediate recommendations for surgery, and with her team of veterinarians and rehab specialists explored what all the options might be, no matter how labor intensive or expensive. Jen wanted the best option for Luce in this particular set of circumstances, not necessarily the most immediate, or the most obvious. While I am sure there are many other veterinarians and rehab teams pursuing non-surgical solutions, the only one we happened to know of at the time, whose whole practice had centered around that kind of rehab, had just retired.

And so began the year long, painstaking, step by step journey to attempt to find the necessary information, resources and protocols to best restore functional integrity to Luce's knee joint without surgery. It wasn't that Jen was opposed to surgery. Her decision regarding the choice of protocol wasn't some flaming anti-surgical flag - far from it. She worked tightly with her comprehensive veterinary team every step of the way. Jen just wanted to see what else might be possible, and had no resistance to the personal investment of the hours and hours of care and physical therapy that such decisions might entail.

I first met Jennifer Carter a few years ago when she and I were both speakers at the 2022 IACP Annual National Conference in Florida (International Association of Canine Professionals), and I had talked her into letting me use Luce as one of the demo dogs in my presentation on movement integrity and its impact on behavior. Jen, on a corollary path was speaking on nutrition and behavior. Jen is super bright, extremely funny, and painstakingly dedicated to learning as much as she possibly can as an owner and dog professional to maximize well-being in her and her clients' dogs.

We stayed in touch after Conference, cross collaborated on a number of cases, and shared education on each other's area of focus. When Luce blew her knee out, Jen called to brainstorm, and kept me apprised as information came in, as she and her vet team decided on their course of action, and as the rehab journey unfolded. Her meticulous attention to detail and the hours of hands-on work were impressive.

Jennifer has brought the same level of meticulous professionalism to the construction of this book. *The Unplanned Obstacle* is not intended to be a medical primer, but rather a detailed diary of one person's deep dive into the often-overwhelming decision-making journey with their dog after a severe canine injury, and the "why" behind those decisions. The goal is to inform the reader of what information is out there that might be relevant to their own considerations with a beloved pet, or a client's dog. She has included information on all the current surgical and non-surgical options and the considerations that might come into play with all of them. Following that, she delves into details of nutrition and supplements that can be marshalled to support healing regardless of whether one opts for a surgical or non-surgical intervention, practical considerations to daily life with an injured dog, and the changing dynamics that may occur to the training relationship between handler and dog precipitated by an injury. From soup to nuts, it's all there. The science, the emotions, the results.

The Unplanned Obstacle is a tremendous resource for both the layperson and the dog professional.

Sheryl "Maryna" Studley Ozuna

Founder, Canine Kinaesthetics™ | Movement Markers™ | The Learning Web™

Arizona Doggy Dude Ranch | May 2025

movementmarkers@gmail.com

How To Read This Book

This book isn't just about managing a cranial cruciate ligament (CCL) tear—it's about guiding you toward the outcomes you want most for your dog, whether you're dealing with an injury or simply striving for lifelong health and vitality.

You'll find chapters focused on weight management, reducing inflammation, increasing mobility, feeding your dog more effectively, incorporating supplements, and gaining a deeper understanding of modalities like Traditional Chinese Medicine.

The goal is to equip you with practical, actionable tools—whether your dog is currently injured, recovering, aging, or thriving.

Throughout the book, you'll notice barking dog heads.

When you see one, stop and tune in: this is the author's way of saying, "Hey, this part really matters." These symbols mark especially important insights, recommendations, or reminders that can make a significant difference in your dog's journey.

Feel free to read straight through or jump to the sections most relevant to you right now. This book is designed to meet you—and your dog—where you are, and to support you both in moving toward better health, together.

Introduction: When The Path Disappears Beneath You

We don't expect it.

We don't plan for it.

And we're rarely ready when it comes.

An injury. A limp. A sudden refusal to bear weight.

The moment your dog looks up at you, pain in their eyes - and something inside you shifts.

Urgently. Irreversibly.

That was the beginning of this journey.

In August 2023, on what seemed like an ordinary day, Luce—my vibrant, athletic, trail-running companion—emerged from our front yard fence line with her right leg held aloft, refusing to put it down.

In that instant, the rhythm of our lives dissolved.

And in its place stood a single, deafening question: *What just happened?*

That question would unravel into one of the most humbling, complex, and transformative experiences of my life.

This book is not just about orthopedic injury.

It's about partnership, advocacy, communication, and trust.

It's about asking not only *how* to heal, but *who* we must become in the process.

It's about choosing conservative management when surgery feels like the only path - and discovering that, with the right plan, the right team, and the right mindset, healing isn't just possible.

It's transformational.

From diagnosis to treatment, nutrition to recovery, and communication to training, *The Unplanned Obstacle* is a comprehensive guide shaped by lived experience.

It's the story of a deeply bonded dog-human relationship navigating pain, doubt, and triumph together—armed with science in one hand and intuition in the other.

Through conservative management, integrative therapies, and unwavering teamwork, Luce regained her strength, her mobility, and, most importantly, her joy.

Each chapter reflects the stages we faced—beginning with injury, navigating tough medical decisions, reshaping her diet and gut health, building a care team, and committing to daily rehabilitation.

Inside, you'll find the details you need to make informed choices: practical checklists, nutritional strategies, training insights, and emotional encouragement.

This journey demanded an extraordinary level of care—physical, emotional, and logistical—and through it all, I learned something vital: you don't need to be a veterinarian or a nutritionist to be your dog's greatest ally.

You just need to show up - every day - with open eyes and a willing heart.

You'll read about how I built a comprehensive rehabilitation plan for Luce – one that included a full team of veterinary specialists, customized therapeutic exercises, targeted bodywork, integrative modalities, and adaptive nutrition.

You'll see how food became medicine, how routine turned into ritual, and how science and soul met in the quiet moments between appointments.

I'll share how I balanced supplements, made environmental adjustments, and managed my own emotions as we navigated setbacks, breakthroughs, and everything in between.

But more than anything, this book is about **relationship**—about how trust is built long before it's tested, how dogs teach us to listen with more than just our ears, and how healing doesn't happen in isolation. It happens in connection.

If you are here because your dog is injured, overwhelmed, or deep in recovery, this book will meet you exactly where you are.

If you're here to prepare—before anything happens—then you're already one step ahead.

And if you're here because you want to do better, be better, and love better... then you're in the right place.

This isn't a story of perfection. It's a story of progress. This book was written not just to educate - but to *empower*.

Injury isn't the end of the road; it's a bend in the trail, one that leads to a deeper understanding of your dog and yourself.

It's a real-world guide through real-life challenges, told from the front lines of canine rehabilitation—where medical plans, emotional resilience, and deep companionship converge.

Join me, and let's walk this path together - over the obstacle, through the unknown, and into the healing.

Jennifer and Luce - May 2025

Chapter 1: Torn

Introduction to Luce

In 2016, I came across an online advertisement for an adorable little black and tan puppy. With her sleek black coat and two charming brown spots above her eyes, she was small, yet her paws were enormous. The family who had her could no longer care for her due to changes in their work schedule and were looking for a new home for her. She was just 12 weeks old; however, they referred to her as a "Chorkie," claiming she was a mix of Chihuahua and Yorkie. I had my doubts about that breed assessment, but I instantly fell in love and decided to name her Luce.

The name "Luce" means "light," derived from the Latin word "lux," which also translates to "light." It's a feminine name in French and Italian, akin to "Lucy" or "Lucia," both carrying the same beautiful meaning.

As it turns out, Luce is a delightful hound mix, known for her adventurous spirit and athleticism. According to DNA tests, she comprises 26% American Foxhound, 18.4% Shetland Sheepdog, 12.3% American English Coonhound, 11.8% Labrador Retriever, 11.4% Beagle, 11.3% Chow Chow, and 8.9% Australian Shepherd. Her diverse genetic background makes her truly one of a kind in appearance, abilities, and personality.

Luce at 12-weeks old

Because Luce was a mixed-breed rescue dog with unknown lineage, I opted for a DNA test to identify any potential genetic health issues. The test, which screens for 180 genetic health risks, showed only two notable results: increased risk for Intervertebral Disc Disease (IVDD) and a low-normal Alanine Aminotransferase Activity (ALT). These two results have no bearing on the events of this book, however, what is important is that you understand that there was no genetic predisposition for the injury we will be discussing.

The DNA test predicted she would reach an adult weight of around 32 pounds and boast a tricolor coat of brown, blonde, and black fur. They also indicated her coat would be smooth, with some longer fur in places, but primarily short. There was *no* sign of Chihuahua or Yorkie in her lineage, turning that "Chorkie" heritage into a running joke. When I took her to the vet for her first check-up, that's when our adventure truly began.

Our family vet chuckled when he heard Luce was a "Chorkie." He pointed out that her paws didn't quite fit that breed, and he guessed she would likely double in size by our next appointment. He was right—she ended up growing far more than that!

Luce was a healthy puppy, which was fantastic news! With her hound and herding background, Luce thrived outdoors, exploring trails, hopping over rocks, and chasing various critters. Over the years, she became an excellent travel companion, making it easy to include her in all our family adventures, near and far. She fits right into our pack effortlessly.

The bond between Luce and me is often described as deeply emotional; I work remotely, so we are together every day. This emotional connection has extended into a spiritual realm, with me feeling a sense of kinship and purpose with her. I have had many dogs in my life, and the connection between Luce and me has always felt different. She and I clicked right away, and our souls enjoy the familiarity.

In August 2023, our life's journey took a twist. For the first time, I had to weigh my spiritual and emotional connection with Luce against the necessary practical and scientific reality that lay before us. How can I be the guardian of this dog and an inquiring scientist at the same time?

Take a deep breath with me. We are going on a journey from injury to triumph, with a tour through experience, observation, communication, and science. By following Luce's lead, I have learned from her how to be a good partner in healing, how to return to a more primal communication long forgotten and how to manifest a successful outcome.

Join us as we take you over the unplanned obstacle into the world of recovery.

The Event Summary

It was a beautiful day on August 14, 2023. My dog, Luce, was in the fenced yard where she had spent the last eight years, running along the fence line eagerly following the neighbors as they drove their golf carts down to the cul-de-sac. Over the years, her constant sprints between the driveway and the corner of the yard had worn a clear path along the fence.

I stood on the deck, watching and listening to her bark as she dashed back and forth. While I could see most of the yard from my vantage point, there were certain areas along the fence that were slightly downhill, making them tricky to observe. I had no idea what had happened until she suddenly emerged from the edge of the hill, holding her right leg up, refusing to put any weight on it.

What just happened? The question echoed in my mind and slipped out of my lips.

With a surge of urgency, I rushed down the 20 stairs to the front yard and sprinted across the grass towards her. Switching into first responder mode, I quickly assessed the situation, in an effort to pinpoint which part of her body was affected so I could provide the best assistance.

Where was she hurting?

It didn't take long for me to realize that she was guarding her right rear leg. She refused to set it down or bear any weight on it. I needed to consider and rule out the various possibilities: Was the injury to her nail, toe, ankle, knee, or possibly her hip? As a first step, I inspected her paw for any foreign objects, gently moving each toe to gauge her reaction. To my relief, she showed no signs of pain.

Next, I examined her ankle—was it fractured, sprained, or twisted? I tested the range of motion and everything appeared normal. Then I delicately palpated her knee, checking for any signs of heat or swelling that might indicate a problem.

Instinctively, I grew concerned it was her knee and feared she might have torn something. I can't explain how I knew, it was just a gut feeling I couldn't shake. Realizing I needed to get her inside and limit her movements, I picked her up and carefully carried her back up the steps to the house.

Calling the vet was my next critical step. With it being Friday afternoon, I had just a few hours before they closed for the weekend. Wanting to avoid an emergency clinic should her condition worsen; I felt a pressing urgency to act swiftly.

When I called the clinic, the staff advised me to bring her in just before their 5 PM closing time, so she could be seen by the vet on duty that day. Although it wasn't our usual vet, I agreed, knowing it was crucial for her to be examined in case of a fracture. I wanted her to find relief and begin treatment as quickly as possible. While waiting to take her in, I performed some first aid—applying ice to her leg and administering natural herbal remedies to help manage her pain, reduce inflammation, and support healing.

I also recorded a brief video of her movements—just a few steps—so the vet could see what I had witnessed right after the incident. From my experience, I know pets often seem fine by the time they reach the vet's office, making it difficult to convey the severity of their condition from just hours earlier. I hoped this video would give the vet a clearer picture of her behavior post-injury.

The wait before going to the vet was excruciating, a mix of helplessness and fear looming over me.

A Leg Up

The time had come. Just a few hours after her injury, I was finally able to take Luce to the vet. My main concern was whether she had a fracture. I carried her in my arms straight to a private room, careful not to aggravate her injury as we waited for the vet to arrive. Luce remained calm and collected, neither panting nor showing any signs of discomfort as she stayed close to me. When the vet entered, she asked me to gently set Luce down on the floor so she could observe her gait. Almost immediately, she noticed the same lameness I had seen earlier.

After carefully palpating Luce's knee, leg, and hips, she reassured me that a fracture seemed unlikely. The knee was now the focus. In humans, the anterior cruciate ligament (ACL) is a thin connective tissue in the middle of our knees that connects our shin and thigh bones. In dog's this connective tissue is called the cranial cruciate ligament (CCL) and it connects the dog's tibia (bone below the knee) to their femur (bone above the knee). Comparing the two, the most relevant distinction is that the CCL is always load-bearing because dogs never unbend their knees while standing. This "ACL in dogs" is thus subject to greater wear and tear than the average human's ACL and a dog's CCL naturally has to withhold greater stress.

To further assess the injury, the vet performed a "drawer test" on Luce's right rear leg to check for any cranial cruciate ligament (CCL) issues. The drawer test for a Cranial Cruciate Ligament (CCL) tear, also known as the anterior drawer test, involves moving the tibia forward relative to the femur to assess for instability. A positive test indicates a CCL rupture, where the tibia slides forward excessively, similar to a drawer opening.

For this test, Luce lay on her side while the vet positioned one hand on her distal femur (the distal femur is the area of the leg just above the knee joint) and the other on the proximal tibia (the upper part of your shinbone, where it widens out to form part of the knee joint). By applying pressure to the femur and pulling the tibia forward, she could assess whether there was a ligament tear. However, if the ligament was only partially torn, this maneuver carried the risk of turning it into a complete tear. The vet suspected a possible ligament tear in Luce's knee but wasn't entirely sure. She recommended I return on Monday to see my regular vet, who had more experience with this type of injury.

No X-rays were taken during that Friday visit. I chose to wait until Monday so my regular vet could handle the X-rays, sparing Luce the stress of multiple manipulations if the first attempt didn't provide clear results. Since he was more familiar with her care, it made sense for him to assess her condition and decide the best course of action.

Before we left, the vet prescribed Gabapentin for pain relief and Carprofen for inflammation. She advised me to keep Luce calm, avoid jumping and stairs when possible, and limit walks to just enough for her to take care of her business outside.

With a follow-up appointment on the horizon, I started to devise a medical care plan for the next few days. I opted for natural remedies and herbs for pain relief to start, while continuing with the Carprofen to manage inflammation in those first few days.

A friend of mine, who is a canine massage therapist, came over on both Saturday and Sunday to help relieve Luce's tight muscles, ease cramping, and reduce fluid buildup. She even lent me a Class 3 laser, a device that helps to minimize inflammation and increase circulation, to help reduce Luce's joint inflammation and promote healing at the injury site. I used the laser on Luce at least twice daily, targeting both the injured and healthy knee. Additionally, I applied ice to the affected area multiple times a day and incorporated other treatment methods regularly.

In the meantime, I spent those two days immersing myself in research on CCL injuries to understand our situation better. It felt crucial to be prepared and informed as Luce and I navigated this journey together.

Years earlier, I had helped our Yorkie, Harley, recover from two torn CCLs - one in each rear leg - which had been corrected using a technique called Tibial Tuberosity Advancement (TTA) surgery done by our family vet. I did at home rehabilitation for her myself. Even with that experience, I decided to approach this injury with fresh eyes, seeking additional knowledge and focusing on treating the dog in front of me.

Over two days, I researched CCL injuries to gain a clearer understanding of Luce's situation. It quickly became clear that we might have to put our physical activities on hold for an extended period, or possibly indefinitely. A wave of disappointment washed over me, along with a deep sense of sadness for both Luce and me. After all, we were right in the middle of peak competition season, with a lineup of Canicross races, obstacle course events, and family trips now hanging in the balance.

The Diagnosis

On Monday, I took Luce to her regular veterinarian, who diagnosed her with a partial or complete CCL tear. X-rays were taken, and the good news was that there were no underlying issues, such as a tumor, contributing to her injury.

There was no sign of arthritis in either leg or her hips, and only a small amount of fluid buildup was found in the injured leg – her left leg looked perfectly healthy.

Although the vet detected some mild hip dysplasia, he assured me it wasn't related to the injury. Figure 1,2,3 and 4 below show the X-rays taken of Luce's Hips and knees just after the injury.

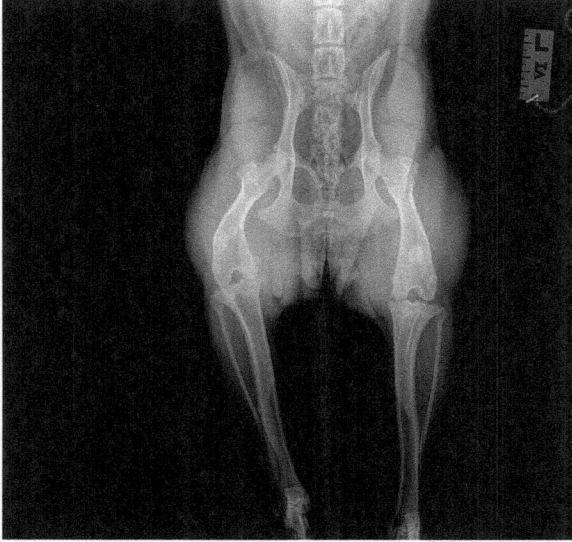

Figure 1

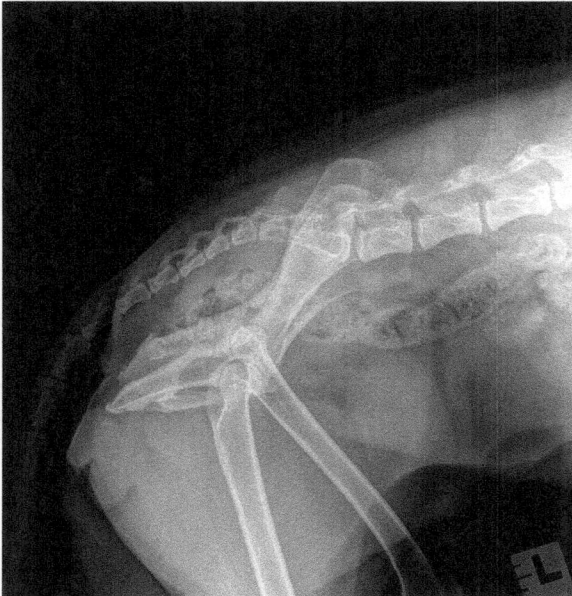

Figure 2

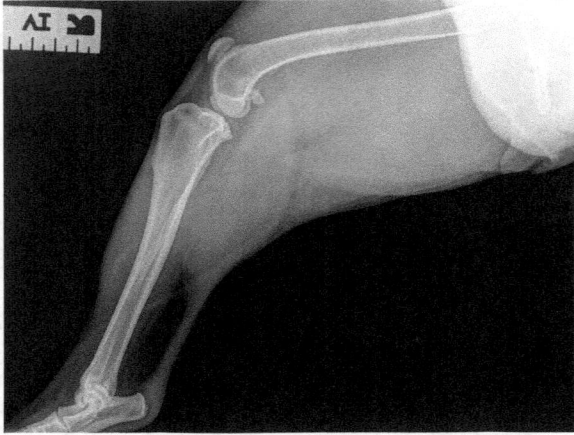

Figure 3

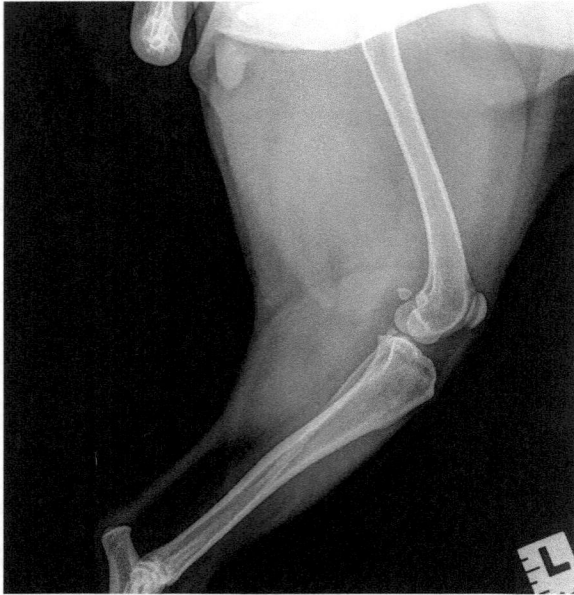

Figure 4

He recommended giving Luce a week of rest and then returning for a follow-up visit to assess any improvement. Additionally, he also suggested consulting with a board-certified surgeon about Tibial Plateau Leveling Osteotomy (TPLO) surgery, as he believed that if there were no improvement after the week of rest, we would need to explore other treatment options. His recommendation for TPLO was based on her size and activity level. There were other potential surgical remedies that could be used to correct this injury; however, the vet told me that TPLO was my only real option. I asked him if we could do the same TTA surgery that we did with Harley and he quickly told me that a TTA procedure would fail due to Luce's athleticism. He also kindly provided me with the names of two reputable local board-certified veterinary surgeons for further consultation.

As the days passed, my attempts to research and seek advice left me feeling overwhelmed - a sensation I wasn't accustomed to. I was determined to make the best choice for Luce but the weight of that decision hung heavily over me. I couldn't shake off the fear of making the wrong move and facing the consequences.

Chapter 2: Ligamentary, My Dear Watson

The first step on this journey is understanding the nature of the injury and your options. This will save you time in your research, give you a starting point for asking the right questions, and even show you some paths you never knew existed. This will give you the confidence to make informed decisions about your dog. My process was to research each procedure individually from reputable sources, I then spent some time reading patient reviews, social media forum discussions, and scholarly article follow-ups.

Knee Couture

The cranial cruciate ligament (CCL), as illustrated in Figure 1, plays a critical role as one of the primary stabilizers within the knee (or "stifle") joint, located in the hind leg. This ligament is comparable to humans' anterior cruciate ligament (ACL).

The meniscus, also shown in Figure 1, is a cartilage-like structure situated between the tibia and femur that forms the crown of the knee. It fulfills several essential functions, including shock absorption, proprioception, and load-bearing. Unfortunately, it often sustains damage when the CCL is injured.

A ruptured CCL causes instability in the joint and this instability causes swelling and pain and is among the leading causes of hind limb lameness, pain, and, eventually, arthritis. A meniscus injury in conjunction with the CCL injury worsens the instability and causes even more inflammation and pain. (See Figure 2)

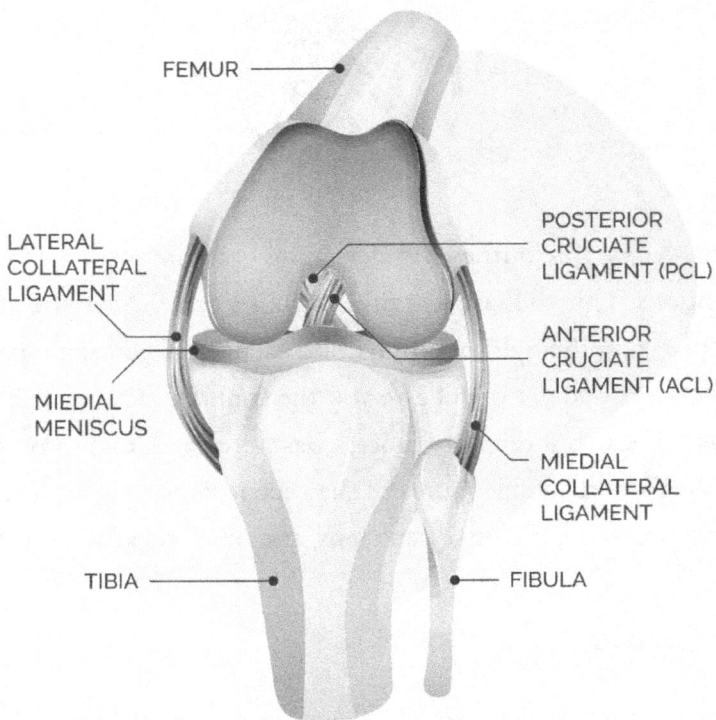

Figure 1: Normal anatomical structure of a canine knee, front view

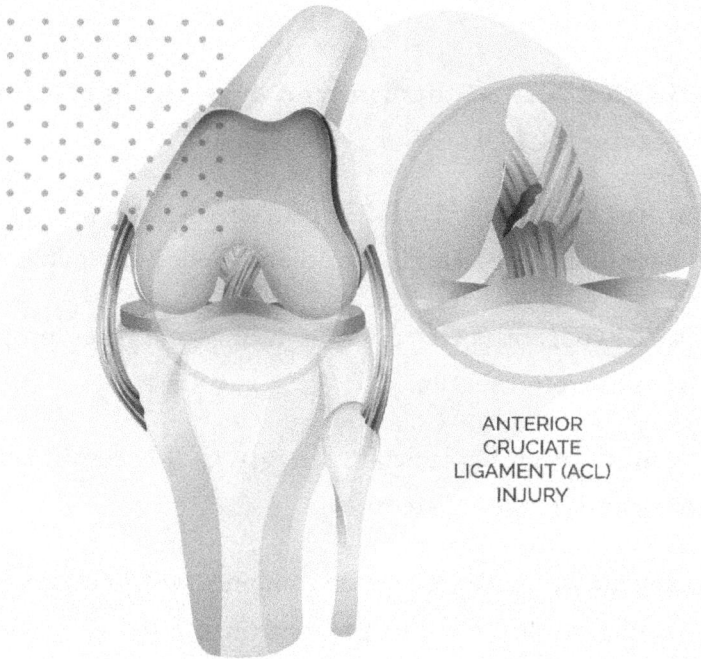

ANTERIOR
CRUCIATE
LIGAMENT (ACL)
INJURY

Figure 2: Anatomical structure of the canine knee with injury to the
CCL (ACL)

In humans, injuries to the ACL typically result from trauma during activities like skiing, football, or soccer. The development of this condition in dogs is far more intricate than in humans. While traumatic ruptures can occur in dogs, they are relatively uncommon. Dogs may experience varying degrees of partial or complete rupture. As a result, veterinarians often refer to this condition as "cranial cruciate disease" (CCLD) rather than simply "cranial cruciate ligament rupture" (CCLR). More often, CCLD arises from a combination of factors, such as ligament degeneration due to aging or overuse, obesity, poor physical condition, conformation, and breed predisposition. In cases of subtle, gradual deterioration, a minor injury to the CCL may develop over months or even years, rather than causing a sudden rupture of an otherwise healthy ligament (The City Vet Clinic, n.d.).

This distinction between humans and dogs highlights three key aspects of canine CCLD:

1. At least half of dogs with CCL issues in one knee will likely experience similar problems in the other at some point in the future.

2. Partial CCL tears are common in dogs and often progress to complete tears over time.

3. While the degree of lameness can vary, CCLD consistently leads to arthritis in the long term.

For active patients, surgical intervention combined with joint supplements is recommended to slow arthritis progression and reduce or eliminate lameness. However, there are also many effective nonsurgical treatment options available.

Cruciate disease can affect dogs of all sizes, (INO Pets Parents Network, n.d.) ages, and breeds. However, certain breeds are more prone to developing CCLD, including Rottweilers, Newfoundlands, Staffordshire Terriers, Mastiffs, Akitas, Saint Bernards, Chesapeake Bay Retrievers, and Labrador Retrievers. Conversely, breeds such as Greyhounds, Dachshunds, Basset Hounds, and Old English Sheepdogs, are less frequently affected. Studies suggest that female, as well as dogs spayed and neutered at an early age, face a higher risk of CCLD, though the exact cause remains unclear (Arizona Canine Orthopedics and Sports Medicine [ACOSM], n.d.).

As previously noted, CCLD often leads to progressive degeneration of the cruciate ligament, ranging from mild partial tears to complete ruptures in more advanced stages. Initially, you may not notice significant lameness, especially if both knees are affected. One telltale sign is when dogs no longer sit "square," instead opting to extend their legs to the side—a behavior dog trainers sometimes refer to as a "sloppy sit."

You might also notice your dog struggling to rise, having difficulty jumping into vehicles, or showing a decrease in activity levels. Other indicators include muscle atrophy (a reduction in muscle mass in the affected leg), limited range of motion, a popping or clicking sound (which could suggest a meniscal tear), and swelling along the inside of the shin bone (resulting from fibrosis or scar tissue). Many dogs instinctively shift their weight away from the injured leg when standing; however, the lameness can be less noticeable during walking, especially with partial ligament tears.

If a partially torn ligament ruptures or the meniscus is damaged, your dog may become non-weight-bearing and begin hopping on three legs. This change can happen suddenly, often without significant trauma—just a minor event that causes the partially torn ligament to give way completely. Dogs in the chronic (later) stages of CCLD typically show symptoms related to arthritis, such as decreased activity, stiffness, reluctance to play, and pain.

Diagnosing complete CCL tears is relatively straightforward for a vet. Your vet will observe your pet's gait, palpate the knee, and take radiographs (X-rays). However, determining whether the tear is partial or complete is more challenging. Advanced imaging techniques, such as ultrasound, MRI, or exploratory surgery, are needed to assess the ligament directly. X-rays are typically performed to check for joint effusion - the buildup of fluid in the joint. They are essential as they help evaluate the degree of existing arthritis, assist in surgical planning. and rule out other conditions like bone cancer.

Certain X-ray views are essential for specific treatments, such as tibial plateau leveling osteotomy (TPLO) and tibial tuberosity advancement (TTA) (Colorado State University Veterinary Teaching Hospital, n.d.), (BoneVet, n.d.). Your surgeon may need to take additional radiographs, even if some have already been completed by your regular veterinarian. Veterinarians use specific palpation techniques, including the "cranial drawer test" and the "tibial thrust test," to confirm a CCL issue. If a dog is painful or tense, these tests may need to be performed under light sedation. These tests help identify abnormal knee movement, which may indicate a rupture. It's important to note that X-rays cannot show the condition of the CCL or the meniscus, as these structures are not visible on standard X-rays. Therefore, the surgeon may choose to evaluate the meniscus and cruciate ligament during the surgical repair, either through an arthrotomy (opening the joint) or by using a minimally invasive camera called an arthroscope - both of which require full anesthesia and shaving the animal.

While CCLD is one of the leading causes of ongoing hind limb lameness in dogs, several other factors can also contribute to pain and lameness in the rear limbs. It's crucial to rule out these additional issues in order to determine the best treatment for your pet. Other potential conditions include hip dysplasia, joint sprains or muscle strains, patellar luxation (which may accompany CCLD), neurological disorders like ruptured discs, cancers affecting bones or soft tissues, fractures, joint dislocations (luxations), Achilles tendon ruptures, panosteitis (an inflammatory bone condition mainly seen in young, large-breed dogs), and osteochondrosis (a cartilage disorder).

The most common complication of CCLD is long-term impairment due to arthritis. Other complications associated with arthritis and CCLD include reduced joint range of motion, muscle atrophy, and diminished limb function, all of which often lead to decreased activity levels. Unfortunately, neither human nor veterinary surgeons can fully restore normal joint anatomy and function. Even after surgery, some arthritis progression is expected.

Try to think proactively. Preventing the onset of arthritis is important as it is much more difficult to try to get rid of it once it has progressed.

The second most common complication associated with CCLD is meniscal tearing. Due to instability in the knee joint, the inner (medial) meniscus is often injured. This damage can occur during the initial trauma or even after surgical intervention for the cruciate ligament. When treating meniscal damage in dogs, the standard approach is to remove the torn sections, which are typically too small to repair. A meniscal tear can be quite painful, and if left untreated, it may prevent the animal from regaining full function. Therefore, your surgeon will remove any damaged portions of the meniscus during the procedure to correct knee instability.

Unfortunately, it is common for a dog who has ruptured one CCL to tear the other within 1 year of the correction of the torn CCL. Whether surgical or conservative management is chosen, strengthening and rehabilitation for both hind limbs is an important part of healing. This is yet another opportunity to think proactively here as we care for the original rupture, we can also care for the other areas of the dog's body hopefully preventing a second rupture.

Numerous treatment options are available for CCLD, with the first major decision being whether to choose surgical treatment or nonsurgical (also known as conservative or medical) management. The best approach for your pet will depend on factors such as activity level, size, age, conformation, and the degree of knee instability.

Surgical treatment is generally recommended for CCLD, as it is the only method that can permanently stabilize the stifle joint and allow for assessment of the internal joint structures. Surgery addresses the two main issues associated with CCLD: the instability of the stifle due to the loss of the cruciate ligament and the damage to the inner meniscus that often accompanies it. Several surgical techniques are available to resolve stifle instability.

If you've been researching this injury, you may have come across the most well-known procedure -tibial plateau-leveling osteotomy (TPLO), often referred to as the 'gold standard' for CCLD, but I will lay out all of the procedures so you can have a starting point for your research on what is best for your dog (DePuy Synthes Vet, n.d.).

Taking it One Step at a Time

To make the information easier to follow I've organized the options for surgical intervention into two main categories: Osteotomy techniques and Suture techniques. As I was wading through all of the information about the different procedures, their nuances were very difficult to keep straight. The details started to blur and all I felt was an overwhelming amount of sensory overload (Embrace Pet Insurance, n.d.).

Osteotomy Techniques

Osteotomy techniques involve cutting the bone (osteotomy). In this case, the tibia is altered to change how the quadriceps muscles interact with the top of the shin bone, known as the tibial plateau. This method stabilizes the stifle joint by modifying the biomechanics of the knee, rather than replacing the CCL. The adjustment can be made either by advancing the attachment point of the muscle (called tibial tuberosity advancement, or TTA) or by adjusting the slope of the shin bone (known as tibial plateau leveling osteotomy, or TPLO). Many surgeons prefer these techniques, especially for larger, more active dogs.

Tibial Plateau Leveling Osteotomy (TPLO)

Tibial plateau leveling osteotomy (TPLO) involves making a circular cut in the tibial plateau and then rotating the bone's contact surface until it is nearly level—about 90 degrees relative to where the quadriceps muscles attach. This new positioning provides relative stability to the knee, independent of the CCL. To stabilize the bone after the cut, a stainless-steel bridging plate and screws are used. These implants are typically left in place after healing unless complications arise. One of the main benefits of this technique is its overall success: improved limb function and reduced progression of arthritis, particularly in younger, larger-breed dogs (Spinalla, Arcamone, & Valentini, 2021).

The main drawback of TPLO is the need for an osteotomy, which requires time to heal. If complications arise – such as implant failure or delayed healing - additional revision surgeries may be necessary, sometimes with less favorable outcomes. Fortunately, these complications are uncommon, especially when an experienced surgeon performs the procedure.

Tibial Tuberosity Advancement (TTA)

Tibial tuberosity advancement (TTA) involves making a linear incision along the front of the shin bone. The tibial tuberosity – the section of the tibia where the quadriceps attach - is then moved forward until alignment forms approximately a 90-degree angle with the tibial plateau. This adjustment stabilizes the knee similarly to that of the TPLO procedure. As with the TPLO, the bone cut is secured using specially designed bridging plate and screws, which may be made of titanium or stainless steel. The choice between TTA and TPLO depends on additional issues, including the surgeon's preference, and the anatomical characteristics of the dog's knee, as not all knees or activity levels are suited to this technique.

The Modified Maquet Procedure (MMP)

The Modified Maquet Procedure (MMP), developed in England and introduced to the US in 2014, is based on principles similar to TTA but offers several advantages. It uses a lightweight, porous titanium implant instead of stainless steel, allowing for a smaller incision and reduced surgical time. Unlike TTA and TPLO, which require multiple screws, MMP places a wedge within the bone that only requires a single pin and staple to secure it. Additionally, this porous titanium alloy promotes bone growth through the implant, leading to significantly faster recovery - typically 4-6 weeks compared to the 10-12 weeks required for TPLO and TTA.

Suture Techniques

Suture techniques can be categorized into intra-articular (within the joint) and extra-articular (outside the joint) (BoneVet, n.d.). In human medicine, the intra-articular replacement of the ACL using grafts is the standard surgical approach. While this method has been extensively researched in dogs, it has not proven successful due to anatomical differences and underlying disease processes. However, many companies and surgeons are now exploring new possibilities. Given the lackluster results with intra-articular techniques thus far, most suture-based procedures are performed extra-articularly. The most widely used method, extracapsular suture stabilization, uses robust suture material placed just outside the knee joint (yet beneath the skin) to mimic the function of the CCL and restore joint stability.

Extra-Capsular Suture Stabilization

Extracapsular suture stabilization – also known as 'ex-cap suture,' 'lateral fabellar suture stabilization,' or the 'fishing line technique,' has been used for many years. While variations exist in suture materials, knot-tying methods, and attachment techniques, the core principle remains the same: externally restoring the function of a compromised CCL. This is typically achieved by placing a strong suture in a position that mimics the original ligament's alignment. The suture must provide stability to the knee joint while allowing normal movement until scar tissue forms and takes over the stabilizing role.

The most common complications following this procedure are suture failure and the progressive development of arthritis. The rehabilitation post-surgery for this procedure is longer than standard TPLO. Suture failure is more likely in larger, more active dogs, which is why many surgeons recommend this technique primarily for small breeds, older dogs, or those with lower activity levels. The key advantages of this method include its lower cost and the fact that it avoids cutting into the bone, thereby eliminating complications linked to bone cuts.

Arthroscopy is a minimally invasive procedure that a clear view of the stifle joint, including the cranial and caudal cruciate ligament structures.

Meniscal surgery is a procedure used to repair or remove damaged cartilage within the joint.

No matter which procedure you may choose, there is the potential of osteoarthritis developing in all cases, leading to some degree of lameness. (BoneVet, n.d.)

There is a lot of information available about the procedures, and as I took copious notes on each, so many questions kept racing in my mind. There are pros and cons to each procedure. What makes one better than the other?

I wanted to share my questions with you as you may be having similar questions from your research. The pressure to do surgery feels rushed. What's the right thing to do for *my* dog? I feel a bit scared as I have never used a board-certified orthopedic surgeon before. I have always used my family vet whom I trust and has known my dog for years. There are many qualified surgeons- how do I pick one? The only experience I have ever had was with TTA and why does Luce not qualify for that surgical procedure?

As I read, I learned about some benefits of each procedure and also the complication (Harasen, 2004). Although not directly caused an individual technique, every procedure seemed to have a complication: some more scary than others. This new knowledge brought more questions.

What about osteosarcoma?

How many dogs reject their equipment, and may need a second surgery to have it removed?

Is removing the meniscus really necessary and what will be the cushion between the bones with it gone?

Why do some procedures use titanium plates and others stainless steel?

Could my dog experience a secondary break in the leg as the screws are put in?

Why are so many dogs needing cruciate ligament surgeries in the first place?

Is my dog doomed to arthritis no matter what I choose?

Do I have to do rehab no matter which technique I choose?

Decision Making

There were many unanswered questions and an overwhelming amount of passionate - albeit sometimes misleading - information about this topic online. I knew I had to take things step by step to find the best path forward. One thing was clear: this injury wouldn't heal on its own without some sort of intervention. That meant "doing nothing" was no longer an option. And if time was indeed a crucial factor, then every moment counted.

I had made my first decision: to fix the leg with some type of intervention.

On to the second decision, which procedure is the right choice? What I knew to be true was as follows: Luce ate a fresh, hydrated diet paired with raw protein, exercised regularly, and maintained a healthy weight of around 30 lbs. She received proactive care through biannual wellness visits, limited vaccinations, and the absence of topical pesticides. She also benefited from regular chiropractic adjustments, acupuncture treatments every six weeks, and bodywork to enhance her mobility, agility, and injury prevention. I had been dedicated to her health from day one, doing everything possible to ward off disease and optimize her well-being. These characteristics made Luce a good candidate for any of the procedures. Her family vet felt that TTA would not work for Luce because of her athleticism. He felt that it would fail and that TPLO would be a better choice for her long term.

And yet, TPLO felt really invasive to me as a first choice. I couldn't shake the fear of making the wrong decision – one that could hurt her instead of help her. Why were so many people in online forums sharing stories of failure? I was still spinning, still unsure of what to do.

It's Not Personal

It felt like the right time to move from research to action, and speak directly with a board-certified surgeon to explore options for Luce and possibly schedule an evaluation. Our family veterinarian gave me the names of three board-certified surgeons, which gave me a helpful place to begin. I contacted each of them, and also reached out to a well-known orthopedic center about three hours away. While this particular clinic wasn't among those my vet had recommended, it had a strong reputation for working with agility athletes nationwide. If surgery became the right path for Luce, I wanted to understand all of the top-tier options.

When I called the orthopedic center, I was greeted by a kind and helpful staff member. I explained Luce's situation and asked to schedule an appointment to discuss the best approach for her. I tried to approach this the same way I would if I were navigating a similar injury for myself.

To my surprise, I was told they could perform the surgery as early as the following Tuesday—less than a week away. I felt encouraged by the quick availability, especially if this turned out to be the right course of action for Luce. I asked when she could come in for evaluation and testing to ensure the diagnosis was accurate and to check for any additional concerns.

I learned that the clinic typically conducts all necessary diagnostics on the day of surgery, just prior to the procedure. I asked whether they could evaluate Luce for a range of CCL repair procedures, depending on what would be best for her specific condition. The person I spoke with explained that their surgeon primarily performs TPLO and that if I was still considering other procedures, it might be worth consulting facilities that offer alternative techniques.

This prompted me to follow up with two more clinics. In both cases, TPLO was also the recommended approach. Several offices mentioned that waiting too long could increase the risk of arthritis or complicate the chance for a successful surgery. I understood their concern and appreciated their urgency. At the same time, I was hoping for a broader discussion of options. It was beginning to feel like only one path was being offered, which left me wanting a more collaborative decision-making process.

When I thought about how similar injuries are treated in human medicine, I kept returning to the idea of starting with the least invasive option. In people, minimally invasive procedures are often recommended first due to benefits like reduced pain, quicker recovery, and fewer complications. This is the framework I'm most familiar with, given my limited personal experience with surgery.

Still seeking a more tailored evaluation, I contacted three more surgical clinics, including two originally recommended by my vet. My hope was that a surgeon could evaluate Luce's individual situation, review her existing records, and determine whether further testing might be necessary to fully understand her condition. I was concerned about the possibility of additional injuries or a misdiagnosis. I wanted to work alongside a surgeon to determine the most appropriate course of action, considering all available options.

However, the clinics I consulted consistently felt that TPLO was the best course—even without examining her in person. Conservative management wasn't really part of the conversation.

This highlighted for me a noticeable difference between human and veterinary medicine in how injuries like this are assessed and treated. In human healthcare, surgery is often not the first-line treatment for similar injuries. Typically, a physician evaluates the injury in depth, considers imaging, and develops a personalized plan, often starting with rehabilitation.

I want to be clear: I am not opposed to surgery. If it had turned out to be the best choice for Luce, I would have supported it fully. For me, cost and recovery time were not barriers—I simply wanted to make the most informed and thoughtful decision on her behalf.

The Tail of the TPLO

Since TPLO was being recommended to me as Luce's best option, I spent a lot of time learning about it. In simple terms, TPLO is a surgical procedure used to treat torn cruciate ligaments in dogs. It involves making a curved cut at the top of the tibia, the primary lower leg bone in the hind leg, rotating the bone to change its angle, and then stabilizing it with a stainless-steel plate and screws.

There are benefits to doing TPLO and they are as follows: the procedure is said to restore normal limb function, minimize arthritic changes in the knee joint, and be suitable for dogs of all sizes and breeds while also reducing recovery time. Bone healing typically takes about eight weeks, with full recovery extending up to six months. These are some great outcomes to consider.

After hearing from so many clinics that they preferred TPLO, I tried to identify what made TPLO the procedure of choice for this injury. What I found was that there is truly no surgical procedure for CCLD which has shown consistent superiority, including TPLO (Boudreau, 2009). Others have pointed out, "Various surgical treatment options have been developed to address this condition; however, a consensus on the most effective technique remains elusive. Although intra-articular and extra-articular surgical methods aim to stabilize the stifle joint by mimicking the function of the intact cranial cruciate ligament and reducing cranial drawer motion, they have not fully restored functionality. Additionally, there is a noticeable gap in comprehensive kinetic and kinematic studies and high-quality clinical trials, which complicates the review and comparison of long-term clinical outcomes" (Wemmers et al., 2022).

When choosing the best treatment for your dog, it's important to consider both the pros and cons of your choice. Some risks are common across all techniques, including anesthesia-related issues, wound problems, infections, patellar (kneecap) luxation (dislocation), failure to regain normal function, and progressive arthritis. Osteotomy techniques, in particular, carry additional risks such as delayed or failed healing of the bone, improper bone alignment (e.g., limb rotation), fractures, and screws or plate failure. These complications can be serious and may require multiple revision surgeries.

I was seriously considering this option for Luce, but my concern was that none of the other procedures required severing and plating the tibia, adjusting force direction, or reshaping the stifle to mimic human anatomy rather than that of dogs (Wemmers et al., 2023), (Harasen, 2004), (Nanda & Hans, 2019). Altering one inevitably affects the other, and a TPLO changes both—irreversibly.

So, let's visit some of the potential concerns regarding this choice. Research shows that up to 30 percent of dogs may experience chronic pain and lameness for years following a TPLO (Wemmers et al., 2022). Within just one year, medium- to large-breed dogs can suffer a reduction in subchondral bone density in the lateral tibial plateau, indicating abnormal loading patterns (Wemmers et al., 2023). Almost every dog that undergoes a TPLO experiences thickening of the patellar tendon, which can lead to pain and restricted movement (Bergh & Peirone, 2012).

Complications arise in nearly one-third of dogs after a TPLO. These can range from swelling and bruising to more serious issues, such as fractures and osteomyelitis (Bergh & Peirone, 2012), (Hans et al., 2017). The process of sawing and plating the tibia not only impacts the bone but can also damage surrounding tissues, including nerves, blood vessels, (Matres-Lorenzo et al., 2018) muscles, and the menisci (O'Brien & Martinez, 2009).

Some of these complications require surgical revisions and may involve removing implants, which adds to the trauma, pain, and financial burden (American College of Veterinary Surgeons [ACVS], n.d.), (Montalbano, Deabold, & Miscioscia, 2021). Additionally, unresolved inflammation, delayed healing, implant instability, and infections can increase the risk of developing osteosarcoma (OSA) (Sprecher et al., 2018). Dogs who undergo a TPLO are 40 times more likely to be diagnosed with proximal tibial OSA than those who don't have the surgery (Selmic et al., 2018).

Additionally, up to 15 percent of dogs may suffer postoperative fibular fractures. These fractures can result from the surgical process, primarily when a jig is not used or drill holes are left unfilled. A fractured fibula compromises overall stability, and in about 45 percent of cases, it does not heal on its own (Zuckerman et al., 2018). This scenario may require a second osteotomy to address the fibula issue.

Knee Haw Partner

Of course, what I have presented here are worst case scenarios. Things can go very wrong and they can go very right. The reason I share both the pros and the cons of this procedure is to help you weigh your choices. With a permanent approach like surgery, you should sit with the potential outcomes for a beat in order to make an informed decision. My grandmother used to say, "Measure twice- cut once."

TPLO is regarded as the "gold standard" of all of the techniques. When presented with the term "gold standard" the tagline felt to me like a marketing tool to sell you on the idea. Here is your gentle reminder to look at the research, testing and time that a process has been in effect and also review the outcomes since it has been employed. Peel the onion back and try to separate information so you can make an informed decision.

Has TPLO been proven effective over time and through research?

Is it the safest and most cost-effective option available?

And does it ultimately lead to the best long-term outcomes?

As I was researching TPLO, I found that research also indicated that smaller dogs can achieve similar outcomes with or without undergoing a TPLO procedure (Kwananocha et al., 2024). In fact, obese dogs that lose excess weight and participate in therapeutic exercise often experience significant improvement within a year (Wucherer et al., 2013). Even if some instability remains, strengthening the surrounding soft tissues can provide better support and protect the joint both mechanically and neurologically (Riemann & Lephart, 2002).

I also came across information that made me reconsider the belief that cruciate ligaments cannot heal. Apparently, they can. Stephanie Filbay, the lead researcher of a study involving 120 patients, noted, "What we found, surprisingly, was those two years after injury, among those who underwent rehabilitation alone, 53 percent showed signs of healing on MRI... Even more surprising was that those with signs of healing reported better outcomes than those who opted for surgery."

What does this mean for dogs? For me, it meant maybe I didn't have to rush Luce into surgery and could give her body some time. I had breathing space to consider a rehabilitation program first. What I learned was that cruciate injuries aren't emergencies, and dogs can develop osteoarthritis whether they undergo surgery or not.

So, let's take a step away from surgical choices and consider a different approach: Conservative Management.

It's Going Tibia Okay

What does conservative management involve, and who is a good candidate?

Deciding whether to proceed with surgery can feel daunting, and this book isn't about arguing for or against surgery versus conservative management. That wouldn't be fair, as every dog has unique circumstances that require individual consideration. What works for one may not be the best choice for another. Conservative management is a choice and I shifted my research efforts into better understanding what this choice entailed.

Sometimes, surgery must be sidestepped for reasons beyond our control. Some dogs may not be surgical candidates due to factors like age, weight, breed-related issues, poor health, fitness levels at the time of injury, or financial constraints. In such cases, conservative management becomes a viable choice.

This subset of patients deserves the same chance at optimal function as prime surgical candidates. An experienced veterinarian can help you manage your dog's CCL injury with conservative treatments, which may include medication, rehabilitation, and a brace.

I would recommend seeking out a veterinarian specializing in rehabilitation. You should not do this on your own. This approach provides a great second veterinary opinion and they can help manage your expectations, guide you through treatment, and give you real feedback.

When managing this type of injury conservatively, several treatment options are typically employed. Medications, such as pain relievers and anti-inflammatory drugs, can help alleviate discomfort. Rehabilitation is key and usually includes physical therapy, hydrotherapy, and targeted strengthening exercises. To support the knee joint, a custom-made or off-the-shelf brace may be recommended.

Adjusting your dog's activity is essential, often involving limiting movement and using a short leash for bathroom breaks. If your dog is carrying extra weight, implementing a weight loss program is crucial. On the other hand, if your dog is at an ideal weight, we must also consider the potential for weight gain while their activity is restricted.

Incorporating dietary supplements like fish oil, turmeric, and glucosamine can further support recovery. Additionally, exploring therapies such as acupuncture, massage, and intra-articular treatments can be beneficial as your dog heals.

Research suggests that this approach may lead to successful outcomes in about two-thirds of patients one year after a CCL rupture. However, without clear guidelines, determining where to begin can be challenging.

One way to approach this is by identifying potential outcomes, which can help guide the choice of treatment modalities and your dog's medical team. The primary goal is to improve your dog's quality of life, ensure their comfort, and help them regain function.

Studies have shown that ligaments heal more effectively with controlled movement and gentle exercise rather than complete immobilization. Encouraging movement not only stimulates healing but also helps maintain joint function.

Early movement is key after a ligament injury, beginning with gentle range-of-motion exercises under the guidance of a rehabilitative therapist. Gradually introducing controlled loading within pain limits, allows the ligament to heal while minimizing the risk of further damage. Strengthening the surrounding muscles enhances stability and supports the ligament's healing process.

I want to share a few important insights regarding a slight difference in recommendations between orthopedic veterinarians and rehab veterinarians: some ortho vets may suggest crating your dog and severely restricting their movement for most of the day. However, when managing a CCL injury without surgery, adjusting activity levels is key. Rehabilitative veterinarians advocate for safe movement during recovery, emphasizing the importance of reducing muscle atrophy through therapeutic modalities while also addressing inflammation and swelling.

It's important to understand that ligaments don't heal well with immobilization. When restricted, they struggle to recover or become stiff and inflexible. Additionally, the injured ligament isn't the only one that needs care – supporting the surrounding ligaments is crucial for overall recovery.

Just like with surgery, a dog's knee will never fully return to its original state after a CCL injury. The body cannot regenerate a new cranial cruciate ligament (CCL), but it compensates by forming scar tissue around the injury site to help stabilize the knee. Additionally, rehabilitative efforts focus on strengthening the surrounding muscles to provide further protection and support to the joint.

Conservative management of this injury requires adjustments to daily routines, such as avoiding stairs, limiting jumping, opting for on-leash walks, and carrying your dog in and out of vehicles when necessary. This is also a great time to consult a qualified canine nutritionist who understands CCL injuries. They can help tailor your dog's diet to prevent weight gain, reduce inflammation, and support healing.

Certain medications, such as Carprofen, can help manage inflammation when given immediately after an injury. However, long-term use may actually slow the healing process. Research suggests that prolonged Carprofen administration can hinder bone healing in dogs that have undergone tibial osteotomy. Therefore, caution is advised when using Carprofen for slow-healing fractures or conditions that may further delay bone repair. (McVey, n.d.)

Your nutritionist can help you explore alternative methods to manage inflammation, alleviate pain, and adjust caloric intake to accommodate reduced activity - all while ensuring your dog gets enough calories for maintenance and recovery. It's more about choosing the right foods than counting calories. Often, they will also recommend other conservative management strategies at the same time. It is ideal for your nutritionist and your rehabilitation veterinarian to work together.

Meanwhile, your veterinarian will determine the most appropriate medication based on your dog's overall health, the nature of the injury, and their pain level. It's important to discuss both the benefits and potential side effects of each option.

Advocate for your dog—don't rely solely on medication to mask the pain. Remember, pain is a signal that something is wrong. If we simply mute that signal, we risk overusing the injured area, leading to further complications.

Taking Strides. Healing Hides

Working with a certified canine rehabilitation therapist is a valuable part of recovery, whether you choose surgical intervention or a conservative management approach. Rehabilitation plays a vital role in both cases.

Typically, a therapist will conduct in-clinic sessions and design a personalized at-home exercise plan. These programs help keep your dog active while supporting healing by reducing inflammation, managing swelling, and improving range of motion, comfort, and overall mobility.

There are a variety of therapies that can assist in recovery from a CCL injury. These include massage therapy, low-level laser therapy, extracorporeal shockwave therapy, therapeutic ultrasound, transcutaneous electrical nerve stimulation (TENS), transformative targeted PEMF/tPEMF therapy, therapeutic exercise, and hydrotherapy such as underwater treadmill sessions or swimming. Another option showing promise is stem cell treatment. Though more costly, it is nonsurgical and uses the dog's own cells to help support tissue regeneration and healing.

It's also important to recognize that, in some cases, doing nothing beyond managing symptoms can be a reasonable choice. Some dogs, like some people, may adapt well with a torn CCL, especially with the help of medications and supportive care such as physical therapy. For instance, with an older dog—such as a 12-year-old Labrador—it might make sense to weigh the benefits of surgery against factors like the recovery period, which can take 6 to 8 months. In contrast, for a younger, highly active or working dog, the decision may lean more clearly toward intervention.

Game of Bones: Ligament Edition

When you sit down to play any game, the first step is always to familiarize yourself with the rules. Understanding these rules is essential, as they shape your strategy and help you recognize your limitations. With that in mind, and now that we have clarity on our situation, let me outline the guidelines I've established for this decision-making game.

Rule #1: Set a deadline. What do I mean by that? A timeline helps drive decisions. Life happens, and time slips away from us when we're distracted. Set a realistic deadline for choosing the treatment that will best help your dog – and make sure to write it on your calendar.

Rule #2: Narrow the List to Two Solid Options. When making decisions, many people will offer advice – your veterinarian, friends, and even

Dr. Google, who presents you with an overwhelming number of possibilities. This flood of information can lead to analysis paralysis, making it difficult to choose.

Ultimately, you can't pursue every option at once. It's best to start with a clear focus and build from there. To avoid feeling stuck, limit your decision to two feasible options that you can realistically tackle before your deadline. Typically, these will be the most straightforward choices. Luce and I narrowed ours down to conservative management or TPLO surgery.

Rule #3: Let Go of Guilt. It's easy to fall into the trap of blaming ourselves or others for a difficult situation, spending precious time dwelling on what went wrong. But no matter what choices led here, the reality is that this injury is costly, and veterinarians charge for their expertise and care.

Most importantly, this is not your fault. Letting go of guilt allows you to focus on making the best decisions for your dog. It's time to accept the situation for what it is – and move forward.

Rule #4: Make a Rational Pro/Con List. Start by listing the pros of each treatment option, then circle the most significant one for each. Next, list the cons – being as realistic as possible – and circle the most important con.

Be practical about your financial situation, mental bandwidth, and what fits your lifestyle. The strain on a caregiver is real, both financially and emotionally, so it's essential to choose a path you can realistically manage.

Rule #5: Keep Your Deadline in Mind. There's a well-known saying: "Sleep on it." You don't need to rush your decision. A good rule of thumb is to trust your instincts – if you feel the same way in the morning, you're likely on the right path.

Take a deep breath. When life pulls you in multiple directions, time becomes your most valuable resource. Spending too much of it overanalyzing can take away from more productive actions. Stay committed to your deadline and move forward with confidence.

Rule #6: Don't Second-Guess Yourself. No one ever wakes up thinking, "I'm going to make a terrible decision today!" You have thought this through and are making the best-informed choice based on the information available right now.

Could another, seemingly perfect option present itself later? Maybe. But it wasn't an option when you made this decision. Trust yourself - you know your dog best!

Rule #7: Be Present. The stress you're feeling comes from a place of love - you care deeply, and that's a good thing. In the end, this decision is yours to make. You may not enjoy the process, but you alone have the power to help your dog. The fact that you're taking the time to research and make an informed choice shows just how great of a pet parent you are!

In any moment of decision, the best thing you can do is the right thing, the next best thing is the wrong thing, and the worst thing you can do is nothing.
-Theodore Roosevelt

Time for me to make a decision. Together, let's quickly review what we know and where we stand in the timeline. Luce's injury happened on Friday, August 19, 2023. That same day, a vet visit confirmed it was a knee injury.

Here are the notes from the vet visit on August 19, 2023: *Non-weight-bearing lameness RR, occasionally touching toes. Reacted mildly upon extension under stress of stifle. Hip, hock, toes no reaction. No crepitus or meniscus; click, but joint seems unstable upon cranial drawer attempt. Acute injury: happened this afternoon.*

It was recommended that we follow up with our regular vet, and on the following Monday, August 21, 2023, Luce was examined, x-rays were taken, and another drawer test was performed. The diagnosis confirmed a torn CCL in her right rear leg.

These are the follow-up vet notes from visit with the regular family vet on *August 21, 2023: Diagnosis: RH- effusion cranial drawer noted 90% NWB. Radiographs: effusion is reported more in the R than the L, slight caudal displacement of the femur is noted as well as indicated CCL damage. Partial vs complete?*

The veterinarian was unsure whether it was a partial or complete tear. So, during the week of rest recommended by my family vet, I continued managing the injury at home while exploring other options – despite my vet's insistence that TPLO surgery was the only solution.

That week, I reached out to board-certified surgeons for additional insight. Meanwhile, amid all this back-and-forth, my canine massage therapist and a friend suggested I consult a rehabilitation veterinarian for a second opinion.

This was the most valuable advice I had received since the ordeal began. Getting a second opinion felt like the wise thing to do since I was considering such a major invasive surgery for Luce. Exploring other options certainly couldn't hurt.

I reached out to Veterinary Rehabilitation Services of Virginia (VRSVA) in Gordonsville, Virginia, where Dr. Katherine Johnson listened attentively to my concerns. She agreed to schedule an assessment and examination for

Luce, which reassured me - I was getting expert input from someone experienced in both surgical and conservative management cases. No matter what path I chose for Luce's recovery, I knew I had made an invaluable connection for the future.

The week seemed to fly by, and on Friday, August 25, 2023, we visited the rehabilitation vet in Gordonsville, Virginia. It had been a week since Luce's initial injury, yet she still wasn't walking normally on all four feet. I had to carry her into the appointment, as she was only occasionally toe-touching with her injured leg.

As we settled into Dr. Johnson's examination room, I shared the information I had gathered from her other veterinarians. I detailed the medications, supplements, diet, homeopathic remedies, and treatments I had been over the week. Prior to our visit, I had sent Dr. Johnson the notes and radiographs from my family vet's office, which she had reviewed thoroughly. She then observed Luce's gait, palpated her leg, and gently manipulated her knee to assess its condition.

Dr. Johnson's notes and diagnosis after her examination: *Luce is in great shape and used to leading an active lifestyle; she's lean, has solid muscle mass, and is a happy, compliant patient. However, there was significant soreness over her T11 area on both sides, as noted during light palpation. The right stifle exhibited instability both medially and laterally, although there wasn't much cranial drawer motion. While manipulating the stifle for examination, a soft clicking sound was present. I noted significant spasms and trigger points when I applied gentle pressure to the iliopsoas muscle. When pressure was applied to the Iliopsoas's tendon and point of insertion on the lesser trochanter of the femur, Luce displayed significant discomfort. Currently, the thigh circumference appears symmetrical on both sides. The radiograph review shows no other causes for the lameness, and there isn't much effusion in the stifle. We discussed the possibility of MRI and ultrasound for further diagnostics if needed.*

Two previous veterinary examinations failed to identify the iliopsoas strain.

A strained iliopsoas can be excruciating and often causes lameness on its own. An accurate diagnosis is essential to treating it alongside the orthopedic issue. Fortunately, I was in the right place – Dr. Johnson, an experienced equine vet with extensive knowledge of this type of injury in both horses and dogs, knew exactly what to look for when others did not.

The failure to diagnose an iliopsoas strain alongside a torn CCL is likely a key reason for the low reported prevalence of muscle injuries in dogs.

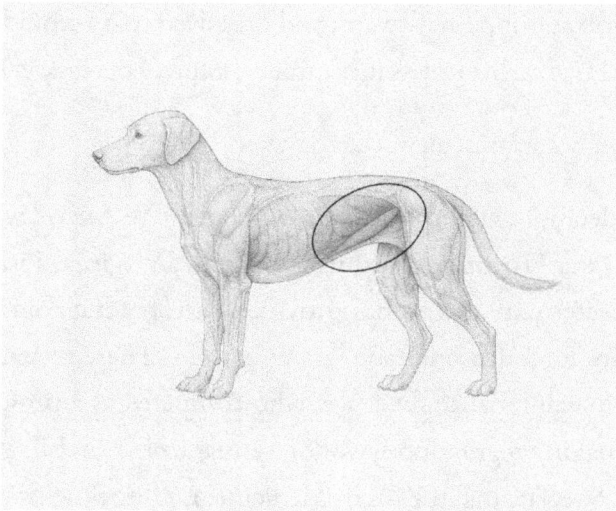

Location of the iliopsoas in the dog highlighted

Through this experience, I learned that rehabilitation can effectively treat iliopsoas strains. Chiropractic adjustments help maintain body balance and minimize subluxations, while acupuncture can aid pain management and promote healing.

After the examination, Dr. Johnson was upfront with me about what conservative management would entail. She explained the level of commitment required and emphasized the need for regular assessments to ensure that Luce's condition didn't worsen. She also recommended an ultrasound to get a clearer picture of what was happening in the knee. Dr. Johnson made it clear that conservative management wouldn't necessarily be cheaper than surgery and that the healing process would take no less than 12 months.

I found myself at a critical crossroads - should I commit to a year of conservative management or follow the advice of three other vets and opt for surgery? In that moment, I made a firm decision: conservative management was the path forward. I pushed aside fear, pressure, and emotions, trusting my instincts that this was the right choice. We embraced rehabilitation as our path forward, and I resolved that I wouldn't consider surgery on Luce's tibia unless it became absolutely necessary.

Dr. Johnson began treatment that day.

With this decision, added another key member to Luce's rehabilitation team: Dr. Jana Froeling. Based in Amissville, Virginia, Dr. Froeling is an equine veterinarian who has provided chiropractic adjustments and acupuncture for Luce since she was a year old. These treatments served as proactive maintenance for Luce, who competed at a professional athlete level, making regular bodywork essential to her mobility and overall well-being. Specializing in Eastern Medicine, Dr. Froeling is well-versed in Chinese herbs, homeopathy, and various holistic healing techniques. Her complementary approach has consistently worked in harmony with our family veterinarian's Western medicine strategy, ensuring well-rounded support for both emergencies and routine wellness visits.

When the injury occurred, I immediately reached out to Full Circle Equine Services in Amissville, Virginia, to schedule an appointment for Luce with Dr. Jana Froeling. Regardless of whether I opted for surgery, this was an obvious choice. I knew Luce's body would be compensating for the injured leg, and I worried that this imbalance might lead to overuse injuries in the other limbs. I also had complete trust in Dr. Froeling and valued her insights, especially since she had worked with Luce for quite some time.

On August 28, 2023, we met with Dr. Jana Froeling. I provided her with Dr. Johnson's notes, reports from other veterinarians, and the radiographs taken by our family vet. To prevent further aggravation of Luce's knee, Dr. Froeling conducted her examination without performing a drawer test. She agreed with Dr. Johnson's diagnosis of both the iliopsoas strain and the orthopedic issue. I also informed Dr. Froeling of my decision to pursue conservative management instead of surgery at this time.

Dr. Froeling's examination and treatment notes: *Something happened in the yard about 10 days ago, and she wasn't putting weight on her right rear leg. Another vet said that she had torn her cruciate. Slovis said torn ACL (not sure if complete or partial). Recommended TTA or TPLO. The third (rehab vet -Dr. Johnson) said she pulled her Iliopsoas. Owner has been lasering both rear legs 2 times a day. Recommend to work on pulling the hip back gently and getting lasering in the femoral triangle. Owner giving Arnica, Vit C, supplement with MSM/Glucosamine/Green Lipped Mussels.*

Had one 7-minute session in the underwater treadmill, laser and fascia work. Has had 2 massages for body. Wednesday will do US (ultrasound) to tell if full or partial tear. Recommend to hold off on the treadmill for a couple of weeks. Owner is using KT tape over the leg. Continue with that. Recommend to do KT tape on both rear legs. Was on Carprofen but owner has stopped it and is giving CBD. Use Body Sore and Tendon/Ligament Formula.

Chiropractic adjustment: right dorsal atlas, C7 body left, right PI, L2, and T9 PL. Acupuncture: white needle at DFM, GB21, GV14, BL23, Bai Hui, Shen Shu, BL40, KID3, LIV3, GB34, ST36, SP9, GB32. Therapeutic US over Iliopsoas on the right at 1.4 watts at 80% duty cycle 1mHz for 15 minutes. Can start functional exercises in a week or two: hip sways, pick up left leg, put front feet on a step and stretch to both sides, to her ribs, then to her hips, stand on balance pad. Dispensed Assisi Loop SN# M18662. Rehab nutritional plan provided by owner attached. Owner has Body Sore and dispensed Tendon/Ligament Formula 90g - Give 3 small scoops 2 times a day.

Luce receiving acupuncture at a visit with Dr. Froeling's office

As I stepped through the door at home, I let out a long sigh of relief. While I knew I had made a decision without any guarantees, my appointment with Dr. Froeling left me feeling reassured that I was on the right path.

As a Certified Canine Nutritionist, I was now ready to confidently manage her diet and supplements. With that foundation in place, I began assembling her rehabilitation team for the crucial twelve months of healing ahead. Time to get to work.

A chance to rehabilitate is a chance to restore.

Chapter 3: Prescription... Nutrition

Congratulations! You've arrived at a crucial chapter in your dog's healing journey. Nutrition forms the foundation of health, and as your dog recovers, what they eat matters more than ever. Whether you've chosen surgery or a conservative path to recovery, their body is hard at work restoring balance, a process that demands energy, nutrients, and time. Now that you've established a treatment plan, it's essential to revisit the basics. Take a close look at everything your dog consumes and remove anything that doesn't actively support their physical or mental healing.

Remember, nutrition goes beyond just physical health - it profoundly impacts your dog's emotional well-being too. By practicing mindful eating for your pup, you'll pay attention to ingredients, flavors, textures, and the overall eating experience of each meal. This approach encourages a healthier relationship with food, reduces overeating or fussiness, and strengthens the vital connection between proper nutrition, physical health, and mental wellness.

Research shows that healing - whether physical or emotional - is significantly boosted when a dog is in good mental health. A positive mindset can improve your dog's ability to cope, increase resilience, and speed up recovery from illness or trauma.

Positive emotions help dogs bounce back from setbacks and manage stress more effectively, which can accelerate healing. Studies have shown a clear link between good mental health and a stronger immune system – an essential ally in physical recovery. When a dog maintains a positive outlook, it's better equipped to regulate stress hormones that might otherwise slow the healing process, allowing the body to focus on recovery. Additionally, dogs that maintain a cheerful attitude are more likely to adapt their behaviors, which is essential for following treatment plans and achieving a successful recovery.

It's also important to remember that nutrition can directly affect behavior. Before the injury, your dog may have been very active – just like Luce - but now, everything has changed. Their environment is different. They're less active, possibly in pain, and they can sense your stress. All this can leave them feeling frustrated and bored. During their recovery, it's not uncommon for your dog to experience mood changes, behavioral issues, or even signs of depression.

Here's a beautiful opportunity to elevate your dog's dining experience - making it nurturing, satisfying, and engaging, while also strengthening their connection to food, an essential part of overall well-being. Imagine being able to give your dog exactly what they need to thrive, heal, and feel their best. This journey isn't just physical - it's reaching all the way down to the cellular level.

Nutrition is essential for our dogs because it powers their bodies and helps them function efficiently. Every cell, tissue, and organ rely on a steady supply of nutrients to perform at its best. Proper nutrition plays a key role in energy production and strengthening the immune system, making its importance in overall health undeniable.

However, this discussion won't cover typical nutrition advice. Instead, we'll focus on what I call *Adaptive Nutrition for Dogs* - a personalized approach that involves feeding your dog whole foods tailored to their specific circumstances and goals. I am using adaptive nutrition with Luce to help manage her weight, reduce inflammation, and improve her mobility, all while supporting natural healing with minimal interference in the body's innate processes.

Moreover, adaptive nutrition considers your dog's evolutionary background, breed, type of injury, other health issues, and current life stage to create a balanced diet with the right mix of meat and vegetables, as needed. Remember, their needs will evolve - so we must reassess along the way!

The prescription here is nutrition. Please have it filled.

Steps in the Right Direction

As I mentioned in another chapter, at the time of Luce's injury, her diet consisted of a dehydrated base mix to which I added raw meat for balance. Since she was a rescue, I'm unsure of her mother's identity or the conditions she faced during her first 12 weeks, including what she was fed in those early days. When I adopted her, she ate feed-grade dry food with various artificial colors, but I immediately switched her to a higher-quality kibble made with better ingredients. Having always fed my dog kibble; I was completely unaware of alternative feeding options until her first birthday. That's when I met some incredible canine enthusiasts at Luce's daycare and training classes, who shared invaluable insights on proper canine nutrition. This introduction motivated me to transition her to the dehydrated base mix and raw protein, which she stuck with for the next seven years.

Like many dogs, Luce faced her share of unique challenges in her first eight years, mostly minor digestive issues, occasional bile vomiting, and persistently low Vitamin D levels that required ongoing supplementation to keep her values in check. As I learned more about available options, I began incorporating frozen raw food, organic meats, and necessary supplements into her diet as needed.

This journey marked the beginning of my path as a canine nutritionist. With two master's degrees under my belt and currently pursuing a Ph.D. at Virginia Tech, I've spent many years studying biological, animal, social, and agricultural sciences.

My background also includes human focused sciences such as phlebotomy, histology, nutrition, and bodybuilding coaching. I worked for several years as a canine nutritionist at a fresh dog food company - an exciting opportunity that allowed me to focus entirely on the animal world, guided by inspiring mentors. I chose to concentrate on dogs and began combining my academic knowledge with hands-on experience.

Every professional opportunity I've encountered has shaped who I am today, from honing my creative and academic writing skills to analyzing data, conducting research, and developing my public speaking abilities.

I've also enjoyed teaching at the collegiate level, sharing knowledge with professionals, and collaborating with teams to reach our goals.

The Role of Nutrition in Rehabilitation

Nutrition plays a crucial role in dog rehabilitation by providing the essential nutrients needed for tissue repair, muscle development, and overall healing. A well-balanced diet tailored to the dog's specific needs can significantly speed up recovery from injuries or surgeries by boosting energy levels and enhancing immune function. Depending on the dog's condition, a rehabilitation diet often includes increased protein, targeted fatty acids like omega-3s, and antioxidants.

As mentioned earlier, proper nutrition is crucial for a canine athlete's physical and mental well-being. A sufficient and balanced diet is essential for both recovery and rehabilitation. Relying solely on a maintenance diet falls short of meeting basic nutritional needs, especially when supporting healing, encouraging new tissue growth, preventing inflammation, or maintaining lean body mass without physical activity. *Rehabilitation nutrition* for athletes recovering from injuries is closely aligned with sports nutrition. Some nutrients, when consumed in higher quantities, can promote healing, while others may not have the same impact.

Both macro- and micronutrients play significant roles in metabolism, energy production, hemoglobin synthesis, and the maintenance of lean mass and bone health. They are also essential for boosting immunity and protecting against oxidative damage.

If we think about nutrition being the foundation of all things, then we need to visualize Maslow's hierarchy of needs as they pertain to the dog. Maslow's Hierarchy of Needs can be adapted to better understand and prioritize a dog's well-being. The Hierarchy of Dog Needs (HDN) is based on the same foundational concept: basic needs must be met before an individual—canine or human—can reach higher levels of fulfillment such as emotional balance, learning, personal growth, or in this case- healing. For dogs, these needs include essentials like food, water, shelter, safety, social interaction, and mental stimulation. While these needs apply to all dogs, special consideration must be given to those recovering from injury.

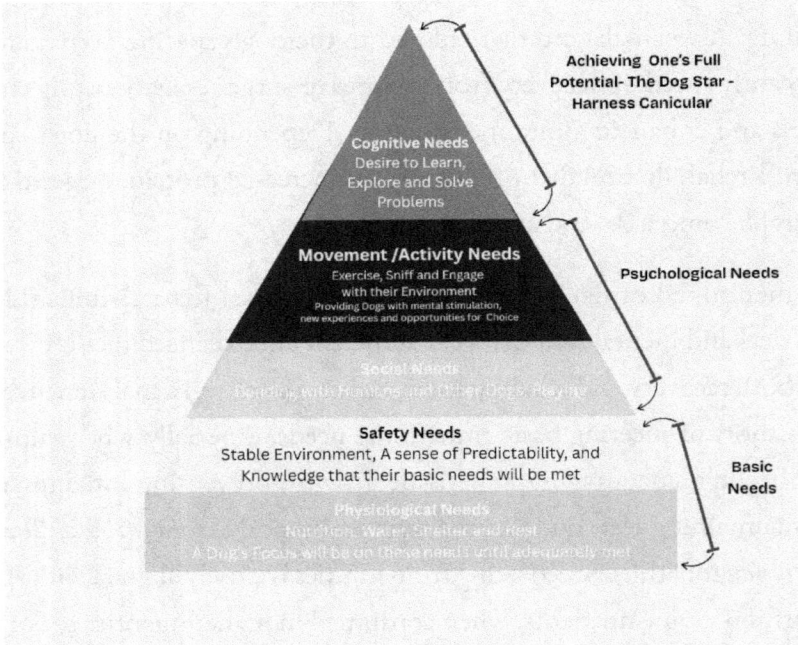

Maslow's Hierarchy of Needs and the Hierarchy of Dog Needs (HDN)

At the base of the pyramid are **physiological needs**, the most fundamental requirements for survival and well-being. For a healthy dog, this typically includes access to clean water, nutritious food, regular exercise, and a safe, comfortable environment. However, for a dog undergoing rehabilitation, these basics require more thoughtful adaptation. It becomes important to evaluate the quality and source of food and water, ensure that the environment is safe for an animal with mobility limitations, and redefine what regular exercise means in the context of recovery.

The next level involves **safety needs**, which generally include a sense of security and consistency within the dog's environment and family structure. A dog in rehabilitation benefits from a predictable routine, consistent caretaking, and a quiet, safe space—ideally separated from other pets—where they can rest and recover without stress or interruption.

Social needs are another key part of a dog's well-being. In normal circumstances, these are met through walks, playtime, training, and interaction with humans and other animals. However, a dog recovering from an injury may not be able to engage in social activities as they did before. Limited mobility, pain, or vulnerability may restrict their ability to interact with other dogs or people. Social needs may have to be met in new ways, such as through short, supervised interactions, passive time near family members, or gentle, low-impact engagement.

Dogs, especially active or working breeds, often benefit from having a **sense of purpose**. These dogs thrive on solving problems, participating in structured activities, or completing tasks. During recovery, these opportunities may be limited, but it's still important to maintain mental engagement. This can be done through creative enrichment such as puzzle toys, scent work, low-impact training exercises, and gentle games that stimulate the mind while protecting the body.

At the top of the hierarchy is **self-actualization**, or reaching one's full potential. In dogs, this might involve confident movement, task performance, balanced behavior, and an overall sense of fulfillment. Achieving this state requires that all previous levels of need are addressed, particularly during the recovery process.

The rehabilitation phase calls for an even more thoughtful and proactive approach. A dog's needs do not disappear because of injury—they simply change. Meeting them requires creativity, presence, and patience. Whether through environmental adaptations, consistent routines, or alternative enrichment, fulfilling these layered needs remains essential to long-term recovery and quality of life.

What is Your Dog's Gut Telling You

Nutrition and gut health play a vital role in the body's healing process. As Dr. Odette Suter explains, an injury can trigger significant changes in the gut – most notably, a shift in the microbiome. Beneficial bacteria often give way to more harmful strains, leading to inflammation and potential complications. This happens because of the powerful link between the gut and the nervous system, known as the gut-brain axis. Remarkably, these changes can begin within hours of an injury and may persist depending on the severity of the trauma.

After an injury, a dog's gut can undergo several key changes (Jona Team, 2025). One major shift is microbiome disruption - when the balance of gut bacteria is thrown off, resulting to a decline in beneficial strains like *Lactobacillus* and *Bacteroides*.

At the same time, harmful bacteria such as *Enterococcus* and *Pseudomonas* may increase. This imbalance can result in heightened intestinal permeability, where the gut lining becomes more porous.

As a result, bacteria and toxins can leak into the bloodstream, triggering an inflammatory response. Gut motility may also be disrupted, causing issues like constipation or diarrhea. As a result, the dog's immune system activates in the gut, releasing inflammatory cytokines that can further exacerbate the condition.

When severe injuries occur, they trigger the release of stress hormones like cortisol and adrenaline, which can directly impact the gut microbiome.

In addition, the gut-brain axis becomes disrupted, leading to altered neurotransmitter signaling that negatively affects gut function. Furthermore, injuries can also reduce blood flow to the gut, further impairing its ability to function properly.

The Impact of gut changes after injury includes:

• **Delayed healing:** Inflammation resulting from disruptions in the gut can hinder the healing process and slow recovery.

• **Pain perception:** Imbalances in gut health may lead to heightened pain sensitivity following an injury.

• **Mental health issues:** The connection between the gut and brain suggests that changes in gut health after trauma may contribute to anxiety and depression.

The health of the gut - and its ability to optimally absorb nutrients - plays a crucial role in nearly every system in the body, influencing healing, inflammation, and overall performance. Growing up, we often heard, *"You are what you eat."* I'd like to take that a step further: *"You aren't just what you eat; you are what you absorb and utilize."* The same principle applies to our dogs. If the digestive system isn't functioning properly, it won't matter much what we put in the bowl.

Regarding the microbiome and chronic joint inflammation, Dr. Steven Marsden, DVM, explains, "Harmful microbes in the microbiome can produce harmful metabolites. A leaky gut and the wrong kinds of bacteria due to poor dietary choices can worsen this issue by allowing these harmful substances to enter the bloodstream. A poor diet can lead to the proliferation of harmful microbes, which can cause inflammation in the joints"(Cracking the Health Code, n.d.a), (Cracking the Health Code, n.d.b).

What preexisting issues am I referring to? As a canine nutritionist, I often encounter problems such as irritable bowel syndrome, low stomach acid production—often linked to antihistamine use—impaired liver function, which disrupts fat digestion and nutrient absorption, and pancreatitis, which affects the release of enzymes and hormones essential for digestive health. Lastly, stress can divert vital resources away from the digestive tract and interfere with normal motility.

When a dog suffers an injury, it can lead to changes in gut health. You have the option to take a proactive or reactive approach. Being proactive means regularly supporting your dog's gut health, which puts them in a much better position to recover than a dog already struggling with dysbiosis before the injury. This way, you're not only addressing the injury itself but also preventing an underlying issue from making things worse. One of the first supportive actions I took when Luce hurt herself was to provide her with a course of Fecal Microbiota Transplant (FMT) capsules.

Being a certified canine nutritionist has been incredibly beneficial - especially when Luce got injured. I recommend working with a certified canine nutritionist who can help you develop effective nutritional strategies. This might include supplementing protein intake when it's lacking and ensuring that your dog maintains muscle mass without gaining excess fat—a challenge that's even trickier for an injured dog, particularly if it was already overweight before the injury.

Just as I tailored Luce's rehabilitation protocols, the same principle applies to nutrition: it should be customized. This isn't a "set it and forget it" situation - ongoing attention is key to a successful recovery.

It's much easier to prevent something from happening by being proactive than to try to fix it after it occurs.

A certified canine nutritionist is essential for customizing a dog's diet to meet its specific needs. This involves carefully considering portion size, feeding frequency, food type, and protein quality. They can also recommend supplements to address inflammation, alleviate pain, and improve gut health.

Since nutrient requirements and calorie expenditure can vary significantly across different breeds, individual dogs, and types of injuries, your dog's care team should include nutrition experts - but that expert isn't your veterinarian.

As I stated earlier, this book focuses on adaptive nutrition for orthopedic injuries. My goal with Luce's injury is to achieve key outcomes through nutrition, such as minimizing inflammation, improving mobility, managing weight effectively, and enhancing healing. Whether you choose a path of rehab or prehab, nutrition and gut health play a significant role in the body's ability to heal.

You can't out supplement a poor diet. What goes into your dog is the foundation of everything.

A Grain of Truth

Nutrition is crucial in preventing and managing orthopedic injuries by promoting joint health and alleviating inflammation. Let's take a closer look at key nutritional elements that can support canine rehabilitation:

Protein:

Opting for high-quality, minimally processed protein is essential. As one of the body's fundamental building blocks, protein is crucial in a dog's diet, especially during recovery or competitive activities. It also plays a key role in numerous physiological and biochemical functions within the body.

Protein for Muscle Repair:

When it comes to recovering from orthopedic injuries, protein is critical as it provides the necessary components for repairing damaged tissues such as muscles, tendons, ligaments, and bones. This helps facilitate a quicker healing process and reduces muscle loss during periods of immobilization or rehabilitation (Hannah & Laflamme, 1998).

Due to decreased activity levels, most injured dogs experience higher protein turnover rates and lower energy expenditure (Hamada et al., 1999). Thus, a diet with higher protein content (over 75 g/1000 kcal) is often recommended to prevent dietary deficiencies. Specific amino acids, such as leucine, can help minimize exercise-induced muscle breakdown in dogs (Drummond & Rasmussen, 2008).

Extensive research in humans shows that leucine stimulates the synthesis of skeletal muscle proteins, and this same benefit likely applies to dogs in recovery. While information on the leucine content of various diets may not always be readily accessible, selecting high-protein diets generally boosts overall leucine intake, as animal-source proteins are typically rich in this amino acid (Drummond & Rasmussen, 2008).

Fats:

Fat is vital for recovery from orthopedic injuries as it cushions and supports damaged tissues, serves as a source of regenerative cells that aid in healing, and may help reduce inflammation when "good" fats are included in the diet. The body's fat plays a role in repairing and reconstructing tissue around injury sites.

Studies show that mild reductions in nonsteroidal anti-inflammatory drug dosing and improved peak vertical forces have been reported with a lower fish oil concentration (about 2.5 g/1000 kcal) administered via a therapeutic joint diet fed for 3 months (Fritsch et al., 2010a), (Roush et al., 2010).

Fat should be the primary energy source in a dog's diet, as it is the most concentrated energy source, providing more calories per gram than protein or carbohydrates. This is particularly important during exercise and rest, making fat the ideal fuel for various canine activities. As a nutritionist, I emphasize the proper inclusion of fats in diets, since some fats can quickly oxidize. Fatty acids travel from the small intestine to the lymphatic system and into the bloodstream (Fritsch et al., 2010a). Essential fatty acids, such as omega-3 and omega-6, are crucial components that should be included in the diet in the right balance. Omega fatty acids play a key role in managing the inflammatory response, with omega-3 acting as a natural inhibitor to help reduce inflammation (Roush et al., 2010).

This becomes especially important when adding certain supplements to the diet of an injured or recovering dog. These fatty acids are vital for maintaining healthy skin, and a deficiency can lead to skin issues and increased water loss through the skin barrier. Additionally, deficiencies in important micronutrients like zinc, magnesium, and vitamin B6 can result in a shortage of fatty acids. Malabsorption problems may arise due to liver disease, biliary disease, inflammatory disorders, or chronic pancreatitis

Healthy fats, particularly Omega-3 fatty acids, are vital for promoting recovery due to their anti-inflammatory properties. These fats help alleviate pain and swelling, which is especially beneficial for dogs undergoing rehabilitation, as they often have concurrent osteoarthritis (Fritsch, Allen, Dodd, et al., 2010b). Numerous studies have shown that modulating fatty acids can significantly impact this condition.

The key polyunsaturated omega-3 fatty acids—eicosapentaenoic acid (EPA) and docosahexaenoic acid (DHA)—are found in certain commercial fish oil products and are known to influence inflammatory processes by promoting the production of less inflammatory eicosanoids. Research suggests that high doses of EPA and DHA (over 7.5 grams per 1000 kcal) lead to the most notable improvements in canine arthritis scores (Fritsch, Allen, Dodd, et al., 2010b). However, it's important to note that few commercial diets meet this high level of EPA and DHA; even diets containing 1 to 3 grams per 1000 kcal have shown positive clinical effects.

Carbohydrates:

In the early stages of recovery, your dog's metabolism ramps up, leading to increased energy demands. This boost is crucial for protecting against tissue damage and maintaining organ function. During this time, carbohydrates play a vital role as they serve as the primary energy source for your dog's brain, nervous system, and muscles—components essential for healing. Carbohydrates supply glucose, which is important since red blood cells depend on it for energy.

Simple carbohydrates are quickly absorbed in the small intestine, providing a rapid energy source. While a small amount can be stored in the liver and muscles for immediate use, any excess is converted into fatty tissue.

On the other hand, complex carbohydrates, primarily recognized as fiber, are processed in the large intestine. These fibers are fermented by the gut microbiome, serving as an important food source for gut bacteria. Without enough fiber, these microbes may start to consume the mucosal layer of the gut, potentially exposing the underlying epithelial cells.

Consuming excessive amounts of refined carbohydrates—such as sugar and processed foods—can lead to increased inflammation in dogs with orthopedic injuries, hindering recovery and intensifying pain. On the other hand, opting for complex carbohydrates from whole grains, fruits, and vegetables can bolster the healing process. These healthier choices provide steady energy without the inflammatory effects often associated with refined carbohydrates.

Refined carbohydrates cause rapid spikes in blood sugar levels, triggering an inflammatory response that can worsen pain and swelling in injured areas. When dogs consume high-glycemic carbohydrates, the swift increase in blood sugar prompts a surge in insulin production, further activating inflammatory pathways.

In contrast, selecting complex carbohydrates with a low glycemic index—like whole grains and fiber-rich vegetables—provides a more gradual energy release, helping to manage inflammation and support tissue repair more effectively.

Managing carbohydrate intake is crucial, and a balanced diet – one that includes adequate protein and healthy fats - is essential for optimal healing after an orthopedic injury.

We don't want to supplement to manage inflammation while quietly feeding it through the diet, undoing all our efforts.

Micronutrients:

Micronutrients are essential to the body's overall function, providing cells with the compounds they need to perform specific tasks. These include vitamins A, D, and K; water-soluble vitamins such as B complex and C; minerals including boron, calcium, chromium, copper, iron, magnesium, phosphorus, potassium, selenium, and sodium; and antioxidants.

Antioxidants:

Vitamin E and other antioxidants help combat oxidative stress, supporting faster healing and tissue repair.

Dietary fiber:

Adequate fiber supports healthy digestion, which is crucial for nutrient absorption and overall well-being.

A dog's body functions as a highly interconnected system that relies on a variety of nutrients to operate at its best. Without these essential compounds, cellular functions can falter, disrupting normal processes like healing. Additionally, systems that help maintain balance—such as inflammation control and the immune response—can become unbalanced, leading to suboptimal health. Our focus here isn't just on general maintenance diets; we're diving deeper into the components of a typical maintenance diet.

Understanding the internal processes that may hinder recovery is essential for tailoring nutrition to support an injured dog. In this context, stress refers to any stimulus that disrupts the body's normal functioning. It acts as a catalyst for adaptation, growth, and change - not just in our lives, but in our dogs' lives as well.

While we often view stress as purely negative, shifting our perspective can change its impact on our pets. The right amount of stress, such as that from exercise, can be beneficial - promoting strength and resilience when applied appropriately. Too little stress won't lead to noticeable effects, but too much can be harmful. Striking the right balance encourages optimal adaptation and enhances performance in our dogs.

When the body encounters stress, it activates both the sympathetic and parasympathetic nervous systems. The sympathetic system prepares the body for action, triggering the fight-or-flight response, while the parasympathetic system promotes rest and digestion. For a patient to heal and recover from an injury, it's crucial that both systems work together effectively.

Cortisol is often labeled the "bad guy" in health discussions, but it actually plays a vital role in the body. "Cortisol is produced by the adrenal glands and is regulated by the hypothalamic-pituitary-adrenal (HPA) axis. It helps maintain homeostasis by influencing glucose metabolism, immune responses, and inflammation control.

While short-term cortisol elevation is beneficial for acute stress responses, prolonged exposure can have adverse effects, particularly on connective tissues such as tendons, ligaments, cartilage, and skin" (Maehrlein, 2025). It helps maintain homeostasis during daily activities and supports normal cellular and metabolic functions. One of its key roles is inhibiting inflammation by binding to glucocorticoid receptors.

However, when cortisol levels remain elevated over time, these receptors can become downregulated or resistant, reducing the body's ability to control inflammation. Additionally, cortisol is crucial for regulating the stress response – not driving it. Chronic stress, therefore, can disrupt cortisol's function and lead to unchecked inflammation in the body (Maehrlein, 2025).

Let's delve a little deeper into what I just mentioned and clarify it further. The question isn't just how much stress is too much - we also need to assess the dog's environment and determine the stress levels they regularly face. Stress accumulates over time as the body's healing response interacts with environmental changes, the owner's stress and uncertainty, and any existing nutritional deficiencies. It's essential to consider all the factors contributing to your dog's stress and explore practical ways to reduce or alleviate them.

Earlier, we discussed how the stress response can redirect resources away from the gut, leading to changes in motility. This means food may either slowdown in certain parts of the digestive tract or move through too quickly. These disruptions can interfere with nutrient absorption and alter the microbiome, especially if food lingers in the wrong areas for too long.

In stressful situations – such as when a dog sustains an orthopedic injury - their body may have a heightened demand for nutrients. Reduced absorption combined with increased nutritional needs can quickly lead to deficiencies. To support recovery during rehabilitation, our approach should focus on increasing the intake of foods and nutrients that specifically promote healing. This helps prevent the body from drawing on its reserves, which can lead to imbalances.

Think of it like fueling a competitive dog: it's not just about providing the right nutrients on competition day – it's a process. Athletes need easily digestible protein to recover from intense training and build muscle. Carbohydrates are a crucial energy source, especially in the days leading up to an event. Proving complex carbohydrates consistently before a competition helps the dog maximize energy stores, while simple carbohydrates on event day deliver quick, accessible energy. Fats are also a fundamental fuel, so it's essential to ensure fat-soluble vitamins are readily available too.

When your dog is undergoing rehabilitation, it presents a new kind of challenge. The body needs extra resources to repair ligaments, tendons, and muscles. Without those resources readily available, healing can be compromised - or the body may pull them from other critical functions.

When comes to the immune system, there are two types of defenses: innate and acquired. Innate immunity includes barriers like skin, mucus, and stomach acid – our dogs' first line of defense. Acquired immunity involves white blood cells, such as monocytes, which can develop into macrophages, neutrophils, basophils, and natural killer cells. Mast cells and cytokines also play key roles in supporting and regulating immune responses.

For our dogs to stay healthy, their immune system needs to function at its best. The idea of *boosting* the immune system is actually a misconception – it's based on a misunderstanding of how immunity works. When the immune system is out of balance, it can trigger immune-mediated diseases. An overactive or overstimulated immune system may lead to autoimmune disorders or allergies.

On the flip side, if it's underactive, the body becomes more vulnerable to infections and increases the risk of cancer. Rather than aiming for an over-the-top immune response, we should focus on achieving a balanced, well-regulated one. Fortunately, there are plenty of nutrients and foods we can include in their diet to support a healthy immune system.

For a long time, we've viewed inflammation as something negative - something to stop, slow down, or prevent in our dogs. But in reality, inflammation plays a vital role in the immune system and is essential for healing. The problem arises when this response becomes dysregulated, turning into chronic inflammation that lingers beyond its helpful phase. This often occurs when the body's initial inflammatory response doesn't fully resolve tissue damage or when the system is overwhelmed. By shifting our perspective and viewing inflammation as a messenger – one that signals imbalances within the immune system - we can approach it with a fresh mindset and find more effective ways to support our dogs' health.

It's essential to ensure the body receives the right nutrients to effectively manage immune and inflammatory responses, while also supporting and regulating the healing process. Just as important, the gut must be able to properly absorb these nutrients - giving the dog the best shot at navigating any imbalances in the system. Factors like stress and disrupted sleep can also interfere with healing.

During rehabilitation, nourishing the gut microbiome becomes especially important. The health of the gut and its bacteria plays a crucial role in influencing nearly every system in the body.

Several key connections, or axes, link these functions together, including:

- gut-immune axis

- gut-brain axis

- gut-lung axis

- gut-bone axis

- gut-musculoskeletal axis

- gut-kidney axis

- gut-thyroid axis

- gut-skin axis

- gut-liver axis

A healthy gut microbiome plays a crucial role in effectively breaking down and digesting nutrients, which is key for proper digestion. It also supports the overall functioning of various systems within the gut. By maintaining a robust and testable barrier, the microbiome fosters the formation of tight junctions, which help prevent the leakage of pathogens, toxins, and dietary antigens into the bloodstream.

Remember, what gets fed survives.

The final component of a well-rounded nutritional strategy is caloric intake. Adjusting it to match a dog's activity level is crucial – providing enough energy for healing while avoiding unnecessary weight gain. During rehabilitation, it's especially important to manage calories carefully to prevent extra pounds from creeping on. Interestingly, the energy cost of sitting and standing can be 30% to 46% higher than lying down (Scott et al., 2013). As a result, dogs that are confined to a crate often need about 25% to 30% fewer calories to maintain an ideal body weight (Shmalberg et al., 2013). On the flip side, energy expenditure may slightly increase during underwater treadmill therapy, especially if the dog exercises at a faster pace during inpatient rehabilitation sessions.

For instance, fit dogs walking in elbow-height water on an underwater treadmill burn about 1.9 kcal/kg^0.75 for every kilometer (Shmalberg et al., 2013). For a 50-pound (22.68-kg) dog, a 30-minute walk at a moderate speed would increase daily energy needs by approximately 1.5%. It's only when exercising at higher speeds for longer sessions that energy expenditure rises significantly - exceeding 5%. Overweight dogs are also at greater risk of musculoskeletal injuries due to the added stress on their limbs. As a result, incorporating weight loss into a rehabilitative nutrition plan can be a vital part of their recovery (Chauvet et al., 2011).

When managing weight in overweight animals, it's tempting to simply reduce their food intake. However, it's essential to focus on calorie restriction is essential *while still maintaining adequate protein levels.* Aim for a gradual weight loss of about 0.5% to 1% per week, as losing weight too quickly can increase the risk of losing lean body mass. Typically, a caloric reduction of at least 33% is required. Diets rich in protein tend to be more effective than those with moderate protein levels. Additionally, lowering fat content can reduce the diet's energy density, as fat contains more than twice the energy density of protein and carbohydrates. Increasing moisture content or adding dietary fiber can also be beneficial.

It's Cruciate to Fix the Root Cause

As a nutritionist, I focus on identifying and addressing the root causes of health issues. Why did the tear happen in the first place? How do we prevent the other leg from tearing? According to the principles of Chinese medicine, the underlying cause of cruciate tears is often linked to circulatory problems. Dr. Steve Marsden, DVM, points out that torn ligaments, including sprains and strains, exhibit hemorrhagic characteristics when viewed under a microscope. One of the vets I spoke to explained to me that ligaments don't heal because of a lack of blood supply to the area.

However, Dr. Marsden explains that the issue isn't a lack of blood supply itself; rather, it's the disorganization of that supply and how effectively it functions.

In Chinese Medicine, circulation lies at the heart of all health issues. Blood vessel function – and overall circulation - is heavily influenced by diet. If your dog consumes a poor-quality diet with a high glycemic load and index, it can cause blood vessels to constrict, making healing even more difficult.

The Glycemic Index (GI) ranks how quickly carbohydrates affect blood sugar levels. Specifically, it measures how fast glucose enters the bloodstream and how much blood sugar rises in pets like dogs and cats after consuming certain carbohydrates.

When discussing the Glycemic Index, we typically divide foods into two groups: low-GI and high-GI foods. Low-GI foods contain carbohydrates that are digested more slowly, helping our pets maintain steady energy levels over a longer period. In contrast, high-GI foods are digested quickly, causing a rapid surge in energy - often followed by a sharp drop.

The Glycemic index (GI) has become a popular tool for evaluating various pet foods on the market. It rates foods on a scale from 1 to 100: Low-GI foods are rated 55 or below, Medium-GI foods range from 56 to 69, and High-GI foods are rated at 70 or above. A higher GI indicates a greater risk of causing unhealthy spikes in your dog's blood sugar levels. For context, raw glucose/sugar has a GI of 100. This index can be a valuable resource when choosing healthier options for your pets and finding the best food to meet their individual needs.

A diet rich in low-GI foods is always ideal, as studies show they offer significant benefits—from boosting energy levels in dogs to supporting weight management and addressing diabetes and other health issues. On the flip side, consuming too many high-GI foods can lead to inflammation, which may contribute to chronic conditions linked to various diseases. When we eat sugary foods, the body releases proteins that trigger immune cells to respond to perceived threats. These sugar spikes can drive up blood sugar levels and fuel inflammation. Additionally, when sugar interacts with proteins or fats, it forms Advanced Glycation End Products (AGEs)—harmful compounds that can further worsen inflammation.

High-glycemic foods can elevate blood sugar levels, which may lead to the constriction of blood vessels. This narrowing increases the risk of cardiovascular disease and can damage vascular tissue. Elevated blood sugar also activates protein kinase A (PKA), an enzyme that enhances calcium channel activity, further tightening the vessels. Additionally, excessive blood sugar reduces the elasticity of blood vessels, making them stiffer and impeding blood flow. This can decrease the supply of blood and oxygen, ultimately raising the risk of high blood pressure. As Dr. Marsden points out, an unhealthy diet can contribute to chronic inflammation - linked to conditions such as hypertension, heart attacks, and osteoarthritis in both humans and dogs. Chronic inflammation, in many cases, is closely tied to our dogs' eating habits.

It's important to realize that chronic inflammation must be actively resolved - it won't simply go away on its own. Dr. Marsden refers to this process as "active resolution," which depends on proper function of the blood vessels. For healing to occur, circulation must be restored, and the blood vessels need to work efficiently.

To effectively address chronic inflammation by tapping into the circulatory system, it's essential to eliminate gaps between cells that allow leakage. This issue, known as endothelial dysfunction, currently has no pharmaceutical cure. By tightening these cellular spaces, we can prevent white blood cells from escaping into the joints and creating chaos. When blood vessels are properly sealed and no longer leaking, optimal drainage becomes possible. While there are no medications that directly fix this dysfunction, Dr. Marsden notes that over the past 30 years, therapies like acupuncture, laser therapy, Assisi loops, and herbal remedies have become vital tools in managing it.

Chronic inflammation: The vet prescribes an anti-inflammatory when your dog gets injured, but then also tells you that the chronic inflammation will never fully go away. The cycle begins: More anti-inflammatories to battle the inflammation caused by the diet choice - the classic Western medicine approach. The problem is not just about the endless use of anti-inflammatory drugs; it's also about the wrong diet approach. You cannot do the same thing over and over expecting a different outcome.

Why should you avoid using prescribed medications long-term? Many of these drugs, like aspirin, inhibit an enzyme that helps seal blood vessels. While plant-derived alternatives such as willow bark also affect this enzyme, their effects are temporary and reversible. In contrast, drugs like Metacam can cause irreversible changes, leaving the blood vessels in a persistently leaky state. The irony, as Dr. Marsden notes, is that the more you rely on anti-inflammatory drugs, the more likely you are to wake up with inflammation the next day. The best approach is to use these medications only as-needed – not as a daily habit.

Dr. Marsden emphasizes the importance of providing dogs with a nutritious diet that includes whole foods, balanced meat and vegetables, and herbal supplements to support healthy circulation. Focusing on these elements has led to remarkable improvements in joint health. By addressing the underlying cause of the initial injury, we can help keep dogs off anti-inflammatories in the long term.

The diet plays a crucial role in laying the foundation for proper vascular function, but it takes time to see results after making changes following an injury. In the meantime, physical therapies can provide immediate benefits.

While waiting for the dietary effects, it's important to fill the gap by using herbs and medications, if necessary.

Dr. Marsden suggests three classes of herbs for CCL injuries:

• **Endothelial support** herbs help counteract leaky vessel issues and endothelial dysfunction.

• **Anti-inflammatory** herbs reduce inflammation without heavily targeting specific enzymes.

• **Pain relief** herbs assist with pain management while supporting overall recovery.

You cannot out-surgery a poor diet. If you don't address the issue that caused the first cruciate tear, you should expect the second leg to tear as well.

By taking the time to heal the torn leg conservatively, you can also strengthen the other leg and reduce the risk of it failing over time.

Food For Thought

It's been a while since we last revisited the timeline. While it feels like a lot of time has passed, many of the events I'm discussing are actually happening simultaneously. Changes to Luce's diet were implemented right away. In the previous section, I provided some background to explain the reasoning behind my nutritional strategy for her. Let's take a quick look at the timeline to see where we stand since her injury.

The original injury occurred on August 19th, 2023. We visited the first vet the same day and saw our regular veterinarian on Monday, August 21st.

On August 24th, we went to the rehabilitation center for a consultation, where we decided to pursue conservative management instead of opting for surgery. Then, on August 28th, we had an appointment with Dr. Jana Froeling, a veterinarian specializing in Eastern medicine, who conducted a further assessment of Luce.

On September 9th, 2023, the rehab vet examined the injured knee. The results revealed not only a complete tear of the CCL but also that the meniscus had torn in two. It was determined that the meniscal tear likely occurred simultaneously with the CCL tear.

After the ultrasound, the final diagnosis included a full CCL tear, an iliopsoas strain, and a complete meniscal tear that appeared to be split into two equal halves. A physical examination confirmed a characteristic, consistent with a meniscal tear. At this point, we had a clear and thorough understanding of the injury's extent.

I then scheduled an appointment for October 2nd at My Pet's Brace clinic in Pennsylvania to have Luce measured and fitted for a custom brace for her injured leg. You'll find more details about this in the chapter on modalities.

We're now all caught up on our journey – it's been about a month since the injury occurred. At this point, it's important to discuss the choices I made regarding Luce's diet and supplementation. These changes were implemented right after the injury and have been a consistent part of her routine over the past month.

I had five goals in mind when I decided to adjust Luce's food and incorporate supplements into her diet:

1. Provide a bioavailable, species-appropriate diet made from high-quality human-grade ingredients with minimal processing and no artificial additives.

2. Manage her weight effectively.

3. Reduce inflammation.

4. Improve her mobility.

5. Heal the root cause of her injury while also promoting recovery and strengthening her body overall.

At the time of the injury, I was feeding Luce a hybrid diet consisting of a dehydrated base mix paired with raw, human-grade protein sourced from a local farm. I rotated her protein sources regularly - beef, duck, rabbit, and turkey – while keeping the base mix consistent. This diet was roughly 25% carbohydrates, primarily from starches and grains, which I felt was too high for her needs. Additionally, the vegetables and grains were not organic and were likely high in Glyphosate. The base mix contained many synthetic vitamins and minerals, and notably, no real bone.

Note: *The concern about glyphosate became very real when I had Luce's urine tested through a third-party lab. The results showed glyphosate levels 10x higher than what's considered acceptable for a 150-pound human. Considering Luce only weighed 30 pounds at the time, the levels were especially alarming.*

While 25% carbohydrates might seem low compared to kibble - which often contains around 60% - I felt it was necessary to reduce the carbohydrate content as much as possible to help minimize inflammation. Starchy carbohydrates convert into sugars, which can fuel inflammation, so I wanted to work smart rather than hard. My goal was to eliminate inflammatory foods from her diet while focusing on reducing the inflammation in her body. With this dietary change, I also hoped to eliminate the primary source of Glyphosate.

I decided to transition Luce to the least processed foods available to boost bioavailability, diversify ingredients in their whole-food form, eliminate synthetics, and lower carbohydrate intake—all while choosing components that would actively support healing. After thoroughly researching various options, I opted for commercially frozen raw food. I selected three companies to rotate based on their ingredient quality, caloric density, and sourcing: Viva Raw, Solutions Pet, and Green Juju. Each brand was chosen for its unique strengths, and by rotating them, I aimed to offer Luce the most balanced and beneficial nutrition possible.

As I mentioned earlier, Luce has a history of bilious vomiting. This happens when her stomach is empty for too long, acid builds up and she is nauseous and vomits only yellow tinged foamy stomach contents. To prevent this, I feed her daily portion in four smaller meals within 8 hours over the course of the day. This not only helps avoid vomiting but also prevents any sharp blood sugar highs or lows. Feeding within 8 hours also allows her to fast overnight and reap the benefits of that practice. As her body continues to heal, it's important to be prepared for unexpected increases in energy demands. Feeding her this way (4x/day) ensures she has a steady supply of fuel – supporting recovery without risking muscle breakdown.

I appreciate that Viva Raw avoids high-pressure pasteurization and steers clear of synthetic vitamins and minerals. It includes a source of real bone, features a single protein source, and contains just 1.3% carbohydrates. The company also provides a transparent, detailed nutritional analysis that's easy for anyone to access. Viva Raw is a raw dog food made from human-grade ingredients, including USDA-inspected meats from humanly raised animals, all free of hormones and antibiotics. The fruits and vegetables are non-GMO, organic, and sourced from the same farms that supply premium groceries stores. These plant ingredients also aligned with my healing goals for Luce, making it an ideal choice. Plus, the food is calorically dense, so I don't have to feed her large portions to ensure she gets everything she needs to maintain her health and continue thriving.

The second company I examined was Solutions Pet. Unlike Viva Raw, their food includes fermented elements, offering a natural way to incorporate probiotics into a pet's diet to aid digestion. I chose their beef and pork varieties. Solutions Pet takes pride in using no artificial ingredients, ensuring humane processing, organic ingredients, and eco-friendly packaging. They avoid high-pressure pasteurization (HPP). Their formulations contain a maximum of 3.45% carbohydrates. I also appreciated that they promptly provided their comprehensive third-party testing analysis when I inquired.

What set these formulas apart was their diverse mix of organ sources, including liver, kidney, and spleen. They also contained raw sheep's milk, real bone, gelatin, fermented okra, and duck eggs. This variety allowed me to broaden the ingredients supporting her healing journey. While some components, like ginger and cod liver oil, were similar to those in Viva Raw, the sourcing and quantities differed in each formula, enabling me to diversify the ingredients even further.

The last company I selected was Green Juju, known for its raw frozen food. Earlier in this book, I mentioned Luce's ongoing issues with vitamin D deficiency. Despite consuming the original dehydrated base mix with raw protein - containing ample vitamin D in the analysis - her body couldn't utilize it effectively. Even when I supplemented with synthetic vitamin D under my veterinarian's guidance, her levels would temporarily rise but never remain stable; each test showed she was deficient. This made me wonder if years of vitamin D deficiency played a role in her cruciate tear. I was determined to address this deficiency during her healing period with proper nutrition, which led me to choose this company's products. The liver in the dehydrated base mix was of lower quality and processed through dehydration into a powder form, whereas Green Juju's offerings are whole food products with limited ingredients, focusing on organ-based nutrition and excluding muscle meat (except for the heart). Like the other choices, Green Juju does not use any artificial ingredients.

The organ portfolio includes heart, liver, and kidney, all prepared using real bone and organic vegetables - specifically limited to kale and kelp. My goal in providing this food was to supply vitamin D in its raw, unprocessed form, with the hope that the body would absorb it more effectively from these nutrient-rich organs.

Green Juju's frozen raw food blends contain less than 3% net carbs. They're also grain-free, gluten-free, and free of fillers and preservatives. All their meats used are humanely processed and human-grade quality. Although Green Juju applies high-pressure pasteurization - which does slightly alter the nutritional profile - it doesn't significantly impact digestibility.

You'll notice that all three companies use only vegetable- and fruit-based carbohydrates in their products, completely avoiding grains. They also steer clear of excessive herbs or added nutrients aimed at detoxification or supplementation. This gives me the flexibility to tailor Luce's meals based on her specific needs. As we discussed earlier, the wrong carbohydrate choices can break down into sugars and contribute to inflammation. These diets give me the option to include grains when needed - I can choose a high-quality, non-GMO, organic grain, and I'm not locked into using it with every meal. I rotate these foods randomly every few days.

It's a Choice, Not a Chance

To heal ligament tears effectively, it's essential to focus on protein sources rich in the amino acid *leucine*. I chose lean meats like turkey and beef, as well as fatty fish such as salmon, sardines, and mackerel. Eggs and dairy products - including Greek yogurt and cottage cheese - are also excellent, providing the critical building blocks for collagen synthesis, the primary protein found in ligaments. Maintaining a steady intake of these protein sources throughout the day is key for optimal recovery.

Creatine supports ligament healing by promoting muscle strength and mass while minimizing muscle loss. It also aids in recovery following surgical procedures, helping prevent the muscle atrophy that often occurs after injury or immobilization. In addition, creatine may help reduce inflammation associated with muscle injuries and can play a supportive role in rehabilitation after joint surgeries like ACL reconstruction (Vandeweerd et al., 2012).

When it comes to animal-based creatine sources, wild game – such as venison, elk, buffalo, and bison - stands out. These meats typically contain fewer calories, less saturated fat, and more lean tissue compared than conventional meats. I've included them in my dog's diet to help build muscle strength, support mass gain, and promote recovery. The higher creatinine content may also contribute to inflammation control.

Protein diversity plays a crucial role for all the reasons mentioned above. As you explore formulas from different companies, pay close attention to the variety and quality of proteins they include.

Food Therapy: Feeding Your Dog with Traditional Chinese Veterinary Medicine Therapy (TCVM)

Food can either nourish and support health or contribute to deterioration and disease in the body. The better the nutrients we provide our dogs, the better their bodies will function.

One of the primary objectives during this healing journey was to minimize processed foods—avoiding sugars and dyes, and keeping carbohydrates to a bare minimum. Feeding real, whole foods is essential for full healing and addressing the root causes of injury, ultimately helping prevent further issues.

In Traditional Chinese Veterinary Medicine (TCVM), understanding a dog's body is framed through the lens of five elements: Wood, Fire, Earth, Metal, and Water. Each element corresponds to specific organs, emotions, seasons, and qualities. By examining the interconnections between these elements within the dog's body, practitioners can uncover and address imbalances.

During this process, I turned to food therapy. In Traditional Chinese Veterinary Medicine, every food carries its own energy. For example, proteins like venison, chicken, and lamb generate heat in the body, while certain fish, duck, and rabbit have a cooling effect that helps dispel excess heat.

Consider this: if you notice your dog moving to a cooler spot on the floor or panting excessively, feeding them a protein that cools the body and restores energetic balance might be a good idea. Conversely, if your dog is burrowing or consistently seeking out warm, cozy spots, adding a warming protein to their diet could help bring things back into balance.

Luce's injury generates a significant amount of heat in the body. When addressing inflammation or working to prevent arthritis, it's important to focus on a diet that doesn't contribute to that existing heat. "Arthritis" literally means joint inflammation. Joints are places where two bones meet, such as your elbow or knee. (National Institute of Arthritis and Musculoskeletal and Skin Diseases, 2022).

Think of it this way: if there's a small garbage can on fire next to your desk, you wouldn't want to pour gasoline on it and risk setting the whole building ablaze.

The seasonal rotation of proteins can help Luce stay in tune with nature. Incorporating warming foods into the diet during winter is beneficial, while cooling foods are more advantageous in summer.

Dogs dealing with inflammatory conditions, in particular, benefit from a cooling protein diet. From a Traditional Chinese Veterinary Medicine (TCVM) perspective, the goal is to reduce inflammation from within (McCarthy et al., 2007).

Food can play a significant role in warming or cooling the body, and it can also act as a Qi tonic to boost energy. In Traditional Chinese Veterinary Medicine (TCVM), Qi represents the vital energy of life. Enhancing energy levels is especially important during the healing process, when the body may feel depleted.

Common Qi tonics include meats like beef, chicken, rabbit, lamb, and tripe, along with vegetables like sweet potatoes and shiitake mushrooms. If you check the ingredients in Viva Raw, you'll notice shitake mushroom is one of them. When used in rotation, I can incorporate this ingredient into the overall diet - just not every day.

Stagnation is a key concept in TCVM, especially when addressing orthopedic injuries. Resolving stagnation is a priority; when the body is healing a region where blood may have pooled or become stagnant, it's important to include foods that promote blood movement and help clear that stagnation. Lamb, venison, crab, shrimp, ginger, and turmeric are just a few examples of foods that can be effective in this regard.

Down the Rabbit Hole

To understand the Chinese body clock, it's essential to grasp the concept of Qi, which represents the vital energy present in all living beings, including dogs. Qi is dynamic and constantly changing as it moves through the body and interacts with the environment.

Over a 24-hour period, Qi cycles through the dog's organ systems in 2-hour intervals, with one key function during sleep: Qi draws inward to help the body restore and rejuvenate.

One particularly important time frame is between 1 a.m. and 3 a.m., when the liver is believed to purify the blood. During these hours, the body begins its preparations for Qi to flow outward again.

The Chinese Medicine Body Clock illustrates when Qi is most potent in different organs throughout the day. By aligning your dog's activities with the natural rhythms of this energy, you can help them achieve greater balance and well-being. The clock is divided into 12 segments; each linked to a specific organ.

Qi flows between paired Yin and Yang organs, progressing from one to another. Each organ system also corresponds to distinct emotions, tastes, sense organs, and even seasons.

In my experience with Luce, I use this body clock to maximize her energy by timing her activities according to when her organs are most energetic. For example, I feed her a healthy breakfast between 7 a.m. and 9 a.m., when her stomach is functioning at its peak.

On the other hand, I avoid giving her dinner too late, as her stomach tends to be weaker in the evening. This mindful scheduling helps her feel her best throughout the day.

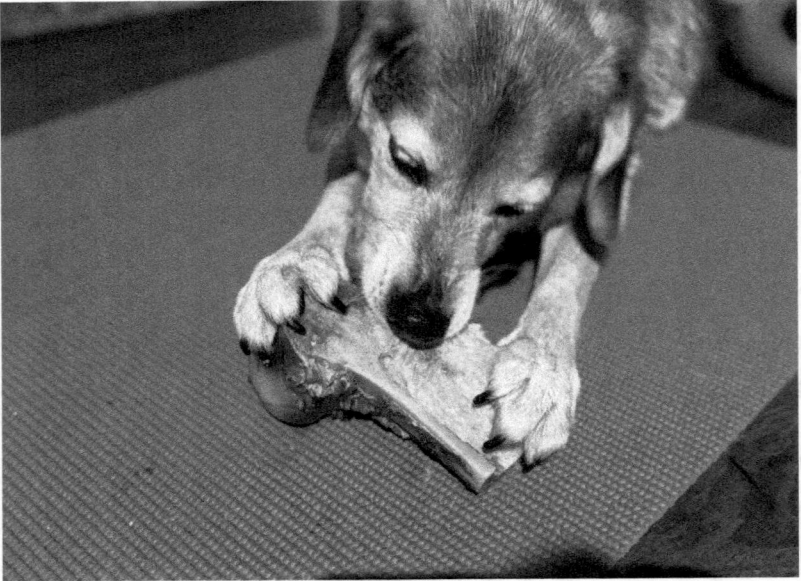

Luce enjoying a bone

The following table shows the organs that correspond to the 2-hour intervals of the Chinese body clock:

Chinese Body Clock – Organ Function by Time

2-Hour Interval	Organ	Peak Functionality
3:00 a.m. to 5:00 a.m.	Lungs	This period is when the lungs are at their peak energy, making it an ideal time to exercise, as opposed to later in the day
5:00 a.m. to 7:00 a.m.	Large Intestine	This period is thought to be the ideal time to give yourself enough time to honor the elimination function of the large intestine.
9:00 a.m. to 11:00 a.m.	Spleen	The spleen is thought to be linked to the stomach, which is responsible for receiving food and drink before ultimately fermenting them. During this period, it's believed that Qi is being propelled upward by the spleen.
11:00 a.m. to 1:00 p.m.	Heart	Because the heart represents peacefulness, it's essential to reduce stress during this period, according to those who follow the Chinese Body Clock.
1:00 p.m. to 3:00 p.m.	Small Intestine	Heavier meals are believed to be better tolerated during this period, as the Qi expands and begins to peak at midday.
3:00 p.m. to 5:00 p.m.	Bladder/Kidneys	It's believed that the kidney is responsible for containing Qi and is directly connected with the bladder. Together, they excrete unwanted waste materials from the body.
7:00 p.m. to 9:00 p.m.	Pericardium	The pericardium is believed to protect the heart. During this period, Qi is thought to be regulated to prevent symptoms such as nausea and vomiting.
9:00 p.m. to 11:00 p.m.	Triple Burner	The triple burner refers to the organ system as a whole, and this period is thought to be when it generates the most heat.
1:00 a.m. to 3:00 a.m.	Liver	Those who follow the Chinese Body Clock believe it's important to give your liver as little to process as possible during this period, allowing it to focus on its cleansing functions. This means eating your last meal of the day early and keeping it light.

According to Traditional Chinese Veterinary Medicine (TCVM), foods function similarly to herbs. They can be carefully chosen to tonify, cleanse, and regulate the body, helping to restore and maintain the balance between Yin and Yang. TCVM categorizes food based on its energetic effects, such as warming and nourishing or cooling and draining. While Western nutrition typically emphasizes calories, carbohydrates, fats, proteins, and vitamins, I applied TCVM principles to heal Luce's body energetically. It's important to note that orthopedic injuries are considered Yang conditions in this framework. By embracing the concept of the Chinese Body Clock, I can potentially make the most of my dog's specific organs and bodily functions when they're at their peak.

In summary, adaptive nutrition is a comprehensive approach to strategically feeding dogs with specific outcomes in mind. It's essential to consider various factors such as the season, the type of injury, the dog's characteristics, breed, age, and any additional health issues. Moreover, the environment, mental well-being, spiritual fulfillment, energy flow within the body, timing of therapies, ingredient choices, sourcing practices, and the time, adaptability and patience required to observe changes and adjust also play crucial roles.

Since nutrition serves as the cornerstone of your dog's conservative healing journey, I highly recommend enlisting the help of a certified canine nutritionist. They can guide you effectively and become integral to your dog's rehabilitation team. It's a worthwhile investment for your pet's well-being.

Chapter 4: You Are Crushing It!

In the United States, many pet parents are turning to supplements to help maintain - or improve - their dogs' health. These products, which come in various forms like pills, powders, and liquids, are widely available without a prescription. You probably have a collection of vitamins, powders, and "Super Foods" in your cabinet that you've gathered over the years. The promise of optimized health for our dogs - sold by supplement companies, influencers, and the wellness industry - can be hard to resist.

However, the use of dog supplements comes with both advantages and disadvantages. On the positive side, they can fill nutritional gaps – especially in highly processed, homemade, or insufficient raw diets - improve health outcomes, enhance performance, and offer convenience. Supplements can help pets meet their daily nutrient needs when their regular diet falls short. Some may lower the risk of chronic illnesses, improve joint mobility, boost cognitive function, and strengthen the immune system. Products like creatine or protein powders can also support athletic performance. For busy pet parents, supplements offer a practical way to provide essential nutrients without making major changes to their dogs' diets.

On the flip side, it's important not to overlook the potential drawbacks of giving supplements to our dogs. One of the biggest concerns is over-consumption - too much of a supplement can lead to toxicity, intolerances, or other health problems. The dietary supplement industry is also largely unregulated, which means some products may contain unsafe or ineffective ingredients. Certain supplements can interact with prescription or over-the-counter medications, potentially causing harmful side effects. Many manufacturers make exaggerated or unproven claims about their products, adding to the confusion. And, of course, cost is another consideration - high-quality supplements can be expensive.

Lastly, supplements may not be necessary if your dog is already eating a bioavailable, species appropriate, balanced, nutritious diet.

From the outset, I want to emphasize the importance of consulting a nutritionist and your veterinarian before introducing any supplements to your dog's regimen. It's essential to check with both, as your vet can advise you on any contraindications related to medications or underlying health conditions. At the same time, a certified canine nutritionist may have more expertise in herbal remedies, Chinese medicine, or homeopathic options. As a responsible pet owner, you must assemble a comprehensive healthcare team for your dog, including experts in all pertinent fields.

When selecting supplements, prioritize reputable brands that follow good manufacturing practices. Just because two products contain similar ingredients doesn't guarantee comparable quality. A side-by-side label comparison won't reveal where the ingredients were sourced or whether the manu-facturer uses a rigorous quality assurance and testing program. Familiarize yourself with the National Animal Supplement Council (NASC) and look for its quality seal. If you're investing in supplements, aim for those that carry the yellow quality seal—this indicates the company has undergone a thorough third-party audit and meets strict compliance with NASC's quality standards. Companies can't simply buy this seal; they have to earn it.

Not every supplement brand has been evaluated by the NASC, but that doesn't mean the product should be dismissed outright. Look for brands that provide third-party testing reports, and consider reading consumer reviews. Some supplements may be contaminated with toxins, heavy met-als, or fillers, which could interfere with the healing process you're hoping to support for your dog. Inappropriate ingredients can overwork the liver and immune system, to leading to inflammation in the body—something we definitely want to avoid.

Many pet owners tend to overestimate the benefits of supplements. Just because a product claims to be 'natural' doesn't automatically ensure it's safe for every dog. Make sure to scrutinize the supplement label and fol-low the recommended dosages. Proper storage is also crucial to prevent spoilage or contamination. And remember - supplements should never replace a healthy, balanced diet.

Based on my experience with supplements, I will always advocate for whole foods when possible. While the chemical makeup of a vitamin in pill form may be similar to that found in food, dogs typically absorb nutrients from whole foods more effectively. Real food offers not just single nutrients but a diverse array of vitamins, trace minerals, enzymes, and proteins that work synergistically in your dog's body. The effectiveness of a supplement depends on its quality, your dog's diet, gut health, and several other factors

- often resulting in ingredients being expelled as waste rather than being absorbed and used effectively.

Supplements can help address nutritional gaps, especially for dogs dealing with health issues or recovering from injuries. Using them for specific purposes is key, and taking breaks allows the body to adjust to its new normal. No single supplement brand should be given to your dog long-term. Rotation and diversity can surprise the body and reinvigorate absorption pathways. You can simplify the supplement process by first providing your dog with the most nutrient-dense food available, then assessing what else is needed. Quality supplements can be expensive - something we often overlook when evaluating our spending on our dogs.

You can't supplement your way out of a poor diet.

Fuel Your Dog's Body, Feed Their Soul

I modified Luce's diet to maintain a healthy balance of protein and fat while reducing carbohydrates. I selected three brands of commercially prepared frozen raw diets, focusing on ingredients that supported my goal of reducing inflammation and promoting a healthy weight - all while ensuring she received the nutrients needed to thrive and heal. Alongside her diet, I incorporated a range of supplements into my Adaptive Nutrition plan, introducing each at different times and for specific reasons.

After an injury, one of the key supplements introduced was **FMT(Fecal Microbiota Transplant) Capsules**, aimed at restoring gut balance and improving nutrient absorption. An imbalanced gut (dysbiosis) can hinder digestion and reduce the effectiveness of food and supplements. A

30-day course of **Legacy Biome FMT Capsules** was used, sourced from raw-fed, plant-rich diet donor dogs raised in eco-friendly, chemical-free environments. These donor dogs are well cared for, with integrative health practices and minimal medical interventions. Pre- and post-treatment gut microbiome tests showed significant improvement in Luce's gut health, aiding inflammation control, healing, and nutrient uptake.

Once we achieved the goals tied to those supplements, we took breaks from them. To keep track, I created a spreadsheet detailing every supplement I gave her, listing the names and all the ingredients, including their respective quantities. I color-coded this chart to easily monitor the total amounts of each ingredient across all supplements. The chart allowed me to monitor how much - and how often - she received a particular nutrient.

We Must Go Back to Go Forward

On August 18, 2023, when Luce first injured herself, I shared some immediate first aid measures I took to help manage her pain, stress, and discomfort. I started with cryotherapy right away to reduce pain and inflammation, and also provided homeopathic remedies to support her through the stress and discomfort.

Many of you may not be familiar with homeopathic medicine, so let's take a moment to clarify what it entails. Homeopathy is an alternative medicine system that uses highly diluted substances to treat various ailments. Since these supplements fall outside of Luce's diet and weren't prescribed by a veterinarian, I've included them in this chapter.

Homeopathy was developed in the late 18th century by German physician Samuel Hahnemann, who believed that the body can heal itself (TNN, 2011). He proposed that small doses of substances that produce similar symptoms could stimulate this healing process. Homeopathic remedies are created by diluting a substance in water or alcohol and then vigorously shaking it. This procedure is repeated multiple times, resulting in only minimal levels of the original substance. Common homeopathic remedies include Arnica for bruises and injuries, Aconitum for colds and flu, Nux vomica for headaches and indigestion, and Opium for pain and anxiety.

Homeopathy is based on the principle of "like cures like." This means that a substance causing specific symptoms in a healthy dog can help relieve those same symptoms in a sick dog (National Center for Complementary and Integrative Health, n.d.). Homeopathic products are derived from a variety of sources: plants like red onion, arnica (mountain herb), poison ivy, belladonna (deadly nightshade), and stinging nettle; minerals such as white arsenic; and even animal products like crushed whole bees.

The process begins by crushing and dissolving these substances in a liquid, typically grain alcohol or lactose, followed by vigorous shaking. This creates what is known as the "mother tincture." Homeopaths then dilute this tincture further by mixing it with alcohol or lactose in ratios like 1 part to 10 (designated as "x") or 1 part to 100 ("c"). After shaking, these diluted mixtures achieve a 1x or 1c concentration.

Homeopaths often dilute these tinctures even further, such as 2 times (2x or 2c), 3 times (3x or 3c), and so on. Many professional homeopaths prefer to use much higher dilutions, operating under the belief that the more diluted a substance is, the more powerful its healing effects become.

Homeopathic products are commonly available as sugar pellets designed to dissolve under the tongue, but they can also be found in various forms such as ointments, gels, drops, creams, and tablets.

One of the key features of homeopathy is that treatments are individualized, tailored to suit each person's unique needs. It's not unusual for individuals with the same condition to receive different remedies. Homeopathy uses its own diagnostic system, assigning treatments based on specific clinical patterns of signs and symptoms, which can differ from those recognized in conventional medicine (Bornhöft et al., 2006).

Homeopathic remedies primarily aim to activate the body's natural healing processes. Homeopaths believe that physical ailments often have underlying mental and emotional components. As a result, a homeopathic diagnosis considers not only physical symptoms, such as fever, but also the dog's emotional and psychological state—like anxiety or restlessness—and their overall constitution. This constitution includes traits like creativity, initiative, persistence, concentration, sensitivity, and stamina. Identifying the proper remedy for a dog's condition involves taking all these aspects into account.

Homeopathic medicine is often used as a complementary or alternative approach to traditional treatments.

One dose of homeopathic remedy usually consists of 1 to 6 pellets (depending on the size of the pellet); the instructions on the container will indicate the target dose. The exact amount isn't critical - just tap the container and use the number of pellets that fall out.

When taking homeopathic remedies, follow these rules:

- Never touch the pellets with your hands.

- Carefully tap or shake the pellets into the cap or a dry spoon. If extra pellets spill out, do not put them back into the container - either use or discard them.

- Place the pellets in the mouth, under the tongue.

- Let the pellets dissolve in the mouth for at least 30 seconds.

- Do not take anything with the remedy or put anything else in the mouth for at least 15 minutes before and after taking it - including water.

- Do not expose the open container to strong odors or other open remedies.

- Take as directed on the container.

When the injury occurred, I gave Luce a homeopathic remedy called *Your Go 2* from Adored Beast Apothecary. I always carry this tincture with me for emergencies. *Your Go 2* is a first-response homeopathic blend designed to address pain, shock, trauma, fever, inflammation, and more - right from the onset.

This product contains two key homeopathic remedies: Arnica 200C (Knuesel et al., 2002) and Aconite 200C. *Arnica Montana* is an herb found primarily in Siberia and Central Europe. The entire plant is used in homeopathy, and its healing properties stem from unique anti-inflammatory compounds like helenalin and flavonoids.

Arnica is especially effective for trauma, bruising, pain, swelling, and inflammation, and even alleviating fear. Aconite, or *Aconitum Napellus*, is frequently recommended for acute conditions and sudden attacks. Its effects are extensive, influencing nearly all areas of the body.

Aconite is indicated for pain, hypersensitivity, fear, trauma, and fever. By administering these two remedies promptly—despite not yet knowing the full extent of her injury—I was able to offer an immediate first aid response that energetically supported her body. One of the major benefits of homeopathic remedies is that they can complement conventional treatments without causing adverse interactions, making them a valuable addition to any first aid kit (Oberbaum et al., 2003).

Homeopathy works by closely aligning with your dog's specific symptom profile following an injury, taking into account important factors like their predisposition to injuries, past weaknesses, or tendency for slow recovery. A well-matched remedy can significantly enhance the healing process. When used for acute injuries, this often means that symptoms like stiffness, pain, and inflammation diminish quicker, helping your dog regain full strength swiftly and without complications.

Additionally, homeopathy is a valuable option for addressing the long-term effects of sports injuries. I've encountered numerous cases where an old injury didn't heal properly and continued to affect a dog's overall health for years. Through homeopathic treatment, I can often resolve these lingering issues and underlying vulnerabilities, helping your dog to return to the activities it truly loves.

After visiting the veterinarian on Friday, just hours after the injury, Luce was prescribed Carprofen and Gabapentin. Carprofen is a non-steroidal anti-inflammatory drug (NSAID) commonly used to relieve pain and inflammation in animals. While effective, it carries a range of potential side effects, including hepatotoxicity, which is more likely during the first three weeks of treatment and with prolonged use. To help manage Luce's pain and inflammation, I gave her Carprofen for two days—Saturday and Sunday—while waiting for an appointment with my regular vet. At that point, I still didn't have a full diagnosis; I only knew she didn't have a fracture and that the issue was related to her knee.

Gabapentin is another medication that veterinarians often prescribe to treat pain, seizures, and anxiety in dogs. It's worth noting that Gabapentin was originally developed for humans, and its use in veterinary medicine is considered "off-label," meaning the FDA hasn't explicitly approved it for pets. The primary side effect to watch for is sedation, which can vary from dog to dog. I decided to hold off on using the Gabapentin for now and opted for some alternative therapies instead to manage her pain. Still, I kept it on hand in case her condition worsened over the weekend.

Here's what I gave Luce alongside the Carprofen over the weekend:

- **Arnica** - 4x/day; started with 30C, then went to 200C, then 1M, and back to 200C.

- **Ruta** - 30C

- **Rhus Tox** - 30C

- **Jump 4 Joynts** (*Adored Beast Apothecary Tincture*) - Contains Arnica, Calendula, Symphytum, and Ruta

- **Vitamin C** (*RX Vitamins for Pets*) - 500 mg, 1x/day

- **Vitamin D** -1000 mg/day

- **Phyto Synergy** (*Adored Beast Apothecary*) - 100% Pure Phytoplankton, 1/16 Tsp/day

- **Doggone Pain (DGP)** –

  - Marine Collagen Extract - 300 mg

  - Boswellia Extract - 30 mg (Reichling et al., 2004)

  - Corydalis Root - 25 mg

  - Wheatgrass - 20 mg

  - Turmeric - 15 mg

  - Feverfew Extract - 6 mg

- ○ Celery Seed Extract - 3 mg

- ○ Proprietary blend (Mucopolysaccharide Complex, Malt Extract, Wild Rosella, Capsicum Extract, Aniseed Myrtle, Mountain Pepper) – 130 mg

- ○ Proprietary enzyme blend (Bromelain 2400 GDU and Papain 6000) – 60 mg

Let's explore why I selected these supplements as the primary support for Luce. I didn't view the right leg as the only injured limb - I also considered how her neck, shoulders, back, and left leg were affected by the injury. It's vital to support the entire body holistically rather than just zeroing in on the injured area. This book will help you understand the importance of addressing compensatory muscle activation and the adjustments that occur in the neck, back, hips, and opposite leg. This holistic approach to the dog's entire body will be a key theme throughout this book. Maintaining balance—physically, mentally, and spiritually—is essential to facilitate true healing.

The "RRA protocol" is commonly recommended for sore muscles and joints. It's a popular homeopathic combination of **Rhus Tox**, **Ruta Grav**, and **Arnica**. This blend can be especially helpful for treating sprains, strains, aches, stiffness, and even the bumps and bruises that result from injuries or accidents.

The remedies in this RRA combination are particularly effective for managing arthritis symptoms. They specifically target issues involving ligaments, tendons, and muscles, making them especially beneficial for athletic or highly active dogs that experience overexertion. Additionally, RRA can aid in recovery from accidents, injuries, and post-surgical situations. It can also enhance the effectiveness of chiropractic, osteopathic, or physiotherapy treatments by helping to ease any lingering aftereffects. You can safely use it alongside conventional pain medications for added support.

ARNICA

Bruises and Swelling: Homeopathic arnica is commonly used to minimize bruising and swelling, especially following injuries or surgical procedures.

Pain Relief: It can help relieve pain associated with muscle aches, sprains, and various orthopedic conditions.

Osteoarthritis: Topical arnica gels or creams may reduce pain and stiffness and improve function in individuals suffering with osteoarthritis - potentially offering results comparable to ibuprofen.

Recovery After Surgery: Specific homeopathic remedies are often used post-surgery to ease pain, reduce swelling, and support smoother recovery - especially after procedures involving tendons, cartilage, joints, and bone coverings.

Sprains and Lacerations: Arnica is also valued for its ability to help stop bleeding and reduce the severity of sprains and lacerations.

RUTA GRAVEOLENS

This remedy is particularly beneficial for injuries involving tendons, ligaments, and cartilage. **Ruta Graveolens** often proves effective in treating connective tissue injuries caused by excessive physical activity, which can lead to lameness or weakness. It's also valuable for injuries to the **periosteum**, the protective layer surrounding bones.

Primarily associated with physical symptoms from injuries, strains, and even certain eye conditions, **Ruta graveolens** is frequently recommended for sprains, strains, and damage to tendons, ligaments, and the periosteum.

Individuals who benefit from this remedy often report stiffness, soreness, and a sensation of bruising in the affected areas. They also tend to prefer cool compresses for relief.

Ruta is commonly used for joint-related conditions, especially those affecting the **wrists, ankles**, and **back** injuries. It's also employed to address **eyestrain, fatigue**, and **bruised or strained eyes**.

Overall, Ruta graveolens can be beneficial for symptoms marked by stiffness, aching pain, weakness of tendons or ligaments, and sensitivity to touch or pressure.

RHUS TOX

Rhus Toxicodendron, commonly known as **Rhus Tox**, is one of the most effective first-aid remedies available, known for its wide range of applications. It's particularly helpful for **sports injuries**, especially those caused by **repetitive strain** and **overexertion**. One key characteristic of Rhus tox is that symptoms tend to **worsen with rest** and at the start of movement, but **improve with continued activity**. Discomfort often intensifies in **cold, damp conditions**, while **warmth** - through bathing or hot applications – typically brings relief.

This remedy is beneficial for various traumatic injuries, including **sprains and strains**, often easing the associated **stiffness** and **burning sensations**.

JUMP FOR JOINTS from *Adored Beast Apothecary*

On the other hand, **Jump for Joints** from Adored Beast Apothecary is another excellent option in my homeopathic toolkit. This tincture blends familiar remedies with new ingredients that support the body in various ways. The unique sourcing and dosage of these homeopathies allows me to diversify and rotate what I administer, enhancing the overall treatment regimen for better results.

The levels of arnica in this tincture effectively reduce inflammation and bruising. This arnica extract includes selenium and arnica ash, which are rich in manganese. These elements act as powerful antioxidants, with manganese playing a key role in maintaining healthy bones, facilitating wound healing, and aiding in the metabolism of proteins, cholesterol, and carbohydrates. This source of arnica, combined with other beneficial plant compounds, may offer strong support during the healing process.

Calendula, known for its high flavonoid content, is a plant-based antioxidant that helps protect cells from damage caused by free radicals. Its use is well-documented in fighting inflammation, viruses, and bacterial infections. When applied topically, calendula promotes faster wound healing by increasing blood flow and oxygen to the injured area. The dried petals included in this tincture are especially effective for treating burns, bruises, cuts, and minor infections.

Symphytum is a homeopathic remedy commonly recommended for injuries affecting bones, cartilage, tendons, and the periosteum. It promotes callus formation and supports the healing of broken bones, earning it the nickname "knit bone" for its remarkable ability to mend fractures quickly. Some vitamin formulations are also vital for addressing fractures and injuries to the bone and the periosteum - the connective tissue that surrounds it.

Ruda, found in this tincture, is indicated for alleviating soreness in bones, tendons, joints, and cartilage. Rudograviolins are beneficial for treating sprains, strains, bruises, and pulled ligaments. They are especially effective for addressing rheumatic and connective tissue issues that often result from chronic overuse, strain, or injury to joints or tendons.

VITAMIN C

Vitamin C plays a pivotal role in maintaining orthopedic health and supporting injury recovery by promoting bone formation, collagen production, and effective wound healing. It may also help reduce the risk of conditions like complex regional pain syndrome (CRPS).

In dogs, Complex Regional Pain Syndrome (CRPS) is a chronic pain condition that can occur after an injury or trauma, particularly to the extremities.

It's characterized by intense pain, swelling, changes in skin temperature and color, and decreased mobility, while not as well-studied in dogs as in humans, the symptoms and potential causes are similar, suggesting the possibility of CRPS in canine patients.

To delve deeper into Vitamin C's benefits:

- **Bone Healing and Formation:** Vitamin C, also known as ascorbic acid, plays a crucial role in the growth and repair of various tissues - particularly bones. It promotes bone formation by supporting the differentiation of osteoblasts and regulating gene expression in hypertrophic chondrocytes. Additionally, vitamin C has been linked to enhanced bone density, which may reduce the risk hip fractures. Animal research also indicates that vitamin C supplementation might boost bone healing and formation.

- **Collagen Synthesis and Soft Tissue Repair:** Vitamin C is essential for producing collagen, a key protein in skin, cartilage, tendons, ligaments, and blood vessels. It not only aids in the healing of tendons and ligaments but also helps mitigate oxidative stress, which can lead to fibrosis and tissue damage. Some studies suggest that it can speed up bone healing after fractures, promote the synthesis of type I collagen, and decrease oxidative stress levels.

- **Wound Healing:** Vitamin C is essential at every stage of wound healing. It plays a key role in neutrophil apoptosis and clearance during the inflammatory phase. As healing progresses into the proliferative phase, vitamin C contributes to collagen synthesis, maturation, secretion, and breakdown - which is vital for proper tissue repair.

- **Complex Regional Pain Syndrome (CRPS):** Some studies suggest that vitamin C supplementation may reduce the risk of developing CRPS, a condition marked by chronic pain and swelling following injury. A meta-analysis of randomized controlled trials found that oral vitamin C intake reduced the likelihood of CRPS type I in orthopedic patients.

- **Other Potential Benefits:** Vitamin C may also help reduce inflammation and swelling --which is particularly beneficial for injuries like sprains and strains that cause discomfort and pain. Research indicates that vitamin C supplementation improves functional outcomes and decreases postoperative pain after orthopedic surgeries.

VITAMIN D

Vitamin D is another crucial nutrient for orthopedic health and recovery. A deficiency can negatively affect bone density, fracture healing, and muscle strength. Supplementation may be beneficial for those at increased risk of non-union fractures.

Here's a more comprehensive overview of the role vitamin D plays in orthopedic injuries and overall health:

Bone Health and Fracture Healing: Vitamin D is essential for maintaining bone health and calcium balance – both critical for effective fracture healing and for preventing conditions like osteoporosis. A deficiency can lead to slower healing, a higher risk of fractures, and an increased risk of non-union, where a fracture fails to heal correctly.

Muscle Strength and Neuromuscular Function: Low vitamin D levels can impair muscle function, increasing the risk of falls and reduce mobility after orthopedic procedures. As I've mentioned, Luce has consistently shown a slight deficiency in vitamin D, confirmed by testing. That's why it's important not to start supplementation without proper testing first.

Research shows that vitamin D deficiency is common among orthopedic patients. Supplementation can be especially helpful for those at higher risk. I recommend regularly monitoring vitamin D levels and considering supplementation for dogs with deficiencies. Some studies also suggest that vitamin D may support post-operative recovery and improve musculoskeletal health.

PHYTO SYNERGY from *Adored Beast Apothecary*

Phyto Synergy (from *Adored Beast Apothecary*) is made from 100% pure marine phytoplankton, which is highly bioavailable to dogs. This single-celled organism delivers essential nutrients, including trace minerals, chlorophyll, essential amino acids, EPA fatty acids, protein, carotenoids, antioxidants, and more. It plays a vital role in nourishing the cellular structure.

Research shows that phytoplankton can reduce muscle damage and help maintain performance during repeated exercise in humans. While it might not seem like an obvious choice, I introduced it early in Luce's healing journey. In sports performance, an athlete's ability to sustain high levels of exertion, technical skill, sound decision-making, and psychological resilience is crucial. A decline in any of these areas can signal fatigue – often worsened by an imbalance between recovery and exertion.

Orthopedic injuries place immense stress on the body – stress that rest alone may not fully relieve. Oxidative stress, in particular, can lead to functional impairments. Since we can't change the demands of healing and injury, I focused on improving Luce's recovery and resilience with antioxidant-rich phytoplankton. My aim was to support muscle function recovery and overall performance. Numerous studies have demonstrated that antioxidant supplementation can significantly reduce oxidative stress, offering strong protection against muscle damage.

DOG GONE PAIN (DGP)

When I began using Dog Gone Pain (DGP), I had already stopped using Carprofen after just two days. Instead, I turned to herbs and homeopathic remedies as an alternate to NSAIDs, believing this approach would be more effective over the long term.

Dog Gone Pain, or DGP, is a nutraceutical made from naturally occurring substances known for their medicinal properties. It's produced in Australia at a facility approved by the TGA, the country's equivalent of the U.S. FDA. According to the manufacturer, the herbs in DGP are cultivated using standardized growing methods to ensure consistent efficacy year after year. Moreover, each ingredient is labeled "human grade" and is grown without pesticides or herbicides.

DGP provides a rich array of anti-inflammatory herbs that support multiple bodily systems—respiratory, circulatory, digestive, thermoregulation, liver, and gall bladder—all of which can become compromised as dogs age. This could explain why many pet owners report a revitalizing effect in their dogs when administering DGP.

Each tablet contains a unique blend of native Australian edible herbs, along with compounds traditionally used in European and other medical practices, including:

• **Feverfew**, known for its anti-inflammatory properties and pain relief

• **Celery seed**, which acts as an all-around calming agent and anti-inflammatory

• **Boswellia**, recognized as a potent anti-inflammatory and analgesic

• **Bromelain** and **papain**, both serving as digestive aids

• **Corydalis**, a tonic beneficial for the circulatory system

• **Cayenne**, which promotes gastrointestinal health

• **Wheatgrass**, packed with nutrients and minerals

• **Turmeric**, a potent anti-inflammatory and digestive support

In addition to its other benefits, DGP is rich in essential minerals like calcium, magnesium, phosphorus, and zinc - all of which are vital for maintaining bone health. It also contains shark cartilage, sourced without harmful solvents, making it an excellent source of chondroitin sulfate and other glycosaminoglycans that support cartilage repair.

The manufacturer advises, *"If your dog is currently on any medication, consult your veterinarian before starting DGP."* This consultation is important because the enzymes in the supplement may affect how medications – such as antibiotics, anticoagulants, and NSAIDs - are absorbed.

Additionally, several ingredients have anti-inflammatory properties that may enhance the blood-thinning effects of anticoagulant drugs.

I introduced this combination of supplements to Luce during the first week following her injury. We visited our regular vet that Monday, just two days after the incident, and a tear was confirmed.

At that point, there was no indication from the vet of possible meniscus involvement or an iliopsoas strain; that understanding came later during our visit with the rehabilitative vet, Dr. Katherine Johnson.

If you take a closer look at all the supplements I was using, you'll see that I was proactively supporting those injuries - even though I was unaware of them at the time.

The first week felt like it dragged on forever. But remember, this section is solely focused on our nutritional strategy. In the next chapter, I'll dive into the physical therapy techniques and various modalities that supported her recovery journey.

Keeping the Relationship Flexible

As we entered week two, our routine included regular visits with Dr. Katherine Johnson, Dr. Courtney Belden and Dr. Jana Froeling. Ten days after the injury, our focus was shifting toward fostering functional scar tissue at the knee, helping the iliopsoas muscle relax and stop spasming, effectively managing inflammation, and ensuring that Luce stayed active.

To support Luce's recovery, Dr. Jana Froeling recommended two combinations of Chinese herbs for her to take consistently. Unlike Western medicine, which often targets symptoms and specific diseases, Chinese herbal medicine—rooted in Traditional Chinese Medicine (TCM)—emphasizes holistic wellness and restoration of balance to the body's energy, or Qi.

Here's a more detailed comparison between Western Medicine and Traditional Chinese Medicine (TCM):

Underlying Philosophy:

Western Medicine operates on scientific principles, with a strong focus on identifying and treating specific diseases or conditions. In contrast, **TCM** is grounded in ancient Chinese philosophy, emphasizing the interconnectedness of the body and the critical importance of maintaining balance and harmony.

Approach to Diagnosis and Treatment:

Western Medicine relies on diagnostic tools such as blood tests and imaging to pinpoint the source of the problem, followed by targeted medications or procedures to treat it. Meanwhile, **TCM** takes a holistic approach - considering the patient's overall health, lifestyle, emotional state, and symptoms to detect imbalances and recommend personalized herbal formulas or other therapeutic techniques.

Herbal Formulas:

In **Western Medicine**, practitioners often choose single-ingredient medications or supplements designed to address specific symptoms or conditions. Conversely, **TCM** uses complex herbal formulas that combine multiple herbs to correct imbalances and support overall well-being.

Focus:

While **Western Medicine** primarily targets diseases or symptoms, **TCM** aims to restore balance and promote holistic health and wellness by addressing root causes rather than just alleviating symptoms.

Examples of TCM Therapies:

Notable **TCM** therapies include *Acupuncture* (inserting thin needles at specific points on the body to stimulate energy flow), *Herbal Medicine* (plant-based remedies to restore balance and healing), and *Dietary Advice* (emphasizing specific foods that support health and balance).

The first herbal remedy we tried was **Jin Tang Body Sore**. We chose the powder version instead of the capsules. This herbal therapy is designed to relieve arthritis pain, particularly in dogs. Its goal is to nourish the yin and promote the smooth flow of *Qi*, which may help calm and balance energy throughout the body.

Ingredients and Their Actions:

- **Dang Gui:** Activates blood flow, resolves stasis, and alleviates stagnation.

- **Yan Hu Suo:** Promotes the movement of *Qi* and blood, helps resolve stasis, and relieves stagnation.

- **Chi Shao:** Eases stagnation and cools the blood.

- **Chuan Xiong:** Alleviates stagnation and stimulates blood circulation.

- **Du Huo:** Helps relieve stagnation while dispelling wind-damp conditions.

- **Mo Yao:** Promotes blood movement and eases stagnation.

- **Qiang Huo:** Alleviates stagnation and stimulates blood flow.

- **Ru Xiang:** Enhances blood movement and relieves stagnation.

- **Bu Gu Zhi:** Supports the back and tonifies *Yang* energy.

- **Chuan Niu Xi:** Benefits bones and limbs.

- **Du Zhong:** Strengthens the back and tonifies Yang energy.

- **Hong Hua:** Breaks down blood stasis and alleviates stagnation.

- **Ji Xue Teng:** Nourishes the blood.

- **Tao Ren:** Breaks down blood stasis and helps relieve stagnation.

- **Tu Si Zi:** Nourishes the kidneys and liver.

- **Yin Yang Huo:** Tonifies Kidney *Yang* and *Yin*

The second herbal remedy from traditional Chinese medicine is **Concentrated Tendon and Ligament**. This formula is designed to nourish the liver, yin, and blood while strengthening the tendons and ligaments.

Ingredients and Their Actions:

- **Sang Zhi:** Soothes the limbs.

- **Yin Yang Huo:** Nourishes both Kidney *Yang* and *Yin*.

- **Dang Gui:** Enriches the Blood.

- **Bai Shao Yao:** Nurtures Blood and Yin while calming Liver *Yang*.

- **Chuan Niu Xi:** Supports the Kidney and benefits the knees.

- **Chuan Xiong:** Promotes blood circulation and helps resolve stagnation.

- **Gou Qi Zi:** Nourishes Liver Yin and Blood.

- **Gui Zhi:** Activates the channels and invigorates the limbs.

- **Shan Zhu Yu:** Provides nourishment to Liver Yin.

- **Shu Di Huang:** Enriches Blood and Yin.

- **Bu Gu Zhi:** Supports both Kidney *Yang* and *Yin*.

- **Wu Jia Pi:** Benefits the ligaments and tendons.

This blend of ingredients works synergistically to support overall joint health and vitality.

Woofs of Affirmation

I decided to incorporate Eastern Medicine alongside Western Medicine to help Luce on her healing journey. Why limit yourself? The only reason limits exist is because of what we don't yet know. Well - that's why you bought this book. I am sharing everything with you so you can expand your knowledge and help your dog by staying open to other ways of thinking.

My goal is to get Luce as close to 100% healed as possible. I'm using every tool in my toolkit to make that happen. Chinese herbal medicine has evolved and matured over centuries. It's rooted in the core principles of Chinese philosophy, particularly the concepts of *Yin* and *Yang* and the *Five Elements*. These ideas emphasize the importance of balance and harmony within the body and recognize the interconnectedness of all living things. At the heart of this system is *Qi* - the vital energy that flows through our bodies and the universe, linking us to everything around us.

I call my approach to nutrition *Adaptive Nutrition* - a highly personalized method tailored to the individual needs of every dog. In much the same way, Chinese herbal medicine honors the uniqueness of each dog, recognizing that no two are alike. Practitioners of this ancient discipline take a comprehensive view of healing, focusing not only on symptoms but also the underlying causes of illness. This holistic approach – one that nurtures the body, mind, and spirit - is a cornerstone of Chinese herbal medicine and aligns perfectly with my supplement strategy.

Everything I am doing is happening in tandem. This isn't a neat, linear strategic plan – it's uncomfortably agile.

Let me explain what I mean by "agile". The mindset behind agile management is a flexible, iterative approach that emphasizes collaboration, continuous feedback, and the ability to adapt to changing needs. It breaks a strategy into smaller, manageable cycles called *sprints*. This methodology is built to flex and shift in response to evolving circumstances, which makes it ideal for something as dynamic as injury recovery.

It also means prioritizing open collaboration and communication with everyone on Luce's rehab team. This approach is constantly evaluated and refined based on Luce's responses and the lessons we learn along the way.

At this stage of Luce's physical rehabilitation therapy, she had started to incorporate side stretches and elevated sit-to-stands into her routine. Additionally, she was doing forward and backward bicycles with my assistance and using the water treadmill twice a week.

Now that she was engaged in more active movement, I adjusted the original supplemental strategy to better support the management of pain, soreness, stiffness, and mobility. Since Luce wasn't on a joint supplement before her injury, I introduced her to Jope.

Jope provides a balanced combination of essential ingredients that promote joint health in dogs. Research suggests that UC-II® is more effective than traditional glucosamine. Several studies have shown that UC-II® is 59% more effective than chondroitin and glucosamine in reducing pain and discomfort in dogs.

One study involving 35 dogs found that UC-II® could alleviate joint pain by 81%. Not only did it outperform glucosamine and chondroitin, but noticeable improvements began within just 30 days and continued for up to 150 days (Gupta et al., 2012).

UC-II®, which consists of undenatured type II collagen, works through a unique mechanism known as oral tolerance. When UC-II® reaches the digestive system, its three-dimensional structure is recognized by Peyer's patches, a component of the immune system. This, in turn, activates regulatory immune cells known as T-cells. These T-cells release anti-inflammatory molecules called cytokines, which help preserve cartilage collagen from breaking down. By promoting oral tolerance, UC-II® reduces inflammation and supports cartilage repair, easing pain and enhancing mobility in dogs.

Two studies have shown that UC-II® significantly improves mobility while alleviating pain and discomfort, demonstrating efficacy comparable to two different NSAIDs (non-steroidal anti-inflammatory drugs). After 30 days, the improvement in relief were similar between UC-II® and Robenacoxib, an anti-inflammatory medication.

Notably, UC-II® is one of the few ingredients in dietary supplements to achieve these results (Stabile et al., 2019).UC-II® is a distinct form of natural type II collagen derived from chicken cartilage through a patented low-temperature extraction process. This method preserves the natural 3D structure of type II collagen in UC-II®, ensuring its health-promoting properties remain intact. Thanks to this unique extraction process, UC-II® operates differently from other supplements, such as hydrolyzed collagen.

The ingredients in Jope were specifically selected for their powerful benefits to the body while avoiding the need for large supplemental doses. Each component contributes uniquely to Luce's overall well-being. According to the company, the most impactful changes should be noticeable after three months.

The manufacturer of Jope recommends separating the administration of glucosamine from the product Jope, because a 2012 study by Gupta suggested glucosamine might prevent the benefits of UC-II® collagen (Gupta et al., 2012).

Therefore, it's best to discontinue the glucosamine or - if that's not something you want to do - give Jope (or any UC-II® product) 8 to 12 hours before or after it. At a minimum, there should be a separation of at least two to four hours.

While waiting, I also decided to include another effective mobility supplement from Wholistic Pet Organics called Joint Mobility GLM. This remarkable product is crafted with top-notch, human-grade, and certified organic ingredients.

Wholistic Joint Mobility GLM™ features a unique blend of premium components to promote joint health. It allowed me to rotate in some of the supplements I was giving Luce and provided additional ingredients to support her holistically – ingredients that weren't included in the Jope product.

After reading everyone's thoughts on bioavailability, I'll be honest here and say I wanted to hedge my bet. I was hoping that, through diversity, something would get in and work.

The Green green-lipped mussel in GLM is rich in glucosamine, glycosaminoglycans (GAGs), and hyaluronic acid - all of which enhance synovial fluid viscosity. Glucosamine is a natural building block for cartilage and plays a crucial role in its rebuilding. Meanwhile, MSM helps maintain normal, healthy connective tissue in joints while alleviating discomfort.

Moreover, the patented Ester C® represents the most effective, Body-Ready™ form of Vitamin C. Vitamin C is vital for cartilage formation and acts as a powerful antioxidant. The Digest-All Plus™ enzyme complex also supports healthy digestive function, contributing to overall well-being.

By incorporating this product into my routine, I was able to reduce or diversify my Vitamin C supplementation while also adding digestive enzymes, glucosamine, MSM, and green-lipped mussels.

In addition to the homeopathic remedies I was using for pain relief, I also incorporated CBD into Luce's regimen. I began with *Calm* from CBD Dog Health and later switched to *Ease* from the same company.

The key difference between these two products lies in their specific targets. I chose CBD Dog Health because they provide a third-party lab-tested certificate of analysis for their products and ensure they meet high standards for quality and uniformity. Their products are tested for pesticides, and the third-party results - showing no heavy metals or pathogens - were shared with me without hesitation.

Initially, I opted for *Calm* because it's an organic, full-spectrum CBD formulated for dogs experiencing anxiety and situational fear. It was especially beneficial for Luce during stressful visits to the veterinarian, where her body was manipulated in unfamiliar ways, heightening her anxiety.

Calm also contains lavender, hemp seed oil, and MCT oil, which help soothe her nerves and allow the CBD to work effectively. Once Luce seemed to have her anxiety under control, I transitioned to using CBD primarily as a pain reliever.

Ease is a proprietary full-spectrum CBD product designed to alleviate pain in dogs, including joint issues, back pain, inflammation, and allergies. Formulated with frankincense and turmeric, it's a natural anti-inflammatory that also helps balance the immune system and soothe aches and pains. Specifically created to target arthritis-related discomfort, Ease supports mobility and helps reduce the inflammation that can trigger or worsen joint pain in dogs.

It's important to note that CBD Dog Health provided a recommended dosage. We did experience a minor setback in this approach to pain management. Luce was taking a fairly high dose of CBD (less than 0.3% THC), and as a result, she experienced a side effect: inappropriate urination.

Between September 9 and September 12, 2023, I worked to understand why this was happening. During that time, I decided to stop all her supplements and reintroduce them one by one, carefully monitoring for adverse reactions. I didn't initially associate this issue with the CBD dosage until I had ruled out other urinary-related problems.

She was drinking a lot of water and eliminating excessive urine. I sent a urine sample to the vet for testing, and the results came back normal. However, she couldn't hold her urine and had accidents in the house, which was not normal behavior for her. I reduced the dosage, but the issue persisted. Once I eliminated the CBD entirely, the inappropriate urination stopped immediately.

On August 30, 2023, I stopped using DGP (to manage pain) and switched to a new product developed by Dr. Marsden: Voltrex (to manage inflammation, which leads to pain). I chose this herbal formula to manage Luce's inflammation more effectively, as it supports ligament healing and helps reduce inflammation in the spinal cord.

Voltrex contains a blend of ingredients, including turmeric root, cinnamon twig, ginseng root, bupleurum root, large-leaf gentian root, white peony root, Pinella rhizome, licorice root, Scutellaria root, ginger rhizome, jujube, and natural flavoring. My primary focus has been keeping inflammation low as an effective way to manage pain.

As I mentioned earlier in the book, while anti-inflammatory drugs can be helpful for treating arthritis and ligament damage in the initial days following an injury, prolonged use of these pain relievers can actually impede long-term healing by restricting blood flow to the very tissues that need to recover.

It's important to remember that short-term strategies should remain just that—short-term. Voltrex supports normal blood flow to joints and ligaments, allowing healing to progress without sacrificing pain relief. As those areas recover over the course of several weeks or months, the need for anti-inflammatory drugs naturally diminishes - ultimately helping to accelerate the healing process.

In Luce's case, I discontinued the anti-inflammatory drug Carprofen after just two days, choosing instead to manage her pain and inflammation with natural supplements.

I also want to emphasize that we're not just addressing the injured leg - we're supporting other joints and ligaments that may be at risk. Using an herbal remedy like this promotes holistic support for the entire body, helping them grow stronger and become less susceptible to future injuries.

According to Dr. Marsden, improvements from enhanced joint circulation typically begin within the first few days. However, complete healing of the ligaments and joints can take several months. The pace of recovery depends on several factors, including whether the dog is a whole-food diet of meat and vegetables, and whether additional therapies are being used to support optimal joint circulation and healing. I used Voltrex initially, continuing until Luce's progress plateaued - then I shifted to a longer-term strategy.

As Luce's physical mobility improved and her exercise routine expanded, I began incorporating Myos into her regimen. Myos is a natural health supplement formulated to support muscle growth and maintenance, while also enhancing mobility in dogs. Its key ingredient, Fortetropin, is an all-natural component that helps preserve healthy muscle mass and reduce muscle loss caused by aging, injury, or surgery. Clinically researched for its ability to promote muscle gain, boost mobility, and accelerate recovery, Fortetropin is derived from fertilized egg yolk. The hens producing these eggs are raised on a diet free from added hormones and antibiotics, and the supplement contains no artificial ingredients or additives.

I've found this product works best when given within three hours of exercise - either before or after.

To promote muscle growth in dogs, it's essential to combine resistance training with adequate protein intake, sufficient sleep, and overall healthy habits that support muscle protein synthesis and repair. Muscles grow in response to challenge – so your dog needs to regularly engage in resistance activities, like bodyweight exercises.

If your dog is mostly inactive and not exerting those muscles, you probably won't see the results you're hoping for. By giving this product within three hours of exercise, you're delivering the protein needed to help rebuild and strengthen the muscles that were just worked.

Additionally, I incorporated fresh eggshell membrane harvested from farm-fresh eggs into Luce's routine. This natural source of collagen, hyaluronic acid, elastin, and other nutrients provides numerous benefits for dogs, primarily in supporting joint health, alleviating pain, and boosting mobility.

Here's a detailed look at the potential benefits of fresh eggshell membrane:

Joint Health

- **Collagen:** The eggshell membrane is rich in collagen, an essential component for maintaining healthy cartilage, tendons, and ligaments, all of which play vital roles in joint function.

- **Hyaluronic Acid:** This substance plays a crucial role in lubricating joints, keeping them flexible, and significantly reducing stiffness and pain.

- **Elastin:** Elastin helps maintain the elasticity of tendons and ligaments, contributing to improved joint flexibility and overall mobility.

- **Glucosamine and Chondroitin:** Naturally occurring compounds in the eggshell membrane, these are renowned for supporting cartilage health and alleviating joint discomfort.

Other Potential Benefits

- **Improved Skin and Hair Health:** The hyaluronic acid in eggshell membrane can boost skin hydration, leading to healthier skin and improved hair quality.

- **Immune System Support:** Some studies suggest that the eggshell membrane may possess immune-modulating properties.

- **Digestive Health:** The sulfates present in the outer layer of the eggshell membrane may may promote digestive health and help reduce gut inflammation.

On September 10th, Luce's only commercial supplements were *Concentrated Tendon and Ligament, Body Sore, Jump 4 Joynts*, and *Joint Mobility GLM*. Once I realized that CBD caused her urination issues, I stopped using it and reintroduced bone broth into her diet. By September 12th, I had added back all her supplements - except for CBD, which I decided to eliminate entirely. With that change, her excessive water consumption also came to a halt.

On September 10th, Luce received her first Adequan shot. Unlike other treatment options, Adequan is the only FDA-approved drug shown to slow down - or even reverse - cartilage deterioration in dogs' joints. Dr. Katherine Johnson and Dr. Jana Froeling recommended Adequan as part of a multimodal approach that includes joint supplements, exercise, weight control, and additional therapies to enhance joint health and recovery. Known for reducing arthritis and inflammation, the goal of introducing Adequan was to protect Luce's cartilage before it could deteriorate beyond repair. These shots are administered subcutaneously rather than intramuscularly, and Luce continues to receive them on a maintenance basis.

Don't Be Super Fish Oil

When it comes to supporting canine joint health and aiding ligament repair, several key ingredients play a crucial role. Glucosamine, chondroitin, omega-3 fatty acids, and MSM (Methylsulfonylmethane) are essential for maintaining joint function, reducing inflammation, and encouraging cartilage repair. While choosing supplements that include these ingredients is important, it's just as critical to monitor daily totals to avoid exceeding recommended dosages. At the end of this book, I've included my supplement chart detailing the products I selected for Luce throughout her healing journey. Some of these supplements contain overlapping ingredients, while others may differ in dosage or include additional components unrelated to her injury but are part of the formula.

Here are a few points to note about my selections:

- All supplements were chosen based on their primary healing properties.

- Rotating products ensured a diverse source of nutrients and allowed for dosage adjustments as needed.

- Each company was thoroughly researched to confirm third-party testing results, ensuring the products were free of heavy metals, synthetic vitamins and minerals, and unnecessary flavorings.

- I selected specific products in response to symptoms or changes in Luce's therapy, as needed.

- I took a layered approach to managing outcomes.

When you look at my chart, you'll notice a variety of supplements along with their associated ingredients. Each product was selected for its specific components. I'm listing the ingredients and their benefits here for your review. If you decide not to use the same companies, you can still reference the ingredient list to ensure you're choosing high-quality options - no fillers, unnecessary synthetic vitamins and minerals, or flavors.

Here's a summary of what I consider key ingredients and their benefits for Luce during her orthopedic injury recovery:

Fecal microbiota transplantation (FMT), often in the form of capsules, can offer benefits for dogs recovering from injuries, particularly those affecting the gastrointestinal tract. By introducing beneficial bacteria from a healthy donor, FMT can help restore the gut microbiome, which is crucial for overall health and can influence healing(Rojas et al., 2024), (Bhadani et al., 2025).

- Injuries can disrupt the natural balance of the gut microbiome, leading to inflammation, impaired digestion, and potentially longer recovery times. FMT can help repopulate the gut with beneficial bacteria, promoting a healthier gut environment.

- A healthy gut microbiome plays a role in the body's immune response and inflammation. By restoring the microbiome, FMT can potentially support the body's natural healing processes and reduce inflammation, which can be beneficial during the recovery from an injury.

- Injuries can sometimes lead to digestive issues, such as diarrhea or difficulty absorbing nutrients. FMT can help address these problems by improving digestion and nutrient absorption.

- The gut microbiome is also linked to various other health aspects, including skin health, immune function, and even behavior. FMT may offer benefits in these areas as well, especially if the injury has affected the dog's overall health.

Glucosamine and Chondroitin (Harvard Health Publishing, 2016)

- **Glucosamine:** Crucial for forming and repairing joint cartilage, glucosamine also helps maintain the fluid that lubricates joints. This promotes smoother movement and less discomfort.

- **Chondroitin:** This compound is known for reducing inflammation and enhancing cartilage elasticity. It works with glucosamine to support the joints' overall structure and function.

Omega-3 Fatty Acids:

- **Benefits:** Omega-3s - typically sourced from fish oil and flaxseed - are celebrated for their anti-inflammatory effects. They help alleviate joint pain and stiffness, especially in dogs suffering from arthritis. When selecting supplements, look for the ones containing *EPA (eicosapentaenoic acid)* and *DHA (docosahexaenoic acid)*, the most beneficial forms.

MSM (Methylsulfonylmethane):

- MSM is a sulfur-based compound known for its ability to alleviate joint pain, reduce inflammation, and promote overall joint health (Versus Arthritis, n.d.).

Other Key Ingredients:

- **Vitamin C:** This powerful antioxidant has been shown to help ease arthritis symptoms in dogs.

- **Manganese:** An essential antioxidant that bolsters the body's natural defenses. It plays a vital role in cartilage production and supports healthy bone development.

- **Vitamin E:** Another powerful antioxidant, Vitamin E helps protect damaged cells and combats the formation of free radicals in the body.

- **Zinc:** Zinc is essential for maintaining healthy joints and contributes to overall health.

Green Chlorella

- **Benefits:** Chlorella contains antioxidants such as violaxanthin, lycopene, and omega-3 fatty acids, which can help reduce inflammation and possibly ease joint pain. Its antioxidants effectively battle free radicals and oxidative stress, factors that can lead to inflammation and joint damage. Additionally, Chlorella is an alkaline food that can help neutralize lactic acid buildup during exercise, which may contribute to joint pain, stiffness, and muscle soreness (Bito et al., 2020)·

L-Carnitine

- **Benefits:** L-carnitine has been shown to possess anti-inflammatory and antioxidant properties, potentially helping to relieve inflammation and oxidative stress in joints. Some studies suggest it may protect cartilage from degradation, a crucial aspect of osteoarthritis management. Research also indicates that L-carnitine supplementation might lower pain intensity and improve the overall assessment of disease status in those with knee osteoarthritis. It may also help reduce synovitis (synovial membrane inflammation) by regulating lipid accumulation and supporting mitochondrial function (Liao et al., 2023).

Coenzyme Q10

- **Benefits:** Coenzyme Q10 (CoQ10) is a powerful antioxidant that may help alleviate joint pain and inflammation associated with arthritis, including osteoarthritis and rheumatoid arthritis, by potentially slowing cartilage degradation and reducing inflammatory markers (Lee et al., 2013).

Resveratrol

- **Benefits:** Found in grapes and red wine, resveratrol shows promise in alleviating joint pain and inflammation, particularly in osteoarthritis, by acting as an anti-inflammatory agent and potentially safeguarding cartilage. (Nguyen et al., 2017).

Bee Pollen

- **Benefits:** Bee pollen has been utilized in alternative medicine for various ailments, including joint pain, due to its perceived anti-inflammatory and antioxidant properties (El Ghouizi et al., 2023).

Digestive Enzymes

- **Benefits:** Enzymes like bromelain, derived from pineapple, are known for their protein-breaking abilities. Some studies suggest that proteolytic enzymes help diminish inflammation in the joints and surrounding tissues by lowering inflammatory substances, such as prostaglandins and pro-inflammatory cytokines. These enzymes may also enhance joint function and reduce pain by breaking down damaged tissue, promoting repair and regeneration.

Bifidobacterium Longum

- **Benefits:** Research indicates that Bifidobacterium longum (B. longum) may benefit joint pain and inflammation by modulating the gut microbiome and reducing inflammation (Oh et al., 2023).

Lactobacillus Acidophilus

- **Benefits:** Lactobacillus acidophilus is a common probiotic that might help with joint pain, especially in conditions like osteoarthritis, by mitigating inflammation and cartilage damage while supporting gut health, contributing to overall well-being (O-Sullivan et al., 2022)

Curcumin

- **Benefits:** Curcumin, the active component in turmeric, shows potential in reducing joint pain and inflammation, particularly in osteoarthritis and rheumatoid arthritis, possibly providing similar relief to NSAIDs but with fewer side effects (Oke, 2009).

- *While turmeric contains curcumin, a compound known for its potential health benefits, it has poor bioavailability - meaning the body doesn't absorb it easily. However, consuming turmeric or curcumin with certain substances, like black pepper (which contains piperine) or fats, can significantly enhance its absorption (Bertoncini-Silva et al., 2024).*

Anchovy Oil

- **Benefits:** Anchovy oil, rich in omega-3 fatty acids (EPA and DHA), may help alleviate joint pain and inflammation associated with arthritis due to its anti-inflammatory properties (Peliushkevich, n.d.).

Turmeric

- **Benefits:** Turmeric, particularly its active compound curcumin, has demonstrated potential in relieving joint pain and inflammation related to osteoarthritis and rheumatoid arthritis, likely offering relief comparable to NSAIDs with fewer adverse effects (Hauser, Matias, & Hauser, n.d.).

Porcine Plasma

- **Benefits:** Porcine plasma is a natural ingredient, and decades of research have backed its effectiveness in modulating inflammation at its source. When consumed orally, the functional proteins in plasma do not disrupt the body's natural immune response but instead help it react swiftly and effectively. Plasma can regulate inflammation both in the gut and systemically, helping to prevent cognitive decline and reducing intestinal inflammation (Quigley et al., 2004).

Collagen

- **Benefits:** Collagen is a key component of cartilage, which cushions joints. Some studies indicate that collagen supplements can help maintain cartilage structure and support its repair. Collagen peptides also possess anti-inflammatory effects, potentially alleviating joint pain and stiffness. Research suggests collagen supplementation can enhance joint mobility and alleviate discomfort during physical activities. Type II collagen, a primary component of cartilage, is often included in joint health supplements (Yu, n.d.).

L-Glutamine

- **Benefits:** L-glutamine shows promise as a safe and effective treatment to slow the progression of osteoarthritis. Glutamine supports gut health by promoting intestinal lining integrity and potentially reducing inflammation. It may help prevent bacterial translocation, which can contribute to gut inflammation. In animal models of Crohn's disease, glutamine supplementation reduces inflammation, prevents weight loss, and improves disease activity. Glutamine may reduce the production of pro-inflammatory cytokines (interleukin-6 and interleukin-8) and enhance the production of the anti-inflammatory cytokine interleukin-10 in the gut (Ma et al., 2022).

Creatinine

- **Benefits:** Research indicates that creatine supplementation, especially with resistance training, can boost physical function and increase lean mass in the lower limbs of individuals suffering from knee osteoarthritis. Evidence suggests that creatine may help alleviate joint stiffness, a common challenge faced by those with osteoarthritis. Additionally, creatine or its by-product, creatinine, might possess anti-inflammatory properties, potentially easing the inflammation linked to joint pain. Creatine is well-known for enhancing muscle strength and promoting quicker recovery, which can be particularly beneficial for individuals with joint issues who may experience muscle weakness or atrophy (Cordingley et al., 2022).

Boswellia

- **Benefits:** Boswellia, derived from the frankincense tree, shows promising potential in alleviating joint pain, especially for osteoarthritis patients. It works by reducing inflammation and enhancing joint function, with some studies suggesting it may rival the effectiveness of NSAIDs, if not exceed it (Lubeck, 2024).

Cod Liver Oil

- **Benefits:** Rich in omega-3 fatty acids and vitamins A and D, cod liver oil may help alleviate joint pain and inflammation tied to arthritis and other joint problems, thanks to its anti-inflammatory properties (Gruenwald et al., 2002).

Green Lipped Mussels (Pollard et al., 2006)

- **Benefits:** Research has highlighted the benefits of green-lipped mussels (Perna canaliculus) in supporting hip and joint health, particularly for dogs. This unique mussel species contains a special nutrient blend that bolsters joint health and mobility. Rich in glucosamine, glycosaminoglycans (GAGs), hyaluronic acid, and chondroitin sulfate, these components contribute to the viscosity of synovial fluid, enhancing joint lubrication. Additionally, these shellfish are packed with valuable omega-3 fatty acids, which promote joint comfort, alongside other elements that support optimal joint function. Our green-lipped mussels are cold-opened and freeze-dried at low temperatures to ensure maximum bioactivity (Abshirini et al., 2021).

Cinnamon Twig

- **Benefits:** In traditional Chinese medicine, cinnamon twigs (Cinnamomum cassia) are believed to have warming and circulation-enhancing properties, potentially aiding in alleviating joint pain and stiffness associated with arthritis and rheumatism. Studies have shown that cinnamon twig extract can exhibit anti-inflammatory and anti-arthritic activities, reducing edema volume in paws of rats with chronic arthritis. Cinnamon twig extract has been shown to have analgesic effects by recovering paw withdrawal latency and suppressing vocalization scores evoked by ankle flexion in arthritis rats. Cinnamic aldehyde, a main component of cinnamon, has been shown to exhibit anti-inflammatory properties in osteoarthritis (OA) synovial fibroblasts via the TLR4/MyD88 pathway (Golden Flower Chinese Herbs, n.d.).

Ginseng Root

- **Benefits:** Ginseng root, particularly red ginseng extract, shows promise in alleviating joint pain and inflammation, potentially due to its anti-inflammatory and antioxidant properties and ability to modulate immune responses and reduce cartilage degradation. Ginseng and its active compounds, ginsenosides, exhibit anti-inflammatory properties, crucial in managing joint pain and inflammation associated with conditions like osteoarthritis and rheumatoid arthritis. Ginseng can help prevent the development of autoimmune diseases by suppressing the excessive secretion of pro-inflammatory cytokines, such as TNF-α, which contribute to joint inflammation and cartilage destruction. Ginseng may help reduce the infiltration of immune cells into the joints, which can further contribute to inflammation and joint damage. Some studies suggest that ginseng and ginsenosides can protect cartilage from damage by inhibiting the degradation of the extracellular matrix, a key component of cartilage (Chen et al., 2023).

Bupleurum Root

- **Benefits:** Bupleurum is an essential herb in traditional Chinese and Japanese medicine. It is frequently prescribed in combination with other herbs to treat colds, fever, malaria, digestive disorders, chronic liver diseases, and depression (RxList, n.d.).

Scutellaria Root

- **Benefits:** Research in animal models of arthritis has shown that Scutellaria baicalensis extracts can reduce pain and inflammation and improve joint function. Scutellaria baicalensis (Chinese skullcap), particularly its root, has shown promise in traditional Chinese medicine for its anti-inflammatory properties, potentially benefiting joint health and alleviating pain and stiffness associated with osteoarthritis. Studies suggest that Scutellaria baicalensis extracts can help reduce inflammation, a key factor in joint pain and stiffness. Research indicates that Scutellaria baicalensis may help alleviate pain and discomfort in animal models of arthritis, with effects similar to ibuprofen and indomethacin.

- Some studies suggest that Scutellaria baicalensis can aid in the recovery of damaged joints and may have a protective effect on joint tissue. A combination of Scutellaria baicalensis and Acacia catechu extracts has been shown to reduce joint discomfort and stiffness in patients with osteoarthritis (Jo et al., 2024).

Ginger Rhizome

- **Benefits:** Ginger rhizome, particularly its active compound gingerol, has shown potential in reducing joint pain and inflammation associated with conditions like osteoarthritis and rheumatoid arthritis, though more research is needed, (Srinivasan et al, 2019).

Jujube

- **Benefits**: Jujube fruit, particularly its extracts and oil, exhibits potent anti-inflammatory properties that may help alleviate muscle aches and joint pains, making it a potential natural remedy for arthritis and other inflammatory conditions (Szymczak et al., 2024).

Hyaluronic Acid

- **Benefits:** Hyaluronic acid (HA), a naturally occurring substance in joints, acts as a lubricant and shock absorber, and HA injections can help alleviate pain and improve joint function in osteoarthritis by restoring the joint's natural lubrication.

Continuing joint supplements after a dog experiences an injury can be crucial in managing inflammation, supporting cartilage health, and potentially slowing the progression of arthritis - ultimately enhancing long-term joint function and comfort (Zhu et al., 2024).

There are numerous advantages associated with long-term joint supplementation. Supplements - especially those derived from highly digestible whole foods - can aid in maintaining healthy cartilage and supporting its repair.

Many contain anti-inflammatory ingredients, such as omega-3 fatty acids, which work to reduce joint pain and stiffness. Components like hyaluronic acid help lubricate the joints, improving mobility and decreasing friction.

While these supplements cannot reverse existing arthritis, they can be instrumental in slowing its progression and managing symptoms. By addressing the root causes of joint issues, they play a vital role in promoting long-term joint health and preventing future complications.

By reducing pain and improving mobility, joint supplements can significantly enhance a dog's quality of life as they age.

Focusing on proactive injury prevention - rather than solely supporting an injured limb - is essential. Orthopedic injuries can compromise a dog's overall well-being, regardless of whether surgical or conservative management is pursued.

Gait changes may occur, potentially leading to degeneration in the opposite leg, and the original injury site often remains a weak point. The body may compensate by shifting weight to different muscle groups, resulting in additional issues.

Prevention involves regular treatments that relieve muscle tension and stiffness, enhance range of motion, and restore function. Ample scientific evidence supports the fact that muscle tension and stiffness can contribute to injuries such as muscle strains or ligament sprains.

Identifying any weaknesses in your dog's body that may lead to compensatory patterns in other areas is crucial.

When compensation persists over time, it can cause tension and tightness, eventually resulting in injury. That's why it's essential to address your dog's muscle stiffness and understand the root cause.

In other words, find out why your dog is compensating and, whenever possible, focus on strengthening overlooked weak areas through a tailored rehabilitation program, a balanced diet, and appropriate supplements.

But Wait, There's More

As we touched on earlier in Chapter 3—when we explored nutrition through the lens of the Traditional Chinese Medicine (TCM) organ clock—I'd be remiss if I didn't revisit that concept here in the context of supplements. Timing matters. Just as certain foods are better absorbed or more beneficial at specific times of day, the same goes for supplements.

I previously noted how some ingredients can interfere with the absorption of others, depending on when and how they're taken. So, if you're aiming to get the most out of your supplements (and who isn't?), let's take another brief step into the world of the TCM organ clock and see how it can guide us in optimizing supplement timing.

Here is a quick explanation again on what the organ chart is so you do not have to go back and look it up in chapter 3. The Traditional Chinese Medicine (TCM) organ clock is based on the idea that *Qi* (vital energy) flows through different organ systems at specific times of the day. Each two-hour window corresponds to a specific organ and its associated meridian, during which its function is at its peak. Understanding the organ clock can help identify imbalances in the body by observing when symptoms or energetic issues arise. TCM practitioners use this timing to understand to assess symptoms and diagnose potential organ dysfunctions.

The 12 Two-Hour Intervals and Their Associated Organs:

Time	Organ
5:00 a.m. to 7:00 a.m.	Large Intestine
7:00 a.m. to 9:00 a.m.	Stomach
9:00 a.m. to 11:00 a.m.	Spleen
11:00 a.m. to 1:00 p.m.	Heart
1:00 p.m. to 3:00 p.m.	Small Intestine
3:00 p.m. to 5:00 p.m.	Bladder
5:00 p.m. to 7:00 p.m.	Kidney
7:00 p.m. to 9:00 p.m.	Pericardium
9:00 p.m. to 11:00 p.m.	Tripler Heater
11:00 p.m. to 1:00 a.m.	Gallbladder
1:00 a.m. to 3:00 a.m.	Liver
3:00 a.m. to 5:00 a.m.	Lungs

What does that mean for the average pet parent? The organ clock can help you determine when to feed your dog, what to feed them, and when to avoid certain foods based on organ activity. It can also offer insight into potential sleep issues and help optimize both your dog's and your own sleep schedule. Timing physical activity to align with the energy flow of specific organs may also enhance results. And because TCM associates certain emotions to specific organs and their time intervals, the organ clock offers a deeper understanding of emotional states as well.

In the Chinese medicine organ clock, the energy associated with muscles and ligaments – linked to the spleen meridian - peaks between 9:00 a.m. and 11:00 a.m. This is an ideal time to support those systems with targeted supplements.

Let's just apply this to the dog's day as an example:

7:00 a.m. to 9:00 a.m.: Stomach Meridian

- This is the primary time for digestion, so aim to feed your dog their main meal during this period.

9:00 a.m. to 11:00 a.m.: Spleen/Pancreas Meridian

- The spleen/pancreas meridian transforms food into energy and nourishes the body.

- This is when the body releases enzymes to help digest food, so ensure your dog has finished their meal by this time.

- It's also a great time for physical activity and tasks that require concentration and problem-solving.

- The spleen meridian is also associated with the emotion of thinking.

11:00 a.m. to 1:00 p.m.: Heart Meridian

- The heart meridian is associated with the emotion of joy.

- This is a good time for rest and lunch.

1:00 p.m. to 3:00 p.m.: Small Intestine Meridian

- The small intestine separates usable energy from waste.

- This is a great time to finish tasks and allow the body to digest.

3:00 p.m. to 5:00 p.m.: Bladder Meridian

- The bladder helps with waste elimination.

- This is a good time to drink and stay hydrated.

5:00 p.m. to 7:00 p.m.: Kidney/Bladder Meridian

- The kidneys are essential for maintaining energy and vitality.

- This is a good time to wind down and prepare for the evening.

To effectively supplement a dog using Traditional Chinese Medicine (TCM) and the organ clock, consider the peak function times of different organs to optimize the timing of food and supplements for better absorption and efficacy.

It's also important to consider the energetic properties of foods. TCM categorizes foods as warming, cooling, or neutral, and suggests eating foods that are in season to maintain balance.

Just like humans, dogs have different constitutions and health conditions, so a one-size-fits-all approach to supplementing Chinese medicine may not be effective.

Here are some examples of TCM supplements and their timing:

- For digestion, consider supplements that support the stomach and spleen, such as ginger or other herbs that aid digestion, during the stomach and spleen hours.

- For energy, use supplements that support the heart and kidneys, such as herbs that promote energy and vitality, during the heart and kidney hours

- For detoxification, choose supplements that support the liver and gallbladder, such as herbs that promote detoxification, during the liver and gallbladder hours.

Chapter 5: Knee-Deep In Recovery

During your dog's recovery from an orthopedic injury, remember that every step forward - no matter how small - is a win. Your dog's strength and resilience are building each day. Instead of striving for perfection, focus on progress and take the time to celebrate your dog's achievements. Setbacks are part of the journey; it's not a question of *if* but *when* they will occur.

Remember, this isn't a reflection of your efforts—it's valuable feedback that helps you adjust your approach and prevent similar setbacks in the future. Embrace the journey; recovery is a process, not just a destination. It's perfectly fine to experience bumps in the road while still recognizing and celebrating those small victories.

Maintaining a positive mindset is crucial. If you find yourself feeling negative, frustrated, or sad, it can hinder your ability to support your dog's healing process. Accept the new normal and channel your energy into positivity. Focus on what your dog *can* do rather than what it can't.

It's easy to fixate on limitations, so shift your attention towards the activities your dog can still enjoy, and explore ways to adapt them. Set realistic goals by breaking your dog's recovery down into manageable milestones - this can help keep you motivated and allow you to track progress effectively.

For those supporting a dog through orthopedic recovery, prioritize creating a safe and nurturing environment. Assist with mobility, manage medications, and care for wounds, all while encouraging rest and a healthy lifestyle. Watch for complications, and remember - your support is vital in this journey.

The first step is preparing your home for safety. For a while, your dog won't be able to navigate slippery floors or stairs, and jumping on or off furniture will be off-limits. With this in mind, consider creating a safe environment.

Start by removing tripping hazards like loose rugs, cords, and clutter. Ensure your dog has easy access to the yard, eating areas, and other essential spots.

Consider setting up a comfortable first-floor room with easy access to necessities like a bed and a door for bathroom breaks, minimizing stairs whenever possible. Stock up on ice packs, bandages, and other essential supplies to be prepared.

Your daily routine will also need to adjust, as you'll be assisting your dog in navigating this new normal. When planning your "getting ready" schedule, add extra time for these tasks. Remember, it's all about working smart - not hard.

- **Mobility:** Assist your dog in getting in and out of bed, the house, and during mealtime.

- **Medication:** Make sure medications are administered as prescribed, and help with wound care if your dog has undergone surgery.

- **Meal Prep:** Prepare your dog's meals and snacks so they're easy to access and require minimal effort.

- **Encourage Rest:** Foster a calming environment that promotes relaxation and sleep. This might include using a crate for some dogs, an X-pen for others, or providing an open space that's easy to navigate.

- **Creative Play:** Think outside the box for playtime. Focus on activities that engage them mentally - brain games over physically demanding ones.

- **Separating Dogs:** If your dog is injured, it's crucial to prevent them from playing with other dogs in the house. Consider separation while allowing safe visual contact and interaction.

- **Monitoring & Seeking Help:** Watch for potential complications. Be alert for signs of infection (such as increased pain, redness, swelling, or drainage) or blood clots if surgery has occurred.

- **Communicate with the Veterinarian:** Keep your vet informed about any concerns or changes in your dog's condition.

- **Know When to Seek Help:** Have an emergency plan ready and know where to go for non-life-threatening concerns.

- **Take Care of Yourself:** Caregiving can be taxing, so prioritize your well-being. Be gentle with yourself, allow space for your feelings, and remember it's normal to feel frustrated or discouraged at times.

- **Seek support:** Don't hesitate to reach out to friends, family, or support groups for assistance.

- **Get organized:** Set up a schedule for medications, appointments, and physical therapy sessions to stay on track.

You've got this! What feels overwhelming right now will soon settle into a familiar routine, and your dog will start to heal. If you opt for conservative management, you're choosing the least invasive route first to see if your dog is a good candidate for that approach. Keep in mind, surgery can always be considered later if needed. Even if your dog has already had surgery, rehabilitation remains essential. It doesn't matter which path you choose—rehab is crucial either way. Skipping this step could lead to complications, such as an injury to the other leg or undermining the time and money you've invested. Your veterinarian may or may not have provided a rehab plan or suggested consulting a rehabilitation specialist. I encourage you to take that step right away!

Finding Balance

I chose conservative management for Luce's full CCL, meniscal tear, and iliopsoas strain. This approach involves activity modification, inflammation and pain management, weight management, muscle atrophy prevention, therapeutic exercises, and rehabilitation.

All of the modalities I'm going to introduce to you are non-surgical. I worked with Rehabilitation Veterinarians Dr. Katherine Johnson and Dr. Courtney Belden from Virginia Rehabilitation Services of Virginia (VRS-VA).

In addition to these two extraordinary Veterinarians, I also continued to include Dr. Jana Froeling on Luce's veterinary health team. It was agreed that Luce would go to VRSVA for rehabilitation two times a week - one visit for a full session including the underwater treadmill and laser, and a second visit for just the underwater treadmill. Luce would see Dr. Froeling once every two weeks for Chiropractic adjustments, acupuncture, and any other therapies as needed.

Over the next twelve months, Luce received a multitude of therapeutic modalities to help her heal (Corbin Winslow & Shapiro, 2002):

1 – Manual Massage Therapy - Massage is not petting. It's a focused, intentional, and deliberate application of various strokes. Massage is a non-invasive way to improve your pet's health through soft tissue manipulation, with goals such as relaxation, stimulation, and relief of muscle issues. It allows the body to function efficiently by increasing circulation and bringing oxygen and nutrients to the tissues (Corti, 2014). Massage can provide relief from many common ailments and also enhance performance.

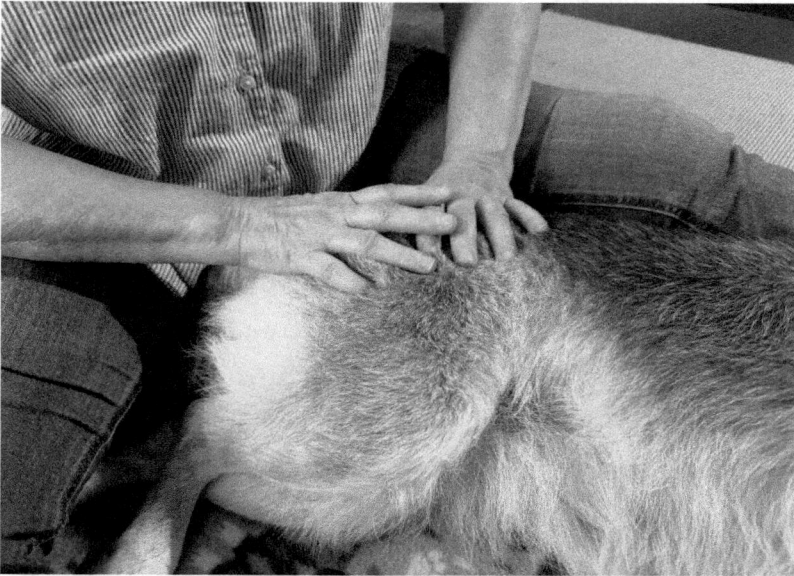

Nancy Lilly providing massage therapy to Luce in between veterinarian visits.

2 – Myofascial Work – Canine myofascial work encompasses various techniques, including massage as well as modalities like acupressure, myofascial release, and chiropractic adjustments. It often takes a holistic approach, considering the interconnectedness of the body, mind, and emotions.

These techniques address soft tissues such as muscles, fascia, and ligaments, but may also focus on the nervous system, joints, and other areas to promote overall well-being. The Masterson Method, which uses a dog's responses to touch to locate and release tension, is one form of bodywork (Beyond Dog Massage, n.d.).

3 – Canine Kinaesthetics™ - This technique, developed by long time dog trainer Maryna Ozuna, was adapted from human craniosacral work to address the specific needs of canines. It involves a gentle but effective rhythmic pulsing movement that works with the dog's neurological system and craniosacral pulse to create lasting changes in soft tissue and bone position and response.

This touch is applied in a series of specific functional locations throughout the dog's body to free up and normalize movement. I used behavioral feedback from Luce, along with changes in the pressure and rhythm of my hands, to create a behavioral "dialogue" with her (Ozuna, n.d.).

4 – Heat and Cold Therapy – When appropriately timed in the rehabilitation process, cold and heat can be very effective in reducing pain and inflammation. During the first 72 hours after surgery or trauma, cold therapy is used to decrease pain perception, reduce blood flow, and limit inflammation. Later in the healing process, heat therapy is introduced to increase blood flow, improve muscle flexibility, reduce pain, and promote healing.

5 – Elastic Therapeutic Tape (KT Tape) – Also known as kinesiology tape, kinesio tape, k-tape, or KT, this elastic cotton strip with an acrylic adhesive is used to ease pain and reduce disability related to athletic injuries and various other physical conditions. (Kinesio Canine Tape, n.d.).

6 – Chiropractic Adjustment - The goal of chiropractic care for animals is to restore clear communication within the nervous system, allowing the body to function at its best. An adjustment may consist of lighter touch energy-type work as well as deeper force impulses into the spine and extremities, stretching work, muscle work, gait analysis, and even lifestyle modification recommendations - depending on the animal's specific needs (Haussler, Hesbach, Romano, Goff, & Bergh, 2021).

7 – Acupressure and Acupuncture (Dry Needling and Electric) - Acupressure takes a similar approach to acupuncture but it's less invasive, using pressure instead of needles to relieve, prevent, and treat various health conditions. It's often combined with massage and is supported by many respected certification programs worldwide. Acupuncture, which originates from Traditional Chinese Medicine, involves inserting thin needles into specific points on the body to promote healing and balance.

It can assist with pain management, arthritis, and gastrointestinal issues in dogs. Electroacupuncture is a form of acupuncture that combines traditional acupuncture techniques with electrical stimulation. It involves inserting thin needles into specific points on the body and then applying a low-voltage electrical current to the needles.

Electroacupuncture is believed to work by stimulating the body's natural pain-relieving mechanisms. The electrical current triggers the release of endorphins, which are natural opioids that block pain signals. Additionally, it may stimulate the release of other neurotransmitters and hormones that have therapeutic effects (Acupuncture for Rehabilitation, n.d.).

8 – Low-Level Laser therapy (LLLT) – Also known as Class III cold laser therapy, Photobiomodulation (PBM), or red-light therapy, is a modality that uses low-level lasers or light-emitting diodes (LEDs) applied to the body's surface. LLLT promotes tissue repair, reduces inflammation, and relieves pain.

Its effects are photochemical – rather than thermal - and occur at the cellular level. Benefits include faster wound healing, increased vascular activity, stimulated nerve function, reduced scar formation, and decreased inflammation (Veterinary Manual, n.d.).

9 – Therapeutic Laser Therapy (Class IV Laser) - Class IV lasers are powerful therapeutic lasers that deliver a high dosage of energy to the tissue over a short period of time.

The effect depends on the wavelength of the light emitted, which is selected based on the type and location of the injury.

These lasers penetrate deeply into tissue and act at the cellular level, specifically targeting the mitochondria to increase cellular metabolism.

This initiates a cascade of events that improves blood flow, decreases swelling, flushes out waste products and toxins, and enhances oxygenation and nutrition of the tissues.

Growth factors increase within the treated area, promoting the development of new blood vessels and nerves and accelerating tissue regeneration. Laser therapy also has anti-inflammatory effects by reducing inflammatory mediators and analgesic (pain control) effects by up-regulating the release of endorphins and bradykinin (Guadagni, 2024b).

Dr. Katherine Johnson doing laser on Luce

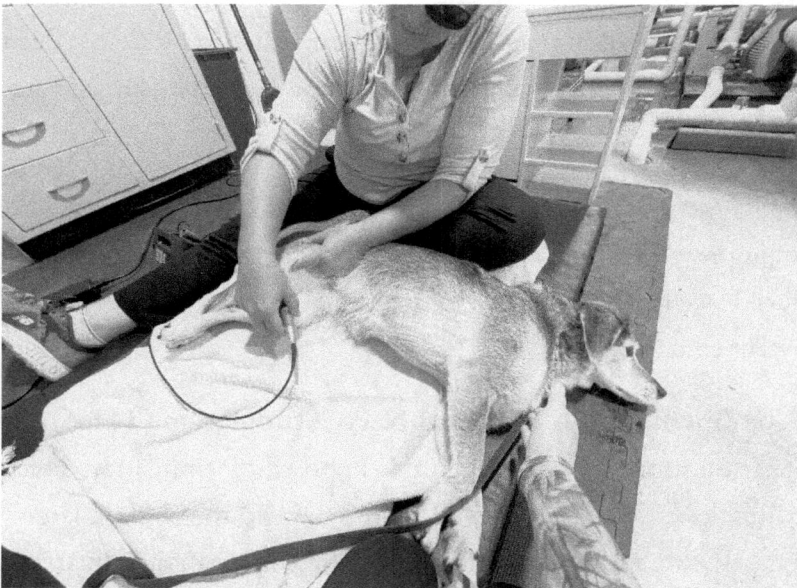

Dr. Katherine Johnson doing laser on Luce's right rear leg

10 – Extracorporeal Shockwave Therapy (ESWT) - ESWT is a non-invasive treatment that uses high-energy sound waves (shock waves) to stimulate healing in various musculoskeletal conditions. The sound waves concentrate in areas where tendon and ligaments interface with bone and can help to increase blood flow, call growth factors and potentially recruit the body's own stem cells to the damaged area.

While this modality may make the patient sorer in the initial 24-48 hours, it has longer term pain reducing qualities. You should consider ESWT if a dog is experiencing chronic pain, especially in the joints or back, ESWT may be a good option. ESWT can help manage osteoarthritis symptoms and improve joint function. If a condition is not responding to traditional treatments, ESWT may be considered (Boström, Bergh, Hyytiäinen, & Asplund, 2022).

11 – Therapeutic Ultrasound - Therapeutic ultrasound uses sound waves to deliver energy to tissues with two primary types of effects. It's primarily indicated in treating chronic scar tissue and indolent decubital ulcers (bedsores), and it may also help relieve muscle spasms and support tendon healing.

Benefits include the delivery of heat energy to tissues, increased blood flow, improved flexibility and extensibility of connective tissue, pain relief, reduced swelling, and muscle relaxation (Boström, Asplund, Bergh, & Hyytiäinen, 2022).

12 – Transcutaneous Electrical Nerve Stimulation (TENS) - TENS is electrical stimulation to the skin, as opposed to stimulation directed at the muscles and nerves. When TENS is applied to the skin, large nerve fibers (A-β) are stimulated. These A-β fibers synapse in the spinal cord and stimulate nerve fibers that block the perception of pain in the brain. This is called the gate control theory of pain.

The frequency of electrical impulses that stimulate the A-β fibers also caus-es the release of endorphins from the pituitary in the brain. Endorphins are natural opiates that produce analgesia when released.

The synapses in the spinal cord also stimulate another nerve fiber (A-δ). A-δ fiber stimulation blocks other nerves headed for the brain and is also involved in the mechanism of action for acupuncture.

The effect of TENS is similar to the effects of acupuncture for pain control (Levine, Johnston, Price, Schneider, & Millis, 2002).

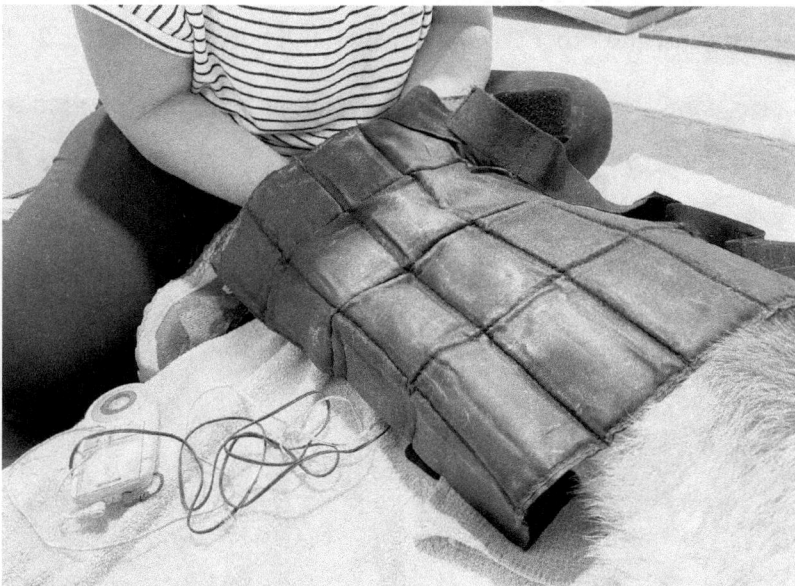

Dr. Katherine Johnson doing TENS therapy with ice pack over top

13 – Pulsed Electromagnetic Field Therapy (PEMF for dogs) - Pets' entire bodies are electrochemical organs and can be effectively influenced by low and safe electromagnetic frequencies.

PEMF uses electromagnetic pulses to gently stimulate and balance the cell function through a pulsating magnetic field that penetrates deeply into tissues and cells. PEMFs are produced through a magnetic field generator and copper coils, which are usually placed in a mat or a pad.

The treatment is painless and non-invasive, and most pets find it relaxing and soothing. The magnetic field stimulates electrical and chemical processes within the cells, helping to increase blood flow, promote the regeneration of damaged tissue, and recharge the cells.

When used on pets, PEMF therapy can help to alleviate pain, reduce inflammation, promote healing, and improve overall health and well-being. It is often used to treat a range of conditions, including arthritis, joint pain, muscle strains, and other types of injuries. (Di Bartolomeo et al., 2022).

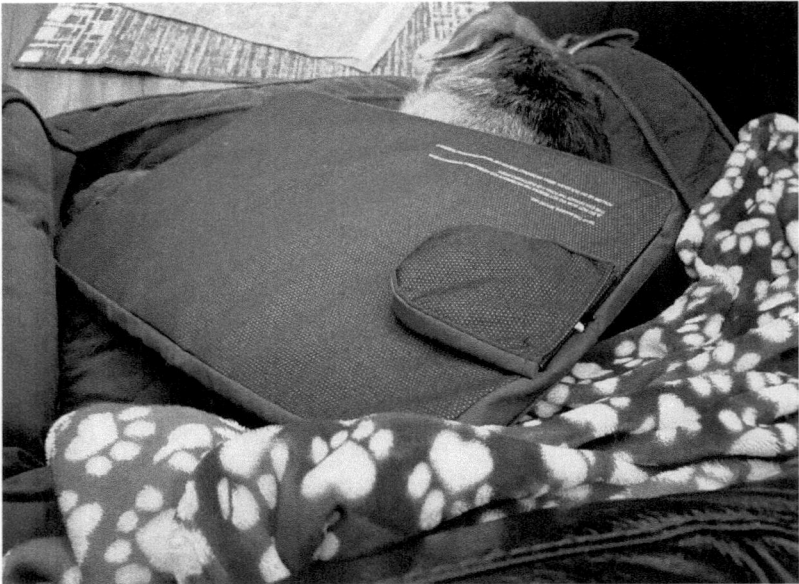

Luce resting under PEMF mat

14 – Targeted Pulsed Electromagnetic Field (tPEMF) Therapy (Assisi Loop) - tPEMF provides a specific signal carried on a series of magnetic field pulses to the treatment site(s).

These uniquely specific energy parameters are transmitted through injured tissue to target the affected area via direct induction. A tiny electrical signal is deposited into the tissue in a way that mimics physiological stimulus that normally occurs in healthy tissue, thereby stimulating cellular repair.

tPEMF is designed to accelerate the body's normal anti-inflammatory activity. Multiple, sometimes concurrent, biological activities occur - from the initial pain and swelling, through new blood vessel formation (angiogenesis), to tissue regeneration and remodeling.

These processes are all linked to an initial step, so accelerating that first electrochemical process should accelerate the entire cascade.

Tissues will respond depending on their current state: acutely inflamed tissue should rapidly respond by reducing pain and swelling, while chronic wounds, for example, should see improvements in blood flow and growth factor production.

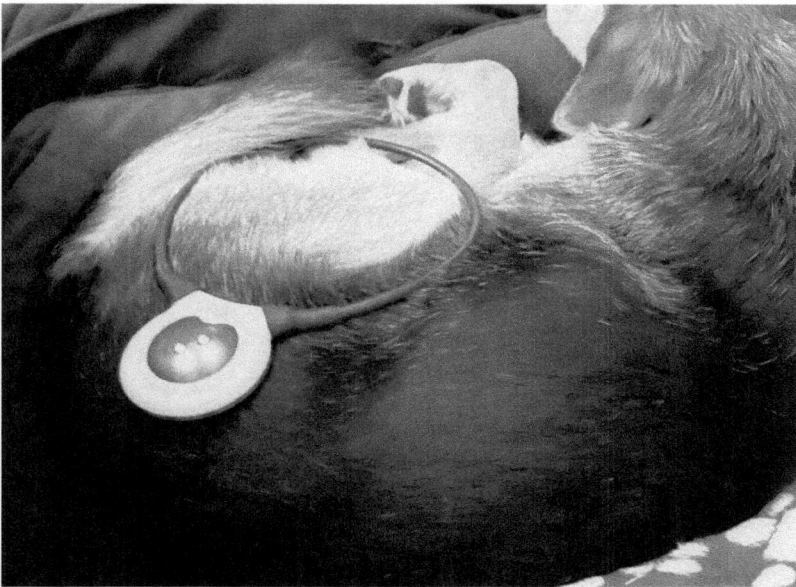

Luce resting with the Assisi Loop on left leg

15 — Therapeutic Exercise - These are exercises that will help increase flexibility, improve range of motion, and build or maintain muscle. Please consult your rehabilitation veterinarian for a home exercise plan that is appropriate for your dog!

- **Controlled Leash Walking:** A simple yet effective way to help dogs recover from injuries, gradually increasing distance and intensity.

- **Stair Climbs:** Encouraging slow, controlled stair climbing can strengthen muscles and improve coordination.

- **Hind Leg Stands:** A classic exercise for canine physical therapy to strengthen hind legs and improve stability.

- **Sit & Stand:** These exercises can help improve muscle strength and coordination.

- **Cookie Stretches:** Using treats to encourage your dog to stretch their head and neck, improving flexibility.

- **Ball Balance:** Using exercise balls or balance blocks to improve balance and proprioception.

- **Extended Paw Touches:** Encouraging your dog to touch their paws to different objects, improving coordination and proprioception.

- **Passive Range of Motion:** Gentle stretching and manipulation of joints to maintain flexibility and prevent stiffness.

- **Gait Training:** Exercises designed to improve a dog's ability to stand and walk correctly.

- **Strength Training:** Exercises like sit-to-stand, walking uphill, or using resistance bands to rebuild muscle mass.

16 – Hydrotherapy (Underwater Treadmill for Dogs or Swimming)
- The underwater treadmill is considered state–of–the–art in pet rehabilitation and has long been respected as a powerful tool for rebuilding strength. The buoyancy takes much of the weight off the joints, allowing movement to occur more naturally and with less pain.

The moving floor encourages walking, while the warm water increases circulation and provides resistance that helps build strength. Free swimming in a pool should be one of the **last** things your dog does during recovery (Guadagni, 2024a), Hodgson, H., Blake, S., & de Godoy, R. F. (2023).

Underwater treadmill used for both horses and dogs

17 – Aqua-Acupuncture (Injection of Liquid, Usually B12, into Acupuncture Points)
- Vitamin B12 injections can address deficiencies, improve energy levels, and support nerve function by helping the body produce myelin, which protects nerve fibers.

18 – Adequan Injections - Adequan Canine helps restore joint lubrication, relieve inflammation, and renew the building blocks of healthy joint cartilage to keep dogs moving. It can be used early, at the first clinical signs of canine osteoarthritis.

19 – Applied Kinesiology (AK) – Applied Kinesiology is a muscle testing system that allows you or your veterinarian to tap into energetic disturbances and weaknesses in the physical, chemical, and emotional body of your dog.

Muscle feedback is influenced by changes in the nervous system, muscle fiber/tissue impairment, toxins, organ stress, meridian blockages, and emotional stress.

In western medicine, we have a thorough understanding of animal anatomy and the intricacies of muscles and organs. Traditional Chinese Medicine (TCM), on the other hand, considers the body as whole when treating ailments.

TCM principles recognize that each muscle in the body is associated with a specific organ, meridian, and chakra.

Kinesiology is a unique modality in that it combines both Eastern and Western methodology with the art of muscle testing.

20 – Iridology: Your dog's iris is complex and contains a large number of fibers connected to every nerve, muscle, and organ throughout the body via the brain and spinal cord.

Through this intricate network, you can observe how each of your dog's systems affects one another.

Luce's right eye - picture of iris

Iridology analyses subtle changes in the iris that manifest as pigment discolorations, eyespots, lines, and textures.

It teaches those imbalances in the body cause rings, spots, and other pigment changes that directly correlate to your dog's organs and tissues - as well as the presence of toxins, chemicals, medications, and heavy metals.

A skilled practitioner focuses on identifying the root cause of your dog's condition, rather than just the illness or its symptoms.

They can help uncover physiological imbalances before symptoms appear, giving you time to adjust your dog's diet, supplementation, and environment - possibly preventing chronic or degenerative illness.

Iridology can also be used to determine whether a current treatment is effective.

21 – Color Therapy: Color therapy, also known as chromotherapy, is an alternative medicine practice that uses color and light to promote healing and well-being.

It is based on the belief that different colors have specific therapeutic effects on the body and mind.

Additional therapies are available, though I haven't used them with Luce. I'm mentioning them here briefly so you're aware of them and can ask if they might benefit your dog:

1 – Platelet-Rich Plasma (PRP) – This therapy shows promise in treating dogs with torn ACLs, potentially reducing pain and promoting healing.

However, it may not fully regenerate the ligament, and surgery might still be necessary in some cases.

PRP therapy involves concentrating a dog's own platelets, which contain growth factors that help promote tissue repair and reduce inflammation (Platelet-Rich Plasma Therapy, n.d.), PRP Therapy in Equine and Canine, n.d.).

2 – Stem Cell Therapy - Stem cell therapy is a form of regenerative medicine with many applications.

Stem cells are undifferentiated cells that can self-renew, regenerate, and differentiate into different cell types, including bone, cartilage, tendon, and ligament cells.

This capability enables the regeneration and repair of tissue damaged by disease or injury Stem Cell Therapy for Musculoskeletal Conditions, n.d .).

Quick point of clarification to help you better understand the difference between an Assisi Loop and a PEMF Mat.

The primary difference between an Assisi Loop and a PEMF mat lies in their delivery method and targeted application.

An Assisi Loop is a portable, handheld device that delivers Targeted Pulsed Electromagnetic Field (tPEMF) therapy to a specific area of the body, while a PEMF mat covers a larger area of the body, often the entire back or body.

Assisi Loop

Delivery Method: A portable loop that can be placed on a specific area of the body for focused treatment.

Application: Often used for targeted pain relief, inflammation reduction, and accelerated healing in specific areas like joints, muscles, or wounds.

Targeted Application: Designed for animals and small animals, but can also be used for humans.

Power: Generally, uses a lower-intensity tPEMF signal.

Purpose: To reduce inflammation, pain, and swelling, and to promote healing in targeted areas.

PEMF Mat

Delivery Method: A mat that delivers tPEMF therapy over a larger area of the body, often the entire back or body.

Application: Used for general wellness, muscle recovery, pain relief, and to support the body's natural healing process.

Targeted Application: Can be used for both humans and animals.

Power: Can use higher-intensity tPEMF signals.

Purpose: To reduce inflammation, pain, and swelling, to promote healing, and to improve overall well-being.

Follow Me to the Other Side of the Joint

Dr. Johnson and Dr. Froeling used a variety of therapeutic exercises in Luce's canine rehabilitation — exercises designed to improve joint mobility, flexibility, strength, and endurance.

Having professionals guide the timing and type of designated exercises was crucial as Luce's body healed.

Dr. Johnson explains, *"Soft tissue injuries often need long rehabilitation that can be frustrating to both the owner and the patient. Doing things right the first time is critical to getting the best possible outcomes in these cases. Soft tissue injury cases with targeted rehabilitation prove to be the best examples of success with rehab -- versus chronic lameness without."*

To illustrate this, please refer to the three figures below:

1. **Image 1 (below)** - shows an injured tendon or ligament. The toothpicks represent a disrupted fiber pattern with excess fluid between the fibers.

Image 1: Injured tendon or ligament

2. Image 2 (below) - demonstrates what happens without structured rehab: the fibers heal in a starburst pattern within the first three months after injury. This structure is weaker and more prone to reinjury when the dog returns to work or sport.

Image 2: Injured tendon or ligament without structured rehab

3. **Image 3** shows an organized fiber pattern, which can be achieved through therapeutic exercise, laser therapy, cross-frictional massage, appropriate use of heat and cold therapy, and injectable therapies such as PRP and stem cells.

Image 3: Organized fiber pattern

Dr. Johnson explains the tendon/ligament in Image 3: *"This tendon or ligament is going to be much more resilient as our patients return to work and sport."*

Ultimately, however, it's the skills and training of the veterinarian and therapist – along with your willingness to learn how to perform these exercises at home – that bring the benefits of therapeutic exercise to our dogs.

There are several factors to consider before using exercise to increase range of motion. Do you want to improve active or passive range of motion? What joint is being treated? Which tissues around the joint are affecting its range of motion? What is the condition of the joint surfaces, articular cartilage, joint capsule, and ligaments? Keep in mind that restoring a "normal" range of motion may or may not be possible, depending on the lesions affecting the joint. When working to increase range of motion in a canine patient, the ultimate goal is to gain function.

Range-of-motion exercises can be performed actively or passively. In an active range-of-motion exercise, Luce was encouraged to perform movements that bring the joint through the desired range. In a passive range-of-motion exercise, the motion is created by the handler or therapist. For example, gentle flexion and extension of the stifle may be used in a postoperative anterior cruciate ligament repair patient.

It's essential to recognize the difference between range of motion and flexibility. Range of motion refers to the movement capabilities of joints, while flexibility involves the elasticity of muscles and tendons. Interestingly, flexibility issues often involve two muscles around the same joint rather than just one. Once these muscles are identified, therapeutic stretching exercises can be introduced.

Like you and me, Luce always warmed up before starting her stretching routine. For non-ambulatory patients, methods like electrical stimulation or therapeutic ultrasound can serve as effective warm-up alternatives. Therapeutic stretches fall into two categories: active and passive. An active stretch is initiated by the dog – treats, for instance, can motivate the dog to reach for certain positions, stretching the targeted muscle.

Active stretching can also include activities like weaving through cones or navigating tight turns. Passive stretches, on the other hand, are performed by the handler or therapist. A good example is extending the forelimb to stretch the latissimus dorsi and teres major muscles. To reap the benefits of passive stretching, it's crucial that the dog feels at ease with the handler or therapist and remains relaxed and cooperative throughout the process.

Building endurance is crucial for canine athletes. Dogs that have been inactive for an extended period often have very low endurance levels. This is because the first muscle fibers to deteriorate during immobilization are the slow-twitch fibers - essential for maintaining posture and resisting gravity. For these dogs, early endurance training may begin with something as simple assisted standing, focusing on strengthening postural muscles rather than boosting cardiovascular fitness.

In contrast, endurance training primarily aims to enhance cardiovascular health in athletic dogs. Various methods - such as land routines, treadmill work, and swimming - can be used to improve strength, speed, and the overall duration of physical activity. Monitoring heart rate, respiratory rate, and recovery time after intense workouts is essential. Adding resistance through weighted vests, sleds, resistance bands, hill training, and water exercises can further enhance the effectiveness of any exercise program.

Strength training centers on building resistance. For instance, Luce's strength training began slowly, with simple movements like transitioning from a down position to a sit, then progressing to a stand - using gravity as the only form of resistance. As Luce became more capable, external resistance was gradually introduced to further develop her strength.

Many dogs undergoing rehabilitation face challenges with body awareness, also known as proprioception. Therapeutic exercise can effectively target this issue in various ways. For patients who are weak or unsteady, proprioception training might begin with assisted standing, gradually progressing to independent standing. During this stage, the handler or therapist introduces gentle movements to challenge the dog's balance. Once the dog can maintain stability despite these perturbations, additional tools – such as rocker boards, wobble boards, and other unstable surfaces - can be introduced to further enhance their skills.

A rocker board features a platform with a rounded underside that allows it to tilt side to side when a dog stands on it. The dog must actively engage their muscles to counteract this movement and stay balanced. Once they excel with the rocker board, the next step is a wobble board, which has a dome-shaped bottom that can tilt in any direction. Increasing the dome's size raises the difficulty level. At home, I already had some FitPaws equipment, including paw pads and an inflatable peanut, which I incorporated into the exercise routine. I also own an Indo Board, originally used to improve my balance for paddle boarding during the winter. This board rests on an inflatable bladder, and users can adjust the air level to vary the difficulty. I adapted the Indo Board to serve as a wobbleboard for Luce, giving her a fun way to work on her balance.

Proprioception exercises can be more engaging by incorporating activities like walking through a pile of PVC rails or navigating Cavaletti rails set at varying heights and distances. Another effective method is walking your dog on an air mattress, which helps enhance proprioception. The more inflated the mattress, the easier it is for the dog. As your dog gains skill on this unstable surface, you can introduce gentle perturbations – either to the dog or the mattress itself. Balance blocks are also useful tools; placing your dog on these blocks and asking them to stand creates challenges. By sliding the blocks apart or moving them forward and backward, you are the one prompting the dog to recapture balance.

It's crucial to work with a rehabilitation veterinarian who can evaluate your dog's condition, determine which parts of the body are affected, and assess the stage of healing. This evaluation helps set clear goals and shapes a therapeutic exercise program tailored to your dog's unique needs. Throughout the recovery process, Luce was assessed at each visit to track progress and make adjustments as needed to address any deficits. The rehabilitation veterinarian plays a key role in recognizing when Luce is ready to progress from foundational exercises to more advanced challenges. Ultimately, the goal is to enhance the dog's functionality and quality of life. Instead of seeking advice from online forums, it's important to remember that each injury is unique - misguided advice could inadvertently hinder your dog's recovery.

Now that I've outlined the various modalities I used during Luce's healing journey, let's revisit the date of her injury. I'll walk you through the immediate steps I took for Luce, and what I did in the days, weeks, and months that followed - all with a timeline in mind. This section will likely be the most intricate, detailing how I applied these modalities and products over time. I appreciate your patience as we navigate through this, just as you did with the chapters on supplements and nutrition.

When an injury like this occurs, the first step is to look around your home for therapeutic tools and supportive products. Having been involved in sports and with Luce for the past seven years, I've accumulated a collection of proper therapeutic instruments. It's only natural for a canine athlete like Luce to experience minor injuries or strains that require home care. To ensure she performed at her best, Luce regularly received therapy from Dr. Jana Froeling, including chiropractic adjustments and acupuncture.

Dr. Jana Froeling, an experienced equine veterinarian, has a deep understanding of horses' mobility needs and has successfully applied that knowledge to dogs as well. As an expert in Eastern medicine, she stands out from other Veterinarians who may have only taken a brief course in acupuncture or chiropractic. Dr. Froeling has traveled to Asia to study these practices in depth, making her highly qualified and providing years of hands-on experience in treating orthopedic injuries in both large and small animals. If you're looking for a veterinarian, she's the one to turn to. While your local Veterinarian could become competent with a few weeks of training, they simply can't match the extensive expertise Dr. Froeling offers.

Luce is accustomed to chiropractic and acupuncture treatments, and she generally enjoys them, so she's usually eager for an appointment. However, when she's in pain, the visit becomes trickier to manage. She often seems apprehensive about being touched, occasionally casting a wary glance at Dr. Froeling and attempting to back away. Yet, despite her hesitation, she allows the treatment as needed.

The injury occurred on Friday, August 18, 2023. After that, we rested for two days while waiting to see our regular Veterinarian for a complete diagnosis. Those two days were filled with pain, inflammation, swelling, heat, and constant stress. First aid is vital for orthopedic injuries, as it can help minimize pain, prevent further damage, and promote quicker recovery while awaiting professional medical attention, ensuring the injured dog's safety and well-being.

Right away, I supported Luce's injured leg by applying ice. Although I wasn't fully aware of the extent of her injury, I knew that cold would help reduce swelling and manage some pain. Ice plays a crucial role in addressing acute orthopedic injuries like sprains and strains, as it decreases swelling, pain, and inflammation by constricting blood vessels and numbing the area, especially when applied within the first 48 hours. When blood vessels leak fluid into the injured area, swelling occurs. By constricting these blood vessels, ice limits fluid leakage and curbs inflammation. Additionally, the cold numbs the area, alleviating pain and tenderness, and helps relax tense muscles, which often respond to injury. By minimizing swelling and pain, ice can facilitate a quicker return to regular activity. I even took a video of her limping right after the injury, just in case she improved before the Veterinarian could see her in that state.

Luce with ice pack on right rear leg

I applied ice for 15 to 20 minutes, taking breaks to prevent skin damage. Using a towel as a barrier between the ice pack and Luce's skin helped avoid frostbite. After icing, I let her leg gradually return to its normal temperature on its own.

I have a few therapeutic tools at home, including a light-emitting diode (LED) device offering red, blue, and infrared wavelengths, a PEMF mat, and an ASSISI Loop. I reached for these because each offers unique benefits. Red LED light therapy promotes collagen production, helps reduce inflammation, and aids wound healing. In contrast, blue light specifically targets acne-causing bacteria, regulates oil production, and alleviates redness and inflammation. Different wavelengths of LED light correspond to various visible colors, each penetrating the skin to different depths.

Blue light affects the top layer of your skin, yellow light penetrates deeper, red light goes further, and near-infrared light reaches the deepest layers. Infrared light therapy effectively penetrates the skin, enhancing circulation and promoting relaxation. It also helps alleviate pain, supports muscle recovery, and aids in detoxification.

On the other hand, Pulsed Electromagnetic Field Therapy (PEMF) modulates inflammatory processes by regulating pro- and anti-inflammatory cytokines at various stages of the inflammatory response. Targeted PEMF therapy, such as the ASSISI loop, provides a noninvasive solution for reducing pain and inflammation. This approach may enhance healing, boost circulation, and promote relaxation by stimulating the body's natural anti-inflammatory mechanisms.

Over the weekend, while waiting for the Veterinarian appointment on Monday, I made sure to use all the products I had at least twice a day with Luce. A few years ago, I bought ramps for my 13-year-old Yorkshire terrier, Harley, to help her get on and off the bed and into the window benches. Since Harley could no longer jump to those heights, I wanted to ensure she didn't hurt herself or feel left out, so I placed 2-3 ramps around the house. Although they were a bit small for Luce, she adapted and used them anyway. Her love for agility and walking on different surfaces really came into play. I repurposed those ramps to give Luce access to the bed, couch, and window bench. She quickly realized that jumping wasn't an option anymore and naturally relied on the ramps whenever possible.

Seeing how well the ramps I already had worked, I decided to invest in three larger ones from the same company to make it easier for Luce to get around the house. I also picked up two car ramps to help her climb in and out of the vehicle. With these new additions, I now had one ramp for the couch, one for the bed, and one for each window, allowing her to hop into the window seats with ease.

Bedroom with ramp to allow access to bed and yoga mat on hardwood floors

Over the past two years, I've replaced all the carpets in my home with hardwood floors. While I laid down a few throw rugs, there was still a lot of bare floors exposed.

One of the first pieces of advice I received was to avoid letting Luce walk on slippery surfaces. Since she enjoys sprinting around the house, the hardwood floors posed a real challenge.

I headed to Five Below over the weekend to tackle this issue and picked up about eight yoga mats. They were cheaper than traditional rugs, provided a good grip, and could be easily rolled up and transported.

I spread the mats across the bare areas of the floor, creating a safe path for her to follow. Instinctively, she took to the covered path, and the slippery floor problem seemed finally solved.

I have 20 deck stairs from my front door to the grass outside. Although I have living space in the lower section of my house, moving there would mean being completely separate from my family, so I decided to stay upstairs and carry Luce up and down the stairs.

At no point did I crate her or limit her freedom to move around the house. Harley, my elderly dog, wasn't interested in playing with Luce, so I didn't have to keep them apart. They were generally quiet while spending time together.

My property spans five acres, but Luce can't yet roam freely everywhere. To give her a safe space, I picked up some fence panels from the supply store and set up a small fenced area around my office.

This way, she could enjoy the grass outside while I worked. She also had easy access through the dog door to the yard and could come back inside whenever she wanted to rest.

Fence panels in yard to limit free yard access, ramps to allow access over stairs. All allowing outdoor space outside my office.

Additionally, I put a gate at the top of the stairs leading from the front door to the yard. Since she couldn't navigate the stairs independently, the gate ensured she could quickly go in and out to bask in the sun through the dog door without having to navigate the stairs.

At this stage, the house was ready for Luce to live comfortably and safely without making too many changes that might unsettle her. I approached the situation this way intentionally, as I wanted to avoid putting her under stress. A stable routine is crucial for a dog's well-being. However, I also had to keep in mind that if I was going to work on her rehabilitation over the next 12 months, I couldn't let it disrupt family life or completely overhaul my daily routine. We occasionally spent time in the lower level of the house, but it was easy to rearrange ramps and yoga mats to create a familiar setup downstairs, just like we had upstairs. Yes, I carried her up and down the stairs as often as she needed it - my personal osteoporosis prevention plan, courtesy of weight-bearing exercises.

It was a crazy time.

On August 19, 2023, I reached out to Luce's therapeutic massage therapist, Nancy Lilly from Whiskers 2 Paws, to let her know about Luce's injury. Luce had received massages from Nancy before, so she was already a familiar face in this ongoing treatment. Nancy wasted no time and came over to perform some muscle work on Luce, focusing on areas around the injury. It's likely that during the moment of injury, Luce twisted and engaged different muscle groups to stabilize herself – something that can lead to painful compensation injuries if those muscles aren't conditioned for that kind of strain.

Nancy approached Luce's treatment with great care, using gentle muscle work to help her body relax and promote the movement of stagnant lymph fluid, lactic acid, and swelling from her limbs. She then applied a Class III cold laser to the tight areas and Luce's injured leg. Before leaving, Nancy taught me how to use the laser, and I began using it on Luce twice a day - ten minutes on the injured leg and five on the healthy one. I decided to stop using my infrared LED light once I started with the laser. It's important to note that while both infrared LEDs and Class III cold lasers are used in light therapy, they differ in light emission and power output. IR LEDs emit a broader light spectrum, while Class III lasers deliver a focused, coherent beam with a lower power output than the Class IV lasers typically used by veterinarians.

> *Caring for the sound leg is just as crucial as treating the injured one. While the therapy may not be as rigorous for the healthy leg, staying ahead of any potential issues is essential - especially if that leg becomes fatigued or stressed. With weight being offloaded, the good leg takes on more work, so proactive measures are key to maintaining its strength and functionality.*

By August 24, 2023, I felt I was making headway in managing Luce's pain – she was improving and becoming more animated. However, she still wouldn't put weight on her right rear leg, which made it increasingly challenging to keep her calm. Observation skills became crucial. I noticed she was shifting her weight onto her left leg by the way her foot splayed; the left foot was noticeably more spread out than the right. I also began spotting signs of discomfort in other parts by examining her fur. There were visible swirls and flips along her spine, neck, and tail. These coat changes - such as hair standing on end and appearing uneven - can indicate underlying fascial tension or myofascial pain, which is relatively common in dogs.

Hair follicles are closely connected to fascia, the connective tissue that surrounds muscles, bones, nerves, and organs. When fascia becomes tight or restricted, it can tug on the skin and hair follicles, altering hair direction and condition.

In addition to changes in coat appearance, dogs with myofascial pain may show signs like excessive rolling, sudden hair flicks, anxious behavior, or a reluctance to be touched or groomed. Thankfully, this type of pain can often be relieved through canine massage therapy, which helps release fascial restrictions and restore muscle function.

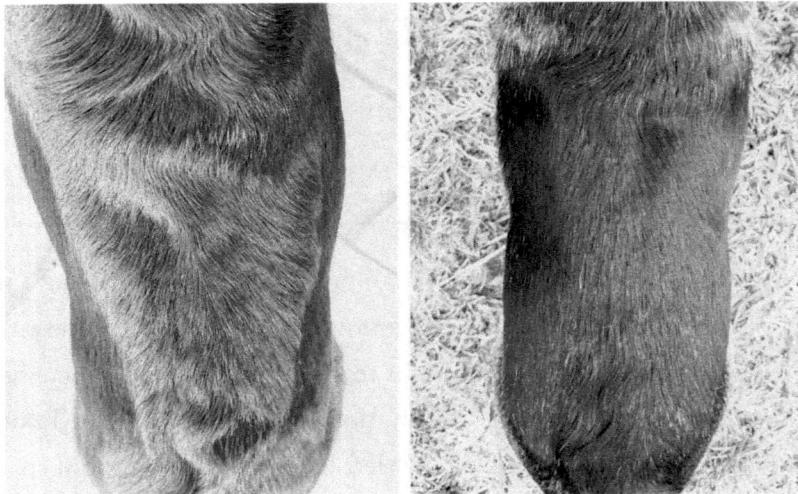

Left: Coat with fascial restrictions patterning; Right: After myofascial work, coat shows normal patterning.

While you have hands on your dog doing myofascial work, take notice if there is heat anywhere along the body as you gently feel for twitches. Feeling increased heat on the skin during myofascial work on your dog could indicate several things, including increased blood flow, muscle activation, or inflammation in the area. Pain or inflammation in the muscles or joints along the spine can also lead to localized heat.

Every now and then, a wave of sadness would wash over me as I silently contemplated the task ahead: calling all the race directors to explain that we wouldn't be able to compete this year because Luce was injured. I understood this would be a long healing journey, and I worried that her days of running on trails might be over. I was anxious - would I be smart enough to help her, strong enough to support her, steady enough to guide her through this tough time?

I share this because many of you might feel something similar. We can't ignore these emotions—they're real and valid. Each morning, I had to choose positivity. I made a conscious decision to manifest our destiny rather than leave it to fate. If I encountered something I didn't understand, I was determined to educate myself. I knew I had to believe in myself to create a successful outcome. Luce was counting on me to lead her through this challenge, and I felt the weight of that trust heavily on my shoulders.

Unbeknownst to me my 13-year-old Yorkshire Terrier, Harley, was in a fight for her life - battling lymphoma at the same time. When Luce's injury occurred, our family was set to go on a cross-country camping trip. My spouse had already hit the road, heading west, and I was supposed to catch up so we could continue together. However, I ran into a problem: the lights on my camper wouldn't work with my truck. Strangely, they worked perfectly with a different truck, and my vehicle functioned fine with another camper - but not with my own. It was a real head-scratcher, and the issue ended up delaying my departure.

The following week, I took my truck and camper to several repair shops, searching for a solution. At that time, I had no idea that Harley was struggling with lymphoma. Although her lymph nodes were swollen and I had already scheduled a veterinarian appointment, the swelling had come on suddenly, and she otherwise seemed perfectly fine.

I kept pushing to make this trip happen despite the setbacks. I was fully packed and ready to go when the Veterinarian delivered the news about the likelihood of lymphoma in my dog. Even so, I decided we would all go - considering it might be Harley's last big adventure and a chance for us to be together. The very next day, after I finally got the camper lights working and was set to leave, Luce injured herself in the front yard. That was the end of the trip. Luce seemed to sense that Harley was in decline and didn't have much time left. She also knew that if she was hurt, I wouldn't be able to travel - so she took one for the team to keep us all at home. Harley passed away just four weeks later.

I want to share this with you because, as you know, injuries like these rarely happen in isolation. If, like me, you have multiple dogs or life circumstances that make it hard to be a full-time caretaker, this message is especially for you. I wrote this book to give you a glimpse into my journey and to help you navigate the decisions you'll face with your dog. My hope is that my experiences will guide you toward a more successful outcome than you might achieve on your own.

Luce has gifted me with an abundance of wisdom throughout this journey, and keeping that knowledge to myself would feel like a missed opportunity. Losing Harley hit me hard - it was a deep emotional setback that made it difficult to be fully present for Luce. Grieving for Harley while staying upbeat for Luce was no easy task, but that's exactly what I did. I channeled all that grief into something positive. Was Harley's departure a nudge to help me focus more on Luce? I may never know. What I do know is that, in their own unique ways, both of them made sure I would be okay.

We're now into the second week since Luce's injury, and we have an appointment scheduled with Dr. Jana Froeling. For the past seven years, Luce has regularly received chiropractic adjustments and acupuncture from Dr. Froeling, so this visit feels like returning to a trusted ally. It's her first session since the injury ten days ago. Ahead of the appointment, I shared all the relevant findings, notes, and X-rays from the other veterinarians so Dr. Froeling would be fully up to speed.

During the examination, Dr. Froeling confirmed Dr. Katherine Johnson's assessment and shared her optimism that Luce's recovery could be managed conservatively – with patience and a well-structured plan. She recommended beginning rehabilitation therapies right away, including a chiropractic adjustment, therapeutic ultrasound targeting the iliopsoas muscle, and acupuncture. She estimated that full healing would take around 12 months. While she expected Luce to start feeling better within a few months, she stressed the importance of staying consistent with therapy and not giving Luce too much freedom too soon. Recover, she reminded me gently, is a marathon – not a sprint.

Additionally, Dr. Froeling advised me to gently pull Luce's hip back and consider laser treatment in the femoral triangle due to the strain in her iliopsoas. She recommended waiting a couple of weeks before introducing the treadmill into her recovery plan. For support, Dr. Froeling suggested applying KT tape not only to the injured leg but also to both rear legs. During the session, she performed a therapeutic ultrasound on the right iliopsoas muscle, setting it to 1.4 Watts at an 80% duty cycle and 1 MHz for 15 minutes. She noted that I could begin incorporating functional exercises in a week or two, such as hip sways, lifting her left leg, having her place her front feet on a step and stretch side to side towards her ribs and hips, and standing on a balance pad.

She emphasized that modifying activity is a crucial part of non-surgical management for a CCL injury. The first 8 to 12 weeks after the injury are vital for limiting activity, although complete immobilization isn't necessary. While initial rest is key to ligament healing, overly restricting movement can actually impede recovery and lead to stiffness and decreased functionality. A balanced approach - incorporating controlled movement and rehabilitation - is essential. During this period, the dog's body is working to form scar tissue around the knee joint, which helps stabilize it while also reducing inflammation and swelling.

Ligaments heal with scar tissue, which lacks the strength and flexibility of the original tissue. Encouraging movement during the healing process can promote the development of more organized and functional scar tissue. In Luce's case, since it's a complete tear, her body won't be able to fully heal or regrow the torn CCL. However, forming scar tissue around the knee can help reduce instability in the joint.

It's crucial not to keep your dog crated all day, every day. Extended periods of immobilization can lead to stiffness and reduce the joint's range of motion. If a ligament injury doesn't heal properly, it may result in joint instability, making the area more vulnerable to further injury. Keep in mind that ligaments aren't isolated - problems in one area can affect other parts of the body. In some cases, incomplete healing can lead to chronic pain and long-term complications.

Restricted movement refers to preventing your dog from running, jumping, engaging in rough play, or spending time off-leash in the yard. It's also essential to avoid letting your dog walk on slippery surfaces and to lend a hand when they navigate stairs.

These activities can be risky during recovery, as the muscle groups supporting the injured knee may not be strong enough to handle the strain, increasing the risk of re-injury.

Dr. Froeling expressed her belief that we could heal Luce's leg to about 85% if we approached the process correctly and remained patient. However, she cautioned that any re-injury could prevent the leg from ever achieving that level of healing again. Each time the scar tissue is damaged, the potential for full recovery decreases. She emphasized the importance of staying dedicated to the initial healing process to maximize Luce's recovery.

Dr. Froeling advised me to switch from using ice to applying heat on the iliopsoas. She also demonstrated how to use KT tape on Luce to support her knee. I had used KT tape on myself before but had never thought about using it on a dog, which sparked my curiosity.

The curiosity led me to enroll in a KT tape certification course so I could learn the proper technique for taping Luce's leg, ensuring she has the appropriate support throughout her recovery and beyond.

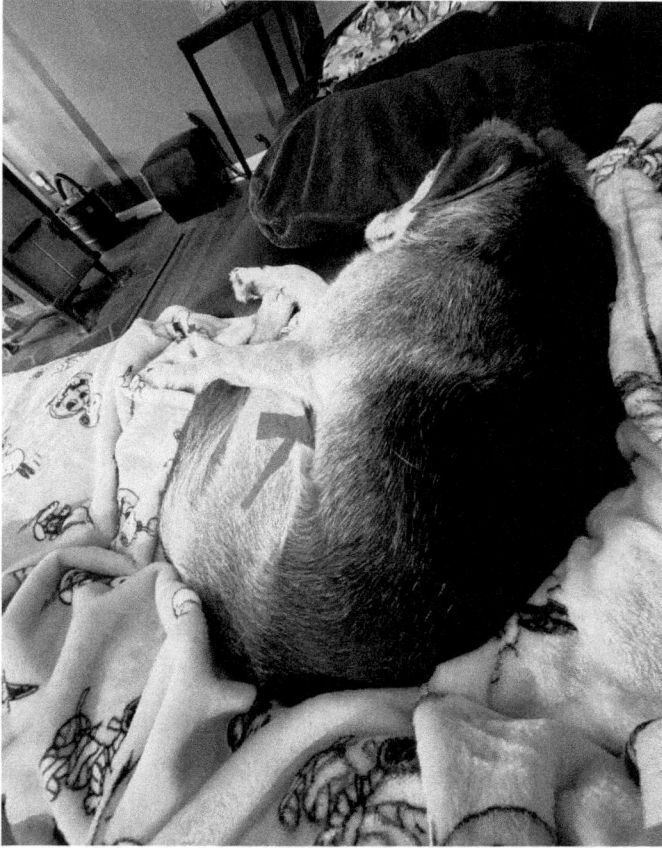

Luce with KT tape on both the left leg (good leg) and the injured leg, both used to support the body while healing.

If you're unfamiliar with KT tape, you might be wondering what it is and how it works. Kinesiology tape, or KT tape, is effective for dogs because it gently lifts the skin, promoting better blood flow and lymphatic circulation. This can help reduce inflammation, enhance circulation, and provide muscle support while alleviating pain.

When applied correctly, the tape has a slight recoil effect, creating tiny spaces between the skin and the underlying tissues.

These spaces allow for improved blood and lymphatic fluid circulation, which can minimize swelling, aid healing, and relieve discomfort.

Additionally, the tape supports muscles, ligaments, and tendons, making it beneficial for dogs dealing with injuries or mobility challenges.

It can also activate receptors in the skin, boosting proprioception (awareness of body position) and aiding muscle activation.

KT tape is known to alleviate pain associated with various injuries, arthritis, and other conditions. It can improve mobility and range of motion in dogs experiencing joint issues or muscle weakness.

By promoting lymphatic drainage, KT tape also helps reduce swelling and inflammation. Additionally, it offers support to muscles, ligaments, and tendons, making it especially beneficial for dogs with injuries or mobility challenges.

During Luce's initial visit to VRSVA, Dr. Johnson recognized that she was reasonably fit and accustomed to an active lifestyle. Luce presented as lean, with well-defined muscle mass, and was a cheerful and cooperative patient. Dr. Belden noted that soreness in her T11 region on both sides.

Upon gentle palpation, Luce exhibited pain in the right iliopsoas area. Additionally, there was lateral instability in her right stifle, though only a slight cranial drawer was observed. Soft clicking occurred during the stifle examination; however, the radiographs did not show significant effusion in that joint. She was described as being 5/5 lame.

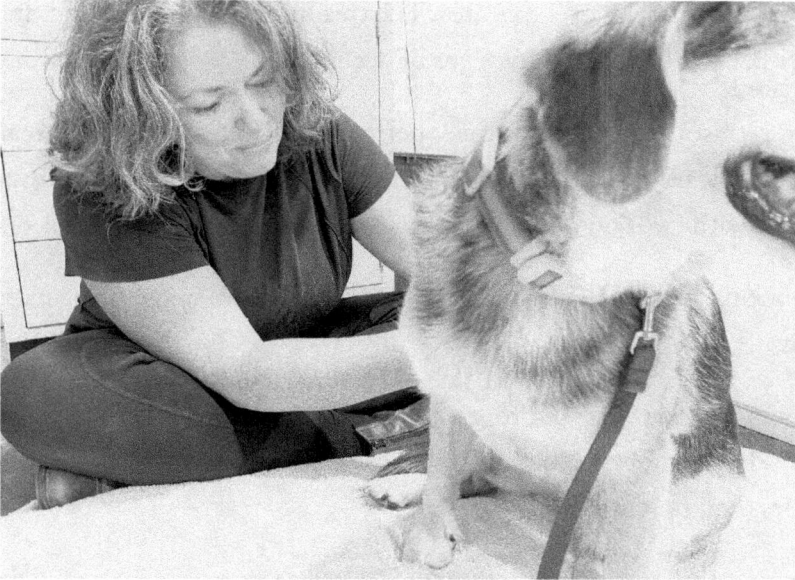

Dr. Belden performing laser therapy on Luce

Dr. Belden performed laser therapy on Luce's right stifle and targeted trigger points along her back, also utilizing myofascial release techniques in those areas.

During the session, gentle bicycle movements were introduced in both directions while stabilizing the stifle.

Dr. Johnson recommended sit-to-stand exercises using a pillow or a Fitbone for Luce to sit on, to elevate her hind end and reduce the strain on her injured area as she performed the exercise.

It's essential to adjust Luce's sitting position if it isn't square and to repeat the exercise up to ten times, three times a day, as long as the quality of her movement remains satisfactory. If her seat becomes unsquared at any point, the exercise should be halted.

Additionally, Luce spent one minute on the underwater treadmill at one mph, then took a 30 second break. The water was at hip height and this was repeated for a total of 7 minutes. The treadmill was stopped and drained once her gait began to show signs of decline.

The ultrasound of Luce's knee, performed by Dr. Johnson, revealed a meniscal tear. It was a complete tear, likely stemming from the ligament injury, with two equal halves present and no small fragments detected.

A clicking sound was also noted in the knee, further suggesting a meniscal tear.

As you all know, I opted for conservative management despite this diagnosis, believing it was better to retain the meniscal padding between the bones than to remove it.

Keeping the meniscus intact, when possible, is generally beneficial, as it preserves the knee's natural shock absorption and reduces the risk of long-term issues like osteoarthritis.

Tears located on the outer part of the meniscus, known as the red-white zone, are more likely to heal on their own due to better blood circulation.

In contrast, tears on the inner section, referred to as the white zone, may necessitate surgical intervention because of inadequate blood supply.

Luce about to have ultrasound done at VRSVA

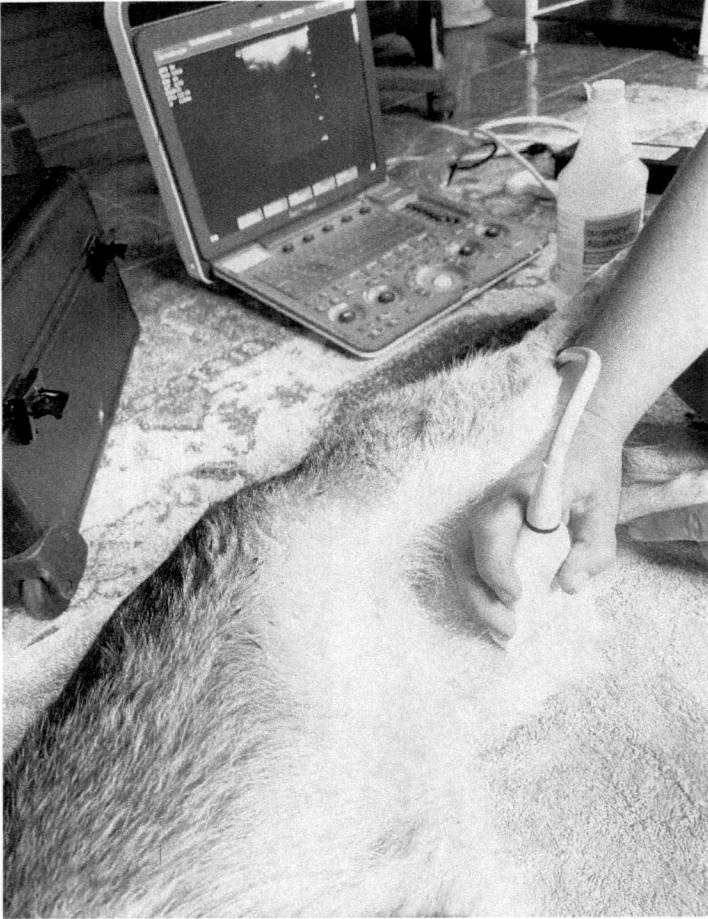

Luce getting ultrasound done at VRSVA

I focused on stabilizing the joint and enhancing blood flow to the meniscus as much as I could. To assist with healing and improve circulation to Luce's meniscus, I implemented gentle massage, controlled range-of-motion exercises, KT tape, and heat therapy - always in consultation with Dr. Johnson and Dr. Froeling.

After two months of this approach, the knee showed signs of stabilization, and the clicking sound had disappeared entirely.

There are specialized tapes designed specifically for dogs, made from light-weight, breathable materials with an adhesive tailored for their fur.

Additionally, medical-grade kinesiology tape developed for veterinary use combines a unique blend of cotton with a breathable, non-allergenic mesh and an acrylic adhesive sourced from plant extracts. I use RockTape, and it is very effective.

As of the end of August, Luce exhibited a grade 4/5 lameness in the right rear leg, with only toe-touching on that leg. There was tenderness upon palpation, along with muscle spasms in the mid-caudal thoracic spine.

The medial stifle also showed tenderness when pressed, along with me-dial-lateral instability, though there was no significant stifle effusion. The iliopsoas muscle felt quieter, but the adductor muscle was notably tight and ropey.

Life Without Acupuncture is Pointless

On September 11, 2023, we had another follow-up appointment with Dr. Froeling. By this point, Luce had been spending 12 minutes on the underwater treadmill with Dr. Johnson.

During this visit, we tried acupuncture with a twist: it was connected to a device that sends a mild electric current to the area around her knee, similar to a TENS unit.

We used a frequency of 20 Hz for 10 minutes, followed by 80 over 120 Hz for another 10 minutes. This method was new for Luce, but she handled it quite well.

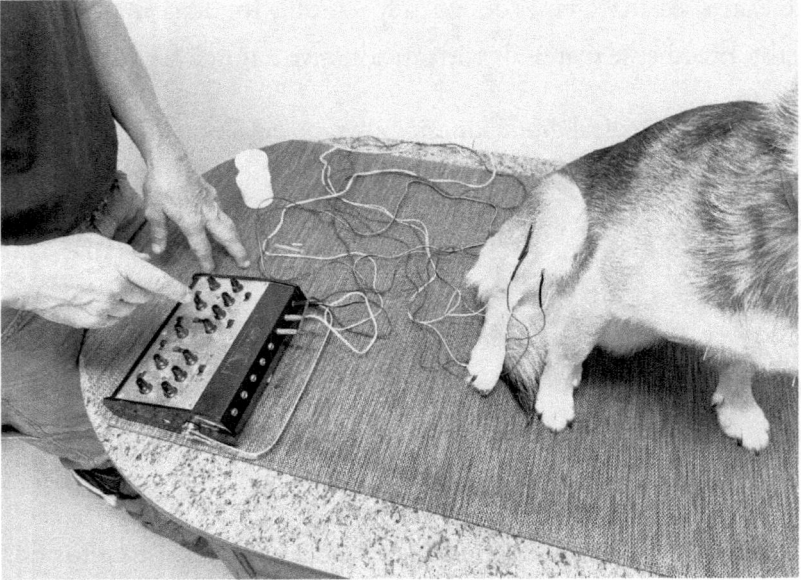

Luce receiving electroacupuncture at Full Circle Equine Services

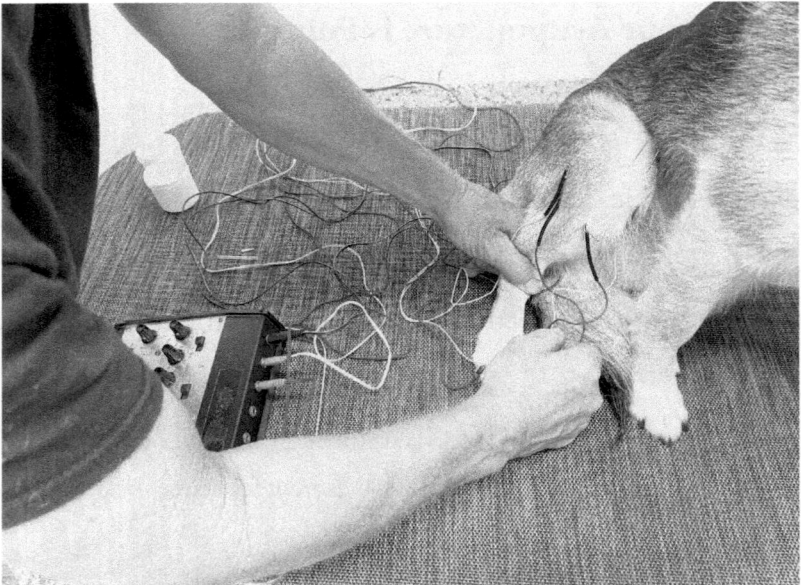

Dr. Jana Froeling attaching electrodes to acupuncture needles already placed on Luce's right rear leg

Dr. Froeling also performed some laser therapy on the iliopsoas muscle. In addition, Luce received her first subcutaneous injection of Adequan during this appointment. Dr. Froeling guided me on how to administer the injections at home, with the plan being one dose every four days for the first seven treatments—this is known as the loading dose. After that, I'll administer a dose once a month for maintenance.

Once injected, Adequan reaches peak levels in the joints within two hours. Hyaluronic acid levels in the joints nearly double over 48 hours, with marked increases observed between 24 to 96 hours. My goal is to protect and support the healing of the injured joint; however, since Adequan is not limited to just one joint, I'm also investing in the prevention and reduction of degenerative joint disease in her healthy leg and other areas of her body.

Adequan is directly integrated into the cartilage, enhancing the joint's ability to withstand compression. It has been shown to support healing and improve the long-term health of articular cartilage, ultimately shortening recovery time by promoting scar tissue formation at the injury site. Additionally, it helps preventing arthritis.

At this point, I've received the green light to proceed with sit-to-stands and was also encouraged to incorporate backward walking for about five steps daily. I was advised to gently push her onto her left side to encourage weight shifting onto her right rear. As she progressed, I was instructed to lift her left rear to promote more weight distribution on the right side, starting with five seconds and gradually increasing the duration as she improves. Additionally, I should continue with leg shakes on the left front and tapping her foot. The final exercise she added was an upward-facing dog stretch.

Take it All Run Day at a Time

Luce is a dog accustomed to running 15-20 miles a week on trails, competing in canine obstacle course races, and participating in 5k Canicross events. Suddenly, Luce had to stop all that and was doing nothing at all. This sudden shift in lifestyle can be harsh on an active, athletic dog. I found myself in a similar situation; I, too, had stopped running and was focusing solely on caring for my dogs.

Injuries are a reality in athletics, whether they're minor sprains or significant injuries that might need surgery, yet we are never truly prepared for the emotional toll they take. Now, imagine your dog is going through this but being unable to communicate how they feel. While we often focus on the physical aspect of recovery, the emotional impact of being injured can be just as significant. There's a psychological response to sports injuries, and it can differ widely among dogs.

Some common reactions I observed in other dogs include:

Depression: When a dog suffers an injury, it can lead to feelings of sadness and hopelessness, especially if the injury sidelines them for an extended period.

Anxiety and Fear: A dog's mental well-being and recovery can be significantly impacted by anxiety and fear of re-injury. This concern not only affects their healing process but can also increase the risk of future injuries. It's important for your dog to regain trust in their leg after it has been hurt.

Lack of Motivation: The thought of a long recovery can dampen a dog's spirits, making it difficult for them to stay engaged in their rehabilitation efforts. When facing a 12-month recovery schedule, dogs may become restless from frequent Veterinarian visits, leading them to form negative associations with the process.

Additionally, dogs that once had a job can experience an identity crisis when they're no longer engaged in meaningful work, leading to frustration.

Moreover, some dogs may not fully grasp the seriousness of their injuries and might attempt to return to their activities too soon. This can exacerbate the injury and is often a reflection of the handler's impatience.

It's essential to recognize that struggling with the stress and anxiety that come with injuries is perfectly normal. For instance, I found it hard to feel comfortable running without Luce, so I simply didn't. This wasn't beneficial for either of us. I realized that keeping her in a positive state of mind was crucial for her healing process. So, I started to think outside the box.

Necessity is the Mother of Invention

It's essential to be creative with your dog's exercise routine during an injury to maintain their mental and physical well-being, prevent boredom, and support their recovery by engaging both their minds and bodies in safe, alternative ways. Dogs need mental stimulation to stay happy, as a lack of it can lead to destructive behaviors. While some injuries may require limited physical activity, alternative exercises can help preserve muscle tone, enhance range of motion, and encourage healing. Although restricting movement may be vital for recovery, incorporating creative exercises can provide the necessary movement without putting undue stress on the injured area.

Even during the recovery phase, spending quality time with your dog through engaging activities not only strengthens your bond but also fosters a positive relationship. While rest is crucial, too much inactivity can lead to deconditioning. Incorporating creative exercises helps maintain muscle strength and overall fitness.

I'm excited to share my portfolio of "things to do," giving you fresh ideas when your own start to feel stale.

Puzzle toys are a fantastic way to engage your dog's mind and provide some mental exercise. Consider options like snuffle mats, food mazes, LickiMats, or interactive games such as hide-and-seek and treat hunts. Teaching new tricks can also offer great mental stimulation.

You might also enjoy a cozy movie night together. While you unwind, gentle massage therapy can improve circulation, ease muscle tension, and promote relaxation outside of structured therapy sessions. Simply laying your hands on your dog can also strengthen your bond.

Don't forget about **PROM** (Passive Range of Motion) exercises. Performing these exercises can help maintain joint flexibility and prevent stiffness.

Weight Shifting Exercises: Setting up an obstacle course at home using simple training tools or everyday items can be a lot of fun. These exercises are excellent for improving balance and proprioception. During one of our trips, I brought Luce's ramps with us.

In our hotel room, I arranged the ramps to form a course between the beds and down to the floor. Luce was guided to navigate the ramps, going up and over them, and once she completed her "agility" tasks, she was rewarded with treats!

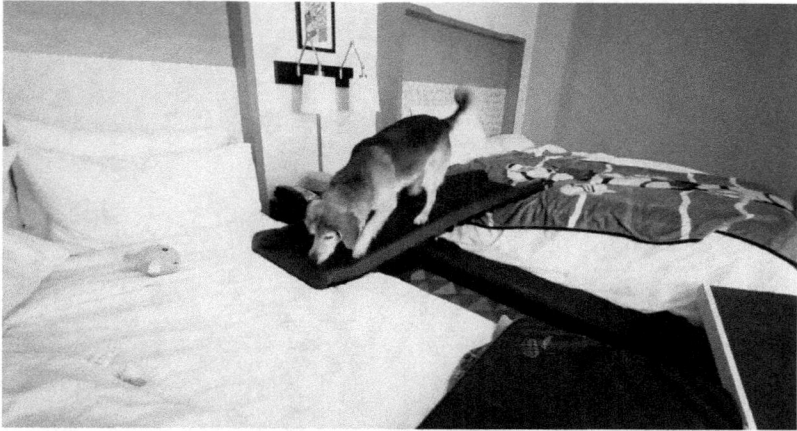

Hotel obstacle course using ramps

Quick Outings: Taking short, supervised walks on soft surfaces or exploring new areas can provide mental stimulation and a refreshing change of scenery for your dog.

Consider creating a sensory garden where your dog can wander on a leash, stopping to sniff, and enjoy snacks along the way.

Recently, Luce and I embarked on a cross-country journey as part of the US National Park Bark Ranger Program.

We visited various national parks, walked their trails on leash, and met with Park Rangers, who officially swore us in. Luce received a certificate, dog tag, or bandana as a keepsake.

Now, Luce proudly holds the title of a sworn Bark Ranger in over 57 National Parks and Historic Sites.

Luce U.S. Bark Ranger

Nose Work Training and Obedience: Why not take advantage of this time to incorporate strength-building exercises into a tricks routine?

It's essential to continue training with positive reinforcement while focusing on basic commands.

Since K9 Nose Work was conducted on-leash, I took Luce to classes that allowed her to engage in the task of finding scent.

She wore her brace, or I brought it along for slippery floors or high hides. Nose Work gave her a way to use her senses and kept her mind active during recovery.

*Luce doing K9 Nose Work competition while
healing.*

Interactive Toys: Use toys that promote problem-solving and encourage engagement.

Cavaletti Walking: This exercise involves setting up poles to guide your dog's movement and can help enhance their strength and coordination.

Cavaletti set up in doorway

Make a "Date" with Your Dog: Dedicate specific time to play with your dog - whether through a structured activity or simply enjoying some quality time together.

Earlier, I mentioned that Harley was struggling to jump onto furniture, so I bought her ramps to ensure she still had access to the parts of the house she loved.

I also got her an all-terrain buggy, which was a game-changer for our hikes. When she got tired, I could put her in the buggy and push her along, allowing her to travel much farther than she could on foot. After her passing, I repurposed the buggy for Luce. I secured her in the harness so we could go out for runs together.

The buggy's wheels are designed like bicycle tires, making it suitable for nearly any terrain without getting stuck.

While we couldn't tackle the challenging trails we once enjoyed, I could run behind it on the road, letting Luce feel the fresh air and wind on her face, giving us that team spirit we cherished.

Plus, the buggy folds up nicely to fit in my vehicle, so I could take it wherever we went.

When Luce was in the buggy, standing up helped her engage her core to maintain balance as we moved. This was an unorthodox way to strengthen her core and encourage her to put some weight on her injured leg while the buggy was in motion.

Luce's buggy

Balancing in the buggy proved to be an excellent way for Luce to shift her weight and engage numerous small muscle groups.

It not only allowed her to remain an active teammate despite being side-lined from her sport, but also enabled her to contribute to the team in new ways.

Moreover, it gave us the chance to get outside and enjoy nature, ensuring our outings weren't limited to veterinarian visits.

One way I got creative was by getting a K-9 Sports Sack.

Since I couldn't use the buggy on the trails that Luce and I used to explore, I invested in a safe dog carrier designed like a backpack. It allowed me to carry her comfortably on my shoulders while we ventured into the woods.

The style I chose has a sturdy frame to support her weight and a waist belt to secure her safely to me.

This method of transportation let us hike up mountains, stroll through parks, and travel around the city—all while keeping her close. Crucially, her position in the sack didn't aggravate her injury.

Luce in K9 Sport Sack ready for me to place her on my back

Luce on my back, front view

Luce on my back, rear view

These creative solutions allowed us to continue our outdoor adventures in between treatments. Even after she was cleared to walk in the woods, we could cover more ground by having me carry her two miles in walk two miles out.

It really helped me maintain a positive mindset and offered a break from the full-time caretaker role. Plus, carrying her gave me a great workout!

Nearly four weeks post-injury, Luce is now spending close to 13 minutes on the underwater treadmill with a smooth gait. The clicking I used to hear and feel during her bicycle exercises is gone, which signals that her knee is stabilizing.

I'm also incorporating new exercises into her daily routine and feel optimistic about her progress at this stage.

That said, her adductor muscle remains very tight and rope-like, though it's responding well to laser therapy.

After her workouts, it tends to tense up again, so I'm supplementing her veterinary treatment with laser therapy at home.

Luce in the underwater treadmill

It's essential to pay close attention to feedback during your sessions. Having the right tools for at-home therapy is a game-changer - it reinforces everything you're working on in rehab. This approach doesn't just help manage inflammation daily, it also keeps costs in check and empowers you to actively support your dog's recovery.

The first two months of rehab brought incredible progress. It almost felt too good to be true – Luce was growing stronger, adding new exercises to her routine, and thriving.

Still, I couldn't shake a lingering worry that something might go wrong. By now, she could take ten-minute leash walks around our property, confidently tackling uphill climbs and easing down slopes. Walking slowly encouraged her to bear weight on the injured leg, rather than hopping or lifting it to move faster.

By month three, our leash walks were stretching into longer ventures over varied terrain – on top of her twice-weekly sessions in the water treadmill.

Keeping the nails trimmed is essential for ensuring proper mechanics when the paw strikes the ground. To further enhance traction and encourage better foot function, I also trim the hair between her paw pads. This simple step helps prevent slipping and ensures she moves with more confidence and control during her recovery.

On September 20, 2023, we faced a particularly tough day in Luce's rehabilitation journey. She was feeling some soreness, which affected her performance. Although she still demonstrated a good range of motion and stride length, there was a noticeable tendency to offload her injured leg during the weight-bearing parts of her stride.

On a positive note, there was no increase in joint effusion, and no clicking was heard during mobilization, which suggested some stability. However, during the physical exam, Dr. Belden observed that Luce seemed quite unhappy during the manipulation and laser therapy sessions. Additionally, her adductor muscle remained tight and spasmodic.

Luce had previously been making significant progress, but during this visit, she managed only 5 minutes of intervals on the underwater treadmill due to her discomfort. After examining her knee, Dr. Johnson reassured me that the joint's stability was intact and that there was still no clicking; she also noted significantly less medial movement. The source of Luce's pain appeared to be not the joint itself, but rather the iliopsoas and her mid-back area.

While I was relieved to hear the joint was stable, it was disheartening to see the dip in her performance on the treadmill. This experience wasn't a setback, but rather a reminder that her body was feeling the strain. Dr. Johnson emphasized that a bit of soreness is standard, but if it lasted more than 24 hours, we should be concerned.

On days when Luce experienced soreness and tension in her adductor muscle, we incorporated additional therapies to manage her discomfort. We often used a TENS machine along with ice on the right leg's adductor muscle. This Transcutaneous Electrical Nerve Stimulation (TENS) machine has been a go-to for pain relief and recovery in humans for decades and has recently found its way into veterinary medicine for dogs as well. The TENS machine delivers low-frequency electrical impulses that stimulate the nerves in the affected area. These impulses work to block pain signals, reduce inflammation, and boost circulation.

When used appropriately, TENS machines can be a safe and effective method to aid in a dog's recovery. In Luce's case, the TENS machine was particularly beneficial for improving her muscle function.

By stimulating the nerves in the affected areas, the muscles were encouraged to contract and relax. This approach was crucial for Luce, especially since she was experiencing some muscle atrophy due to her limited activity and injury.

Throughout our sessions, we consistently used laser therapy on Luce's legs, back, shoulders, and other areas where her muscles felt particularly tense. With her long back, Luce often experienced soreness in the thoracic region.

The second month brought a few challenging moments, likely due to the introduction of more demanding exercises. I noticed that when she got tired, she would sometimes forget to lift her feet properly, which led to tripping or her nails hitting the bar during Cavaletti exercises. On some days, she would lift her injured leg to indicate she was in pain.

By the end of month two, we decided to take a full week off from everything. We used heat and ice to help calm her body, and I made sure to use the PEMF mat while she relaxed in the evenings.

While most of our rehabilitation sessions went well, there were a few tough days along the way. However, after that week of rest, Luce seemed to regain her strength and was able to walk on the underwater treadmill for nearly 15 minutes.

While it's common to say a 5-minute swim in an underwater treadmill is roughly equivalent to a 5-mile run, the exact mileage equivalent for 15 minutes is not a precise measurement. It's more accurate to say that 15 minutes of underwater treadmill work is equivalent to a significant amount of land-based exercise, offering similar benefits like building muscle, improving endurance, and providing a cardiovascular workout.

She began month three on a strong note, and after a week of rest, she quickly got back on track. It's important to emphasize that merely addressing pain without tackling the underlying issues can put your pet at a greater risk for further injury.

An effective pain management strategy includes a combination of diet, supplements, rehabilitation, and medication to achieve three key goals: relieve pain, reduce inflammation, and support cartilage repair.

I adjusted her diet, supplements, and therapies based on her performance during rehabilitation sessions. This exemplifies an iterative and agile approach to the overall strategy.

On October 3, 2023, I traveled with Luce to Morgantown, Pennsylvania, for her leg brace fitting at My Pet's Brace. I chose to make the four-hour drive from home to the company's headquarters so that they could take the measurements themselves. This way, they could create her custom brace on-site and have it ready for me to pick up the very next day.

Knowing the correct measurements would be taken gave me confidence that the brace would fit well, allowing for any necessary adjustments before we headed back to Virginia.

The custom knee brace is designed to help Luce bear more weight on her injured leg while providing comfort throughout a range of motion. This not only minimizes the load on her healthy left leg but also aids in her recovery. The anterior knee strap applies pressure to the tibial crest, helping to prevent cranial drawer motion.

Over time, the support from the brace, along with the prevention of this motion, will assist in the development of stable scar tissue. This will allow Luce to gradually return to her normal activities and regain any lost muscle mass as she begins to use her leg again.

Measuring adjustments to Luce's new brace from
My Pet's Brace

The custom brace was definitely on the pricier side, but it would be specifically tailored and fitted for Luce. After carefully weighing my options and comparing various brace companies, I concluded that this particular product was the best fit for her leg.

I wanted something that wouldn't shift around or cause chafing, could withstand moisture without deteriorating, and would protect her leg from twisting to avoid re-injury during more active moments.

This brace featured lightweight, comfortable straps designed to secure it around her leg, along with an ankle sleeve to prevent slipping.

I appreciated that they offered complimentary follow-up appointments to refit the brace as Luce's leg changed due to muscle development and healing.

They also provided a warranty covering her entire rehabilitation period, including any defects, breakages, or the need to replace Velcro straps or padding.

The company's general protocol recommended that Luce wear the brace all day for nine months, except when she was crated or sleeping. Dr. Froeling and Dr. Johnson advised that Luce should wear the brace on slippery floors, rugged terrain, or during vigorous activities.

However, they also noted that it wasn't necessary for her to wear the brace all the time. They suggested leaving it off during underwater treadmill sessions, slow walks, and stretching exercises.

Their goal was for her to use her leg without support most of the time, putting the brace on only when conditions called for extra protection.

Since Luce was never crated, that concern didn't arise, and she didn't wear the brace while sleeping. My Pet's Brace echoed the importance of following my veterinarians' advice.

Luce was surprisingly cooperative; she let me put the brace on and take it off without any fuss. Since she had never worn a brace like this before, I made a concerted effort to ensure the experience was positive for her.

This liberating technology helped protect her and allowed me to have peace of mind that her injured leg wouldn't twist awkwardly or knock against her knee.

With the brace on, our walks stretched to over 45 minutes in the park and along the trails, letting us enjoy our time outdoors together.

When I bought the brace, I had the option to choose from a variety of patterns and colors. I applied some principles of Color Therapy when making my selection.

While I'm not entirely convinced of its significant impact, I figured that if it could have any positive influence, it was worth taking advantage of.

In Color Therapy, each color is linked to a specific vibration and energy that can affect our mood, emotions, and even physical health.

By exposing ourselves to particular colors, we can help balance these energies and promote healing.

Here are some commonly used colors and their associated benefits:

- **Red:** Boosts energy, circulation, and motivation.

- **Orange:** Sparks creativity, fosters optimism, and aids digestion.

- **Yellow:** Elevates mood, sharpens focus, and improves sleep.

- **Green:** Calms the mind, alleviates stress, and supports healing.

- **Blue:** Eases anxiety, encourages relaxation, and lowers blood pressure.

- **Purple:** Amplifies intuition, nurtures spirituality, and enhances sleep.

Since Luce was going to wear her brace every day, the choice of color could provide her with ongoing exposure to the therapeutic benefits of a specific hue. I decided on green for her brace.

Luce's new brace. Harley in her K9 Sport Sack cheering her sister on.

By the end of October 2023, Luce weighed 30.6 lbs. She actively participated in K9 nose work classes while wearing her brace and seemed to be thriving. During this period, she also enjoyed one- to two-mile walks, both with and without the brace, and continued to handle these outings well.

However, Dr. Froeling advised that we reduce the length of her walks and ensure she had ample rest days. During this visit, Luce underwent electro-acupuncture at a frequency of 20 Hertz for 10 minutes, followed by a session at 80 over 120 for 10 minutes.

We also applied laser treatment over the right iliopsoas at three watts for four minutes using the large cone.

In Luce's rehabilitation session with Dr. Johnson and Dr. Belden, we observed improvement in her right iliopsoas, although her left side appeared much more tense and uncomfortable this time around. There was a noticeable decrease in toe touching, and her right adductor seemed less agitated. However, some tender spots in the thoracic area of her spine were still present.

Luce on the Assisi Mat getting ready for laser therapy

I Knee-d a Break

Three months into rehab, Luce and I were taking a stroll in the front yard. It was November 4 when the mailman appeared down the street. Luce absolutely loves this part of her day; the mailman always stops to let her race along the fence with him, full of excitement.

Today, however, she was on a leash, and I was holding her flat buckle collar - the same one she's worn for the past eight years. Suddenly, in a burst of energy, Luce twisted around to bark at the mailman, and in that split second, she slipped out of her collar.

Without her brace, she took off like a shot, sprinting 200 yards down the fence line. I felt as though I had stopped breathing.

All I could think was that running could ruin everything we had worked so hard for over the last three months. I felt like a terrible pet parent. I'd read countless stories online about dogs slipping their collars and always thought, *'come on... just be more careful.'* And yet, here I was, becoming one of those stories.

In an instant, she was out of sight, racing over the hill and toward the corner of the yard, completely unrestrained.

She came back up the hill with no visible running issues with either knee. She trotted back to me normally, full of herself and happy as a clam. I finally allowed myself to breathe. She was okay. Wow, that was lucky.

I immediately applied ice to her right leg, and I'm pleased to report there was no limping or lameness. My initial step was to ice the injured leg while using a laser for five minutes on the healthy leg, focusing on both the outside and inside of the knee.

Then, I switched the laser back to the injured leg for another five minutes on the inside while icing the good leg. The next morning, I dedicated 10 minutes of laser treatment to the injured leg.

I also treated her left shoulder and thoracic spine with laser therapy for 10 minutes. When she ran, she moved straight ahead before making a left turn, then straight again, and turned left once more - consistently turning on her stronger side. This could have been a significant setback.

You'll likely face similar challenges in your journey. I mentioned before that you might encounter moments like these.

The key is to do your best to prevent them, but if they do occur, return to the therapies you're familiar with and update your veterinarian about what happened. They can't effectively help your dog unless they're aware of these incidents.

On a side note, I went ahead and purchased a martingale collar.

Luce had an appointment with Dr. Froeling shortly after the incident to ensure everything was still okay. During her evaluation, she was found to be 1/5 lame at a walk on her right rear leg. At that point, she typically was wearing a brace while working and had been gradually working up to 10 minutes on the underwater treadmill with Dr. Johnson.

During this visit, she received electro-acupuncture again, along with laser treatment using a large cone at 7 watts for 3 minutes on her right iliopsoas and from T5 to T10. I was advised to continue strengthening her right rear leg and to have her practice balancing on that leg using a balance pad or by standing on a step.

Dr. Froeling demonstrated how to massage and move her leg, as well as how to shake her toes or tap them. At this visit, Luce weighed 31.2 pounds.

Surprisingly, at her rehab appointment with Dr. Belden, her right adductor had improved, felt softer than before, and she was using it well. However, she still showed some tenderness in the thoracic area of her back.

We haven't yet touched on the topic of muscle atrophy. With reduced activity, muscle loss can occur. Our goal is to keep the dog moving as much as possible during the healing process to minimize muscle atrophy and control weight gain. It's not ideal to let the muscles weaken, as recovering from that can be a long journey - especially for an older dog - making it much harder to rebuild strength.

I wish I had measured Luce's legs prior to the injury, as I now regret not having those baseline figures. I'll never know if one leg was smaller than the other before the injury. Dr. Johnson noted on Luce's first visit that her muscularity appeared to be the same on both legs. It wasn't a measurement, but it was still informative.

Since then, I started closely monitoring her musculature and taking measurements myself to track any differences and observe the recovery process. From August to October, there was just a 6% change in muscle atrophy.

The status update at the end of November indicated that Luce was making significant progress. She was using her right hock more effectively to dig in when pulling, and her lameness had improved considerably. Dr. Belden noted that while the right adductor was still a bit tense, there was a marked improvement overall.

On December 5, 2023, Dr. Johnson took additional measurements of Luce's legs- the thigh circumference at 70% of way from the stifle to the hip joint. The results revealed that her injured right leg measured 25.5 cm, while the healthy left leg measured 28 cm.

From October to December, muscle atrophy had increased, showing a 9. 8% difference. This indicated a noticeable disparity in muscle development between the two legs. We continued to monitor any changes as we moved forward.

On December 14, Luce had a visit with Dr. Froeling, where she weighed in at 32.2 pounds. She had undergone rehab with Dr. Johnson and Dr. Belden the day before, working a bit harder than usual but handling it well when she got home. Dr. Belden noted that her adductor was tight and twitching after the treadmill session. Her back felt generally quiet, except for a few sensitive spots in the cranial thoracic region. Luce was putting weight on her left hock, which seemed very strong in that area, but later that evening, she appeared to be limping slightly. I used the PEMF mat and a CC Loop, which helped her, and by morning, she was doing fine again.

During her appointment with Dr. Catherine Johnson, Dr. Courtney Belden observed that Luce was twitchy around her thoracic and cervical areas and had used the laser during her therapy session the day before.

A chiropractic adjustment by Dr. Froeling revealed mild to moderate spasming in her right iliopsoas, especially near the femoral triangle. Electro-acupuncture was performed during this visit, along with laser treatment on the right iliopsoas for three minutes and 35 seconds at 7 watts.

With the holidays around the corner, therapy took a break at the end of December, which meant all the care fell on me during that time.

We decided to switch things up a bit, and instead of our usual running routine, we enjoyed leisurely leash walks on the beach in the Outer Banks. Walking on the sand offers numerous advantages for dogs. It not only strengthens their muscles and joints but also engages different muscle groups, providing a low-impact way to exercise. Plus, it adds an element of fun and stimulation to our outings.

Navigating the sandy terrain requires more effort than walking on solid surfaces. For Luce, the sensation of sand between her paws, the soothing sounds of the waves, and the delightful smells of the ocean created a rich and immersive experience.

Additionally, walking on the sand serves as a natural exfoliant for a dog's paws, helping to remove dead skin cells and keep them in top shape.

When Luce was first injured, she weighed 29.6 lbs. and was in excellent athletic condition. It's crucial to monitor her weight since reduced activity can lead to body changes, including shifts in fat and muscle. We wanted to avoid muscle atrophy and prevent fat from taking its place. That's why we decided to modify her diet by cutting out carbohydrates, which also helped address inflammation. Sugars can convert into stored fat if not burned off.

On January 15, we visited Dr. Froeling, and Luce had gained some weight, now at 33.2 lbs. She appeared noticeably more muscular, and Dr. Froeling noted that there was less compensation in her left shoulder; while it was tight, it wasn't nearly as bad. Luce accomplished her longest walk since the injury—a 4-mile trek without a brace. She felt slightly sore afterward, but bounced back quickly the next day.

After a 4-week break from all therapies due to vacation, Luce received a favorable report at her 5-month check-in. Dr. Froeling noted that she was getting stronger each day. Notably, Luce had also gained an additional 4 lbs., which is significant for a medium-sized dog.

Since it was winter, this weight gain falls within her "winter" range, but I kept a close eye on it. I wanted to avoid any extra weight on her joints, as it could hinder her healing process.

Two days later, on January 17, Luce began her rehab and had a fantastic session. She was allowed to go upstairs but not down, and she could walk as far as she wanted, albeit slowly and on a lead.

I also introduced a new exercise to help shift her weight by gently lifting her rear paws one at a time while her front feet were elevated.

On January 29, Luce was cleared to walk downstairs. Finally, I wouldn't have to carry her up and down anymore! Strangely, I felt a bit nostalgic about that.

On February 22, Dr. Johnson conducted the next leg measurement for Luce. Her right leg measured 28 cm, while the left measured 30 cm.

The good news? We've narrowed the difference in circumference from 2.5 cm in December to just 2 cm, reducing the gap to a 7.2% difference. We were definitely headed in the right direction.

Luce's progress was so encouraging that Dr. Johnson said she could run freely in the yard with her brace on. Each run should be limited to about 15 or 20 minutes in an open field. Luce absolutely loved it and seemed to thrive; she was delighted to feel like herself again and couldn't contain her excitement, clearly getting the zoomies afterward!

By the end of January, Luce was sound at the walk and trot, with her adductors palpating quietly along with her back.

Over the next few months, Luce continued her routine of underwater treadmill sessions, therapies, adjustments, acupuncture, and various exercises.

By this point, Dr. Johnson had reduced her underwater treadmill sessions down to just once a week. I used a brace for any long walks, and she managed well that way. While I was still performing laser and PEMF mat therapies at home, it wasn't on a daily basis anymore.

During a recent visit, Dr. Froeling noted that Luce was still offloading weight onto her left rear and left shoulder, but she was definitely making strides in her recovery. We gradually increased her walking, and running was permitted in a straight line while she wore the brace, which finally I let us hit the trails.

New exercises were introduced that challenged her entire body, such as raising the height of the Cavalettis, performing weave Cavalettis, pivoting on the wobble board, and starting 25-yard recall exercises up to five times in the yard.

By the end of March, I decided to reintroduce Voltrex into Luce's diet. She hadn't had it since February 28, but as I ramped up her exercise routine and she began working harder, I wanted to use it to help minimize inflammation. I had initially taken a break from it earlier since she wasn't experiencing soreness during those initial months.

At this point, we were now eight months into Luce's healing journey, and on April 24, 2024, we retook her leg measurements. Her good leg measured 28 cm, while the bad leg was at 27.5 cm. That meant we were down to just a 2% difference—pretty amazing!

Luce's body was strong, although she was still carrying a few extra pounds, now at 34.6 kg. Despite this, all of her doctors were optimistic about her recovery.

On June 25, 2024, Luce reached an exciting milestone – she was granted limited Free Run time in the yard without a leash. This was a big step forward for her. While I was thrilled to see her gaining more freedom, I couldn't shake the worry that something might go wrong, leading to a re-injury or a new issue. If you're feeling the same way, just know you're not alone in this.

On July 21, Luce was cleared for free swimming and spent seven and a half minutes in a friend's open pool with a floatation device. It's crucial to wait until the end of rehabilitation before introducing swimming, and a flotation device should always be used, even for strong swimmers.

Swimming too soon after an orthopedic injury can slow down healing and increase the risk of re-injury or complications, primarily due to the repetitive motions and potential strain on the affected area. Dogs tend to thrash around in the water, which can lead to setbacks, if not carefully managed.

For dogs, 30 minutes of swimming is generally equivalent to approximately 120 minutes (2 hours) of running. This is because the resistance of the water makes swimming more physically demanding for a dog than running on land.

For safety and to encourage proper swimming technique, a rehabilitating dog should always wear a flotation device, like a life jacket, during open swimming. This precaution helps prevent exhaustion or panic, especially if the dog is still recovering from an injury.

As fatigue sets in, a dog's form can deteriorate, leading to additional complications. Early swimming can place undue stress on an injury that hasn't fully healed, potentially risking further damage or delaying the recovery process.

Luce swimming over winter in a dog pool

Swimming is a physical activity that involves repetitive motions, which can strain muscles and tendons. If a dog has an underlying orthopedic issue that hasn't been properly addressed, the risk of injury increases significantly.

For instance, a dog with an orthopedic injury might compensate for pain or weakness by altering its swimming technique, which could lead to new injuries or exacerbate existing ones.

Depending on the nature of the injury, swimming may need to be avoided altogether, or it may require a careful, monitored reintroduction to prevent complications.

For example, swimming after a knee injury could cause problems if the knee hasn't fully regained strength and range of motion. Therefore, taking a gradual approach and having a rehab professional oversee the return to swimming is essential for ensuring proper healing and minimizing the chances of re-injury.

A flotation device is essential for keeping a dog buoyant and ensuring their head stays above water, especially when they tire out or become disoriented while swimming.

Even the strongest swimmers can quickly fatigue, and using a flotation device helps conserve energy and prevents overexertion, which might lead to muscle soreness or, in the worst-case scenario, drowning.

A well-fitted life jacket promotes a horizontal swimming position, allowing the dog to use all four paws for propulsion.

Additionally, in rehabilitation scenarios, it also facilitates controlled, low-impact exercise, aiding in muscle strengthening and improving range of motion without placing unnecessary stress on their joints.

On August 8, 2024, after a year since her injury, Luce's leg measurements showed her left and right legs both at 34 cm - marking the first time they've had equal muscularity!

However, her weight had increased to 34.4 lbs., which was a bit concerning. Dr. Froeling reassured me that her weight would likely decrease as she continued to heal, but I couldn't shake the feeling that it was a bit heavy for her.

We had been going on runs a few days a week using her Canicross harness. While she did get some off-leash time, it was limited. Luce had also made great strides by going up and down the stairs on her own, which was a huge milestone.

However, she was still not allowed to play with other dogs at that point. In between veterinary visits, our therapy sessions were now "as needed."

Luce had been swimming regularly for about 10 minutes each session, and she was doing well with it.

Additionally, she continued her rehab, including underwater treadmill sessions every three weeks. It was recommended that she add side shuffles, small circles on both sides, and serpentines to her exercises.

At this stage, Luce had returned to nearly all her activities. She was actively participating in Rally Obedience, Nose Work, and Canicross and enjoys her swims in the pool and running in the yard.

The only thing we were holding off on was her playtime with other dogs. Most of these activities were taking place without her brace.

At this point, we were training for our first 5k in October, and back at the end of August, she successfully ran a 5k distance with me. While she felt a bit sore afterward, she bounced back by the next day with no signs of lameness.

She continued to see Dr. Froeling for maintenance visits and check-ins every six weeks, just like she did before her injury, as we progressed in our training.

We were still incorporating the underwater treadmill into her routine at VRSVA, but we only used it every three weeks instead of bi-weekly as we initially did.

Each week, we were hitting the trails to work on building her overall strength and endurance. After intense workouts, I provided necessary therapies, and we kept adjusting her supplements to ensure her body got the support it needed.

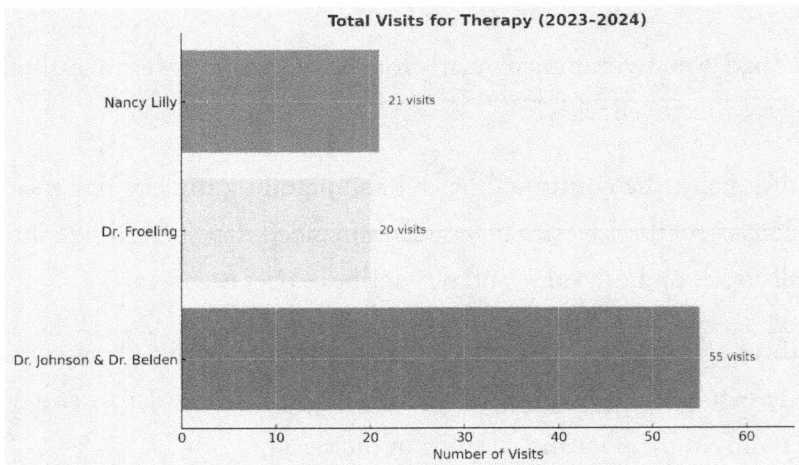

Total Visits for Therapy 2023-2024

Chapter 6: Training – It's Less Me and More We

Training dogs is essential for their safety and well-being, as well as for fostering a strong bond with their human companions. It equips them with vital life skills necessary for cohabiting with humans and encourages positive behaviors. Well-trained dogs are less likely to stray, chase cars, or engage in actions that could jeopardize their safety. Moreover, training enables dogs to respond calmly and appropriately in various situations, whether meeting new people or encountering other animals.

We often think of training for all these reasons, but we rarely consider it in a proactive sense - training to prevent or manage injury. When training your dog for this purpose, use every opportunity to deepen your relationship with them. Most important is helping your dog feel comfortable being touched, examined, treated, and rehabilitated. That's what we're going to explore here.

This chapter will explore the importance of building trust with your dog before an injury occurs. Engaging in activities like obedience training, agility, Nose Work, or even trail walking and running helps forge a strong bond. While these activities are fun on the surface, they also create opportunities for deepening your relationship. Simply managing your dog's behavior isn't enough - you can't expect them to let you or a stranger near if they're hurt. It's vital to learn their way of communicating and to help them understand yours. If your dog doesn't feel safe with you, they may see you as a threat when injured.

Basic obedience commands such as "come," "sit," and "stay" are crucial for managing your dog in various environments. Training provides mental stimulation and helps dogs channel their energy in positive ways, reducing boredom and the risk of destructive behavior.

When dogs successfully learn and apply these commands, it boosts their confidence and reinforces your value as their handler. A consistent training routine also gives dogs a sense of purpose, helping them understand their role in your household - and in your life.

Dogs express themselves through their behavior, and learning to interpret these signals is key to understanding how they feel in different situations. Training helps both you and your dog communicate more effectively, fostering a deeper connection. Through consistent training and positive interactions, you build trust and respect that strengthens your bond.

It's important to distinguish between managing a dog and nurturing a meaningful relationship with one. Management focuses on meeting basic needs and ensuring obedience, while a true relationship is built on trust, emotional understanding, and a strong connection grounded in mutual respect and affection.

Training is more than just teaching commands - it's about forging a connection. The trust developed during training forms the foundation of your bond and guides your journey together.

"Trust is built on training long before it is needed in the field."
-Field & Trial

Luce's injury required extensive hands-on care from both me and her health team, which included veterinarians, technicians, rehabilitation specialists, and others. It demanded a great deal of patience, as she had to endure unusual physical positions that left her feeling vulnerable or uncomfortable.

That's Bubble Trouble

Everyone has their own personal space bubble. These bubbles can vary not only by individual preferences but also based on factors like age, gender, health, and even species. German psychologist David Katz introduced the "bubble" concept in 1937 (Blackburn, 1938). Leslie Hayduk from the University of Western Ontario offers one of the most widely accepted definitions of human personal space:

"We can define personal space as the area individual humans actively maintain around themselves into which others cannot intrude without arousing discomfort" (Hayduk, 1978).

It shouldn't be a surprise that dogs have their own personal space bubbles, too. Even though they're domesticated, dogs are still highly aware of how close humans and other dogs get to them - and they adjust their behavior accordingly.

Often, we don't realize when we're infringing on that space. We tend to act based on what we want or need, without always being mindful of how it affects them. Compared to us, dogs are incredibly attuned to movement and body language. That's why learning to be observant is so important - their behavior speaks volumes.

In this discussion, I'll explore some of the terms used to describe a dog's reaction to an invasion of personal space, such as fight or flight. These terms are also commonly used to describe a dog's defense drive - their instinctual response driven by self-preservation and protection. This drive can prompt dogs to defend themselves, their pack, or their territory from perceived threats, with behaviors ranging from barking and growling to more aggressive displays.

In discussions about space, a key term is *flight distance* - the distance at which a dog will attempt to escape from a perceived threat. This is the zone where the approach of another animal or human triggers the dog's instinct to flee.

A dog's primary drive is survival and the continuation of its species, rooted in its ability to avoid danger. This results in a state of constant vigilance, as the dog stays alert to detect and evade potential threats. By maintaining a safe distance - or "bubble" - the dog aims to protect itself from whatever may be approaching.

Each dog has its own comfort level when it comes to how much personal space it's willing to share. Even if it feels uneasy, a dog may still allow someone into that space if it trusts them not to cause harm. But that trust often vanishes when injury is involved.

An injured dog instinctively reacts because it feels vulnerable - regardless of whether it's domesticated or wild. Cornered animals lose the ability to gauge a safe distance from an approaching human. When they can no longer maintain their personal space, they're left with two options: to submit or to fight, as McBride noted (McBride, 1971). Hediger referred to this scenario as *fight distance.*

On the other hand, *social distance* refers to interactions within a group of similar species and does not involve maintaining physical distance. Hediger defines social distance as "the maximum distance an animal will move away from its group" (McBride, 1971).

For both animals and humans, personal space tends to be larger in the front than on the sides. Likewise, flight distances often take on an elliptical shape, as McBride and James (1963) outlined (McBride & James, 1963). In humans, research shows that we respond more strongly to individuals approaching from the front than from behind - but we perceive someone as closer when they are facing us rather than turned away (Jung et al., 2016).

Hediger noted that reducing or eliminating the instinct to flee is crucial to successfully domesticating a species. Artificially shortening the flight distance between animals and humans is a key result of the taming process. In fact, animal psychology can be defined as the reduction of flight tendencies in the presence of humans (Hediger, 1955).

As a domesticated species, dogs show a strong willingness to adapt. Their flight distances are situational and can vary significantly. Since behavior modification can help reduce flight distance, training for specific outcomes becomes especially valuable.

I highlight these points because investing time in building trust and a strong bond with your dog is crucial. Without that connection, transitioning from public expectations of space to social, personal, and eventually intimate space becomes much more difficult.

If a dog is injured, that's not the ideal moment to establish intimacy – especially if a relationship hasn't already been built. While you might find yourself in that situation out of necessity, navigating it is much easier if you've done the groundwork.

Humans often fail to respect dogs' personal space in the way dogs would prefer. We tend to assume they want our petting and touching. Even when we try to be considerate, our ways of showing love can still overwhelm them.

We often express affection through closeness and hugging – behaviors many dogs interpret as restraint or intrusion. As their caregivers, we also sometimes perform intrusive tasks or bring them to strangers who handle them in ways they might not welcome.

Don't Pressurize - De-Stressurize

There's still a widespread expectation that dogs should naturally like - or at least get along with - people and other dogs. But dogs who are selective, fearful, shy, or introverted often struggle under this societal pressure. It's important to remember that even the most outgoing dog has a personal space we need to learn to respect.

The first step is recognizing that we exert various types of pressure on dogs - then comes understanding *how* we do that. For instance, humans tend to make direct eye contact. In our world, eye contact can foster a sense of connection, and the same can be true for dogs – but not always. Some dogs don't care to lock eyes with their humans or other animals. For them, a glance away can communicate volumes.

We must be careful not to stand stiff or still and face a dog head-on. This body language can be intimidating. Be conscious of how you engage with a dog and avoid standing tall or leaning over, especially with smaller dogs, as this can make them uneasy. It can trigger the dog's defensive drive, making them feel the need to create space.

We have all experienced someone reaching out with the back of their hand to let a dog sniff them, crouching down to get in their face, or walking into a dog's space, which may feel intrusive. Even petting can be perceived differently based on the dog's comfort level.

Several human behaviors can be particularly intrusive and challenging for dogs. For instance, crowding too many dogs and people into a space that isn't spacious enough can be overwhelming.

Additionally, using a training method that involves physically forcing a dog into position and applying body pressure can be stressful for them. Most veterinary exam rooms are small, with furniture like an exam table or chair. Now, add a vet, an owner, and a technician - and you can see how that can change a dog's perspective on space.

Confining a dog to a crate or any small space without proper conditioning can also have negative effects. Not allowing a dog to withdraw from human interaction or preventing them from finding a hiding spot when they feel overwhelmed can increase their stress levels.

Additionally, think about how a short leash can prevent them from getting away. You may think you need to hold them tighter so they don't leave, but this can be counterproductive when they try to distance themselves. Lastly, keeping a dog still or restraining them - whether for management, discipline, or medical procedures - can be distressing.

During rehabilitation, certain procedures may cause pain. While some discomfort is only temporary, it is often a necessary part of the treatment.

Training should be a positive experience. The use of discomfort, pain, or fear during training - such as startling tactics, intimidation, applying body pressure, causing pain, using loud noises, or flooding (which involves deliberately restraining the dog and exposing them to something frightening or painful) - may elicit an unintended response, and the training should be adjusted. A dog in distress, or one that has not had its basic needs met, is not learning.

I mentioned earlier that we often invade dogs' personal space without even realizing it. With their keen sense of smell, dogs experience a rich world of sensations that we can't fully grasp. Just as visual and auditory stimuli can influence their perception of space, certain odors that suggest a threat can have a similar effect. Chemicals are released in the presence of fear from other animals and humans. These chemicals alarm the dog and can trigger a defensive state.

The best approach is to use techniques like desensitization and counter-conditioning to foster positive associations or shift unpleasant ones to neutral. This can help a dog better manage these unavoidable intrusions.

Many people misinterpret or overlook a dog's body language. Countless videos online showcase dogs clearly expressing their discomfort, while their owners insist that the dogs are happy. Stress responses such as panting, yawning, raising a front foot, lip-licking, a tucked tail, and head turns all scream, 'Help me cope.'

If we don't make an effort to understand dog body language, our attempts to respect their space and preferences will not be successful. We'll miss the signs that indicate they're feeling stressed. Therefore, continuously observing and learning about the dogs we live with is essential. In rehabilitation scenarios, distinguishing between a dog's typical behavior and their current signals will empower us to advocate for them effectively in the moment.

To help illustrate this, I use the following example. While there isn't a specific association between back-end pain and dog-dog aggression, or neck pain and human-dog aggression, pain can contribute to aggression in dogs. Remember, dogs gather information about other dogs from their rear end, and humans are usually at the head end of the leash.

A dog in pain may be more likely to react aggressively, especially if they are being touched or handled in a painful area. If aggression that never existed before starts to appear, the first thing to consider is whether it's pain-related, and get the dog checked.

Forced Family Fun

As we've discussed in previous chapters, dogs thrive on familiar routines because they provide comfort. If your dog lacks a daily schedule and faces constant changes, they may struggle to trust you. The unpredictability can leave them unsure of what to expect. Establishing a consistent routine can greatly enhance the trust between you and your dog.

To create a routine, aim to do daily activities at the same time. Consistently feeding, grooming, walking, exercising, and playing with your dog can help establish this structure while you're building your relationship. While it's important to stick to a schedule, try not to be overly rigid, as your dog might become anxious if things are off by just a few minutes. Finding a balance is key.

Building a strong bond with your dog is an excellent way to establish trust. The most effective way to nurture this connection is by engaging in activities you both enjoy. Regular training sessions, exercise, and playtime can capture your dog's attention and help you develop positive feelings together.

To make the most of this bonding experience, having a dog you can take with you wherever you go is essential. Starting with basic obedience training sets the groundwork for successfully introducing your dog to new environments, people, and other dogs. This ensures your dog can respond to commands when needed, keeps everyone safe, and helps everyone enjoy the outing.

Exposing your dog to different situations creates new training opportunities that further strengthen your bond.

This isn't about you strolling along a trail with your eyes glued to your phone while your dog meanders off in all directions, dragging you behind. Instead, be fully present with your dog. Pay attention to their body language, make necessary adjustments, advocate for their needs, and truly enjoy the experience together. Engage in the activity alongside them - not just near them.

This is not about your dog experiencing the world like they would in daycare. Quality bonding time is meant to be just between you and your dog, without the presence of other dogs. You can certainly supplement your moments together with some time apart, but this book focuses specifically on those activities that involve *you*.

You can also strengthen your bond with your dog by allowing them to rest close to you while you watch TV or work. These quiet moments together help your dog feel relaxed in your company and build trust in you. They also offer a chance for gentle touch, gradually desensitizing them to handling in sensitive areas—and helping you learn which areas are more sensitive.

Over the past year, I've gained a wealth of knowledge with Luce. Just when I thought we couldn't get any closer, her injury built our trust like nothing else. It was like going through the trenches together - *Relationship 2.0!*

The idea that everything we do today impacts our future with our dog isn't just a popular belief - it's a fundamental truth. Our current actions have lasting effects that shape what's to come, making thoughtful choices all the more important. This understanding shows how our decisions create ripple effects, influencing not only our relationship with our dog but also our connections with others.

The choices we make each day for our dogs, regardless of their size, have a profound impact on their future well-being, relationships with both humans and other dogs, and overall life path. We touched on this concept in the nutrition section.

For example, if we fail to recognize our dog's selectiveness around other dogs and push them into uncomfortable situations, believing they'll simply adjust, we're not advocating for their best interests. Instead, this could lead the dog to take matters into their own hands, ultimately resulting in an unpleasant situation for everyone involved. This is never the outcome we want.

Not advocating for your dog - breaks their trust.

Understanding the potential long-term effects of our actions encourages us to be more mindful and intentional in our decision-making, helping us create a brighter, more rewarding future for our dogs.

For example, putting effort into training today can pave the way for a stronger, more satisfying bond with our canine companions down the line. Training is an investment, just as nutrition is an investment in our dog's future.

I adopted Luce when she was just 12 weeks old, and we've been training together since she first arrived on my doorstep. We've both been learning about each other throughout this journey. Initially, my training centered around formal obedience, which was the foundation of my upbringing. When I was in my twenties raising dogs, obedience training was the primary way to communicate with dogs and encourage desired behaviors, all while having a blast competing in events with others who were learning the same skills.

Since I started walking the earth with Luce in 2016, I have expanded my sports portfolio and have ventured into rally obedience, agility, tricks, hiking and running together, nose work, rodeo dog, and finally, canine obstacle course racing. Each of these activities requires its own unique skill sets, observation techniques, and communication styles between Luce and me.

Over the past eight years, I've prioritized exposing her to various activities and environments, pursuing the ones she enjoys the most while letting go of those that don't spark her interest.

I never really considered how much our time spent training, exercising, and playing together would come into play when Luce got injured. I hadn't thought about the possibility of her getting hurt or what it would take for us to tackle that challenge together.

When the day of her injury arrived, it became crystal clear that everything we had experienced together had a significant impact on how we would navigate the following year. I hope to share the lessons I learned, so that if you're just starting your relationship with your dog, you can incorporate some of these ideas into your training routine—ideally, so that you won't need them. And if you find yourself on a rehabilitation journey, there are still skills you can work on that might ease your dog's path to recovery. Since Luce's injury was orthopedic, it highlights the importance of proprioception and its role in healing.

I'm on a Roll

Everything your dog does is tied to proprioception. But what exactly is it? Proprioception in dogs refers to their awareness of their body and limb positions and movements; in other words, it's their understanding of where their body is in space. This sense is essential for maintaining balance, coordinating movements, and navigating their surroundings. Proprioception creates a neurological connection between their paws and brain, enabling dogs to walk and stand normally.

When dogs experience proprioceptive deficits, you might notice signs like dragging their limbs, tripping, reduced coordination, or abnormal paw placement. These deficiencies can result from injuries, neurological disorders, or spinal surgery, often leading to unusual body postures or movements.

Signs to watch for include knuckling with their paws, dragging their feet while walking, stumbling, difficulty maintaining coordination, poor paw placement, challenges with spatial awareness, circling or pacing, and showing less interest in play or activities.

A conscious proprioception test is a simple assessment where you gently turn the dog's paw upside down and observe its reaction. A healthy dog should quickly flip the paw back to its original position. However, when

Luce was injured, her family vet performed this test, and she didn't move her paw back as expected.

You can also conduct a walking test to assess the dog's gait and stability on different surfaces. To evaluate lateral walking movements, observe how the dog shifts its weight to one side. When Luce walked, her right rear leg would sometimes knuckle, and you could notice abnormal weight distribution and a change in how she collected herself.

If you notice any of these issues in an otherwise healthy dog, it's important to start working on improving proprioception right away. For dogs recovering from an injury, closely observing how these issues change throughout the healing process is crucial to helping them regain normal body movement. Proprioceptive problems can cause improper weight distribution, abnormal gait, and overreliance on certain muscle groups - putting extra strain on tendons and ligaments and significantly raising the risk of re-injury.

Luce has always had a slightly weaker core. Through her chiropractic adjustments, I've gained insight into the areas where her body tends to overcompensate, where she experiences pain, and where strain builds up. Even years before her injury, I was intentional about strengthening her core.

Hopefully, by now, you're beginning to see how interconnected the body truly is - and how understanding those connections can help you better solve the puzzle of your dog's health.

Certain exercises can be highly effective in improving proprioceptive function. If you're concerned your dog might be showing signs of proprioceptive issues, it's a good idea to consult a rehabilitation veterinarian for an accurate diagnosis and tailored treatment recommendations.

I took a class with trainer Maryna Ozuna, where I learned about a unique program called Movement Markers™. The program explores a wide range of postural, conformational, and movement-related cues that reveal a dog's physical and behavioral health, attitude, reactivity, drives, and overall mental and temperamental balance.

Of all the components we covered, the insights on proprioception stood out to me. Knowing how a dog should ideally move and behave – and comparing that ideal to their current state – makes you more observant and empowers you to create positive changes.

I applied these techniques from Maryna's class to help Luce on her healing journey (Ozuna, 2023).

Here are some of the Movement Markers™ I learned to notice, along with the questions I needed to ask to further my assessment of her:

Symmetry and balance from side to side:

Q: What barriers exist to acquiring and retaining equal development side to side?

Conjunctive and disjunctive elements of the body:

Q: What mixed signals might be communicated to other dogs?

Center of balance:

Q: Where are the equilibrium points of arousal, impulsion, and collection?

Integration of the body from front to back:

Q: Is there a connection between the brain and the body?

Whether movement is "through" from front to back:

Q: How effectively and quickly will new information be processed and integrated?

The leg flight pattern:

Q: Is the dog balanced, or leaning toward physical or behavioral instability?

The condition of footfalls:

Q: How much tension is present in the body? How much stability - or instability - exists?

The degree of flexion, or its absence, in the body:

Q: What capacity does the dog have to manage pressure or assimilate stimuli?

Areas of rigidity in the body:

Q: How much resistance to physical integrity and learning capacity might there be?

Areas of dysfunction within the body:

Q: What obstacles impede learning and affect physical or behavioral stability?

The angulation and rotation of the shoulders:

Q: How much stress is the dog displaying?

The rise and fall of the chest:

Q: Where does the chest position fall on an aggression scale from 1 to 10?

Suppleness - or lack thereof - in the hindquarters:

Q: Where does the stiffness or flexibility in the hindquarters fall on an aggression scale from 1 to 10?

Integration of the forequarters:

Q: Is the impulsion anchored in stability?

The smoothness - or absence of it - in the connection between forequarters, neck, and head:

Q: How easily can this dog regain balance after experiencing stimuli?

The proportion of topline to underline:

Q: What is the inherent balance point and temperament of the dog?

The ratio of topline to leg length:

Q: How much has that original balance been either reinforced - or disrupted - by nutrition, development, training, or its absence?

These are just a few pieces of the Movement Markers™ puzzle that Maryna examines. Each component can work individually or in harmony to shape your dog's behavioral profile. By sharing that I took this course, I'm not suggesting you need to become an expert in everything. My point is this: knowledge is empowering.

Whether you take a class in bodywork or find an expert to join your dog's team, you might never know these options exist if someone doesn't share them. There's real value in spending time observing your dog's typical behavior when they're not injured, asking the right questions, and learning how to *really* see your dog. That awareness makes it much easier to spot changes. And ultimately, bringing the right healers onto your dog's team is key to achieving success.

Luce and I participated in a multi-day Canine Kinaesthetics™ class, also taught by Mayna Ozuna, which turned out to be a valuable experience. The foundational skill in Canine Kinaesthetics™ is the Pulsing Touch - a gentle yet effective rhythmic movement that works with the dog's neurological system and craniosacral pulse to create lasting changes in soft tissue and bone position and response.

According to Ozuna, this touch is applied to specific functional locations throughout the dog's body to help normalize and free up movement. I learned how to use behavioral feedback from the dog, along with shifts in the pressure and rhythm of my hands, to create a kind of behavioral "dialogue." This not only improved communication – it also supported lasting behavioral change (Dog Body Care, n.d.).

I gained a deeper understanding of Luce through the body work we practiced. Armed with this knowledge, I was able to help her maintain balance in her body more effectively.

For me, learning how to observe her, touch her, and engage in purposeful body work in rhythm with her neurological system allowed me to *feel* with my hands – and, through energy transfer, release parts of Luce's body from tension, pain, and stress in a way I never had before.

You don't know what you don't know. So, take the time to learn. Stay open to new ideas and discover something new about your dog every single day.

I Don't Trust Stairs: They're Always Up to Something

Establishing trust with your dog *before* any injury or medical procedure is essential for a positive experience - for both of you. When your dog trusts you, they're more likely to cooperate and feel less anxious in potentially stressful situations.

A strong bond helps your dog understand and accept your actions, making it easier to manage them, administer medication, or carry out necessary procedures.

For example, say you're investing in a chiropractic adjustment or canine massage - if your dog is tense throughout the treatment, it may not be as effective.

Building trust with your dog is essential for several reasons:

1. Enhanced Cooperation and Lower Stress

Trust helps your dog remain calm and reduces anxiety when approached, making it much easier to manage them during potentially stressful situations.

This doesn't just benefit your dog - it also reduces your own stress. A more cooperative dog is easier to handle and less likely to become injured or scared.

2. Greater Understanding and Acceptance

A trusting dog is better able to grasp your intentions and is more open to your actions, even if they're unfamiliar or a bit uncomfortable. They're less likely to interpret your movements or expressions as threats, which leads to fewer misunderstandings and a smoother overall experience. Trust creates a sense of safety and reassures your dog that you genuinely have their best interests at heart.

3. Decreased Fear and Anxiety

When dogs trust their humans, they're far less likely to feel anxious or fearful in unfamiliar environments - like the vet's office or during medical procedures. That trust gives them confidence that you're there to protect and care for them, which can make a huge difference in their behavior and ability to cope with stress.

4. Easier Handling and Dosing

A dog that trusts you is far more likely to let you handle them, give medications, supplements, or homeopathic remedies, and perform necessary procedures without a struggle. This makes caring for them during an injury or illness much simpler and safer. A cooperative dog is also less likely to bite or scratch, protecting both of you from harm.

5. Increased Confidence and Security

A trusting dog feels more confident and secure in your presence. They're able to relax, seek out your attention and affection, and feel safe in your care.

This not only strengthens your bond – it builds a solid foundation for a lasting, trusting relationship. This newfound confidence can help them navigate tough situations and tackle challenges more effectively.

At this point, we've covered the importance of bonding with your dog, effective communication, keen observation, and understanding their normal behavior.

It's essential to recognize that *every* experience—good or bad—contributes to your growth. Mistakes and setbacks aren't just bumps in the road; they're stepping stones for personal and intellectual enrichment.

Adopting this mindset encourages lifelong learning, as you continue to embrace new knowledge and skills over time. Even experiences that feel negative in the moment can provide valuable lessons that support personal growth.

This perspective fosters resilience - helping you to view setbacks not as failures, but as opportunities to learn. In turn, it promotes adaptability and sharpens your problem-solving abilities.

Cumulative learning refers to the process where each experience builds on previous knowledge, leading to a deeper understanding of the world. By embracing the principle that *nothing is a waste*, you being to see life from a broader perspective - recognizing how different experiences are interconnected and contribute to overall growth.

When Luce got injured, it felt like I was suddenly "called up to the big leagues." I had to draw on everything I'd learned about dogs, using that accumulated knowledge to devise a strategic plan for her recovery. I took all my insights and applied them for her benefit.

Luce and I spent years training together, exercising side by side, exploring new sports, and traveling to different places. All that time and effort brought us closer than ever. Each experience challenged us to navigate new environments, manage stress, celebrate triumphs, and sometimes endure pain.

Different sports required varying levels of independence and confidence, and we leaned on each other as teammates to find the best versions of ourselves.

In the following section, I'll share our journey through the sports we participated in and how each played a crucial role in helping me support Luce over those 12 months. I remained flexible, adjusting our strategies as needed, so that even as our "new normal" shifted from the highly physical to more emotional and intellectual challenges, we continued to maintain a sense of purpose.

Life Off the Leash

Maybe you've done the same sports with your dog as I have with Luce – or maybe some of them are totally new to you. The whole point of this section is to share what we did and open up your sporting world, just as others once did for us.

Let's dive into the world of agility! Dog agility training is an exciting sport where dogs learn to navigate a series of obstacle courses. It blends physical challenges and mental exercises, pushing both dog and handler to their limits.

Engaging in agility can significantly boost a dog's physical health, provide valuable mental stimulation, and strengthen the bond between a dog and its handler. It's also a fantastic way for dogs to socialize and build confidence in a supportive environment.

Agility training offers dogs a fun and challenging way to exercise while also providing essential mental stimulation. It strengthens the bond between dog and handler by fostering clear communication and teamwork. When a dog successfully navigates obstacles, it gives them a chance to build confidence in their abilities.

Typical agility courses include jumps, dog walks, teeter boards, tunnels, weave poles, A-frames, and various other challenges. Dogs learn to respond to their handler's verbal and nonverbal cues as they maneuver through the course. This sport demands a high level of trust and communication between the dog and its handler.

Agility trials and competitions offer a popular outlet for dog owners to showcase their pets' skills.

For Luce, agility training taught her to navigate different heights safely, develop awareness of her back end for better stability on obstacles, and gain confidence on various surfaces.

I quickly learned just how much my body position communicated information and ultimately influenced her performance. She was not listening to the words I was saying as much as she was watching my feet.

Agility provided a platform for Luce to feel more comfortable in her everyday world, even with routine tasks like getting on an exam table.

The command "table," learned during her agility training, meant the same thing in the vet office - helping her feel confident and at ease when it was time to jump up and stay off the ground for a period of time.

When Luce needed to use ramps instead of jumping onto furniture, saying "A frame" or "dog walk" signaled that she was about to tackle a narrow, inclined obstacle - just like the ones we practiced in agility.

This made it easy to introduce a new term at home and in the car by simply using the word "ramp" when I need her to ascend.

At first, I rewarded her with targets, just as we had during our training sessions, so she learned to expect a reward upon completing the obstacle.

Eventually, she began navigating the ramps effortlessly, recognizing that her reward was reaching the window seat, the car, or the bed.

It was a win for everyone: she stayed safe and confident during recovery, and I didn't have to keep her off the furniture – or move my sleeping arrangements to the floor, as some people do.

Luce and I participated in agility for several years, during which she earned titles through the United States Dog Agility Association (USDAA). Unfortunately, due to her injury, we may no longer be able to compete in this sport.

The rapid twisting movements (torsion) required to navigate between obstacles could pose long-term risks for her knee, increasing the likelihood of reinjury.

However, we still train and work with agility equipment – we've simply stepped away from competition.

Canicross is an exciting and physically demanding sport where a person runs cross-country alongside their dog, with the canine doing the pulling.

Essentially, it's cross-country running with the added thrill of a dog leading the way on a bungee leash, often positioned ahead of the human athlete.

The dog is connected to the runner through a waist belt and a flexible bungee line, providing shock absorption and enhancing control.

Luce and I running in the 2024 Rehab Rover 5K Canicross and Trail Race

Originating in Europe as a training method for sled dogs during their off-season, Canicross has grown into a popular sport in its own right.

Canicross is perfect for both recreational enjoyment and competitive events, making it a versatile option for dog lovers looking to stay active.

Canicross is an excellent way to boost your exercise routine, strengthen your bond with your dog, and enjoy the great outdoors. It offers a fun and challenging activity that helps dogs build endurance while addressing issues like pent-up energy, separation anxiety, and boredom.

Before getting started with Canicross, ensure your dog has basic obedience training and feels comfortable on a leash.

Start with short, low-intensity runs and gradually increase the distance and intensity as both you and your dog get more accustomed to it.

Teaching your dog commands like "go," "stop," "left," and "right" will also make it easier to navigate your runs together.

What's most important in Canicross is that your dog stays in front of you, able to follow cues verbally without needing to turn and look at you.

During winter, when harsh weather made outdoor conditions less than ideal with snow, rain, or ice on the ground, or in summer when temperatures soared or air quality dropped, Luce would hop onto the treadmill. This wasn't a special dog treadmill - just a regular one that I used for the same reasons.

I took the time to teach her how to run correctly on the treadmill, getting her accustomed to the noise and movement so she could still exercise when the weather didn't cooperate.

This training proved invaluable when she needed to use the underwater treadmill for rehabilitation.

Although she had never encountered an underwater treadmill before, her familiarity with the regular one made the transition much smoother. She adapted effortlessly, whether on a small dog-sized underwater treadmill or a horse-sized one.

Canicross evolved into Canine Obstacle Course Racing (OCR) for Luce and me. In this exciting sport, competitors run alongside their dogs, tackling a variety of physical challenges, including climbing, crawling, carrying heavy objects, and navigating through mud or water.

The sport is rapidly gaining popularity, with events varying in distance, difficulty, and whether they are timed.

OCR is a unique blend of running, endurance, and strength, making it both challenging and rewarding.

Participants work their way through a course while overcoming various obstacles - either natural or man-made – that test their strength, agility, endurance, and mental grit.

Events can range from short, action-packed courses loaded with obstacles to longer endurance races that push your limits.

Here are some examples of obstacles you might encounter:

- Scaling giant A-Frames, walls, or maneuvering over tire mounds.

- Crawling beneath fence panels, through tarps, or navigating tunnels.

- Carrying heavy items like my dog, sandbags, or logs.

- Making your way through mud, water, or challenging terrain.

- Leaping over barriers like barricades or swimming in water pits.

- Climbing atop cars and buses.

- Swimming in open water, whether in pools, rivers, or creeks.

OCR training typically combines running, strength exercises, and agility workouts. To prepare effectively, it's important to strike a balance between endurance and strength to tackle the variety of challenges ahead. OCR provides a demanding workout for both humans and their dogs, pushing everyone to their limits.

Conquering obstacles not only builds physical strength but also fosters mental toughness, teamwork, and resilience.

Additionally, OCR events often feature a supportive community where participants cheer each other on. Many see OCR as an exciting and adventurous way to stay active alongside their dogs.

OCR training allowed me to interact with Luce in a way that was completely different from any other sport. Obstacle course training required me to enter her personal space and build trust - especially when helping her navigate obstacles.

This meant using a gentle touch and adjusting my pace to match hers. Some challenges even required me to pick Luce up and carry her in various positions for a set period of time.

This skillset of carrying her became crucial after her injury, when I needed to carry her up and down 20 deck stairs daily to access the yard or lift her in and out of the car.

At the top of the deck, I would give her the command to wait. Then, I'd carefully enter her space by bending down or reaching toward her, lifting in a way that protected her spine and limbs.

Next, I'd direct her to "be still" as I cautiously navigated the stairs. Once we reached the bottom, I'd ask her to wait again while I gently set her on the ground.

Carrying Luce across a log over water in the Midwest Canine Obstacle Course Race

Carrying Luce up and down the 20 stairs that lead to our home

It was essential to execute this process slowly and deliberately. If she were to jump from my arms onto the pavement without being steady on all four limbs, it could create a seriously unbalanced situation and risk injury. Training for this kind of personal space invasion required breaking it down into manageable steps. Along the way, an incredible amount of trust was established between us. Just think about it—I could easily trip or accidentally drop her, and the consequences would be catastrophic, whether in a competition or real life.

I applied the skills I developed while training for the obstacle course race to help her navigate the stairs safely. I never anticipated that my training would come in handy for other tasks. This approach also prepares you to carry your dog in case they get injured on a trail. It's important to understand that the first time you practice an emergency carry should not be when they're already hurt.

When I began training dogs in my twenties, I quickly gravitated toward obedience training as my preferred sport. This discipline not only teaches dogs essential commands but also sharpens their focus and deepens the bond between dog and handler.

Engaging in obedience training helps dogs manage distractions, socialize with people and other dogs, and provides both mental stimulation and physical exercise. In basic obedience, dogs learn vital commands like "sit," "stay," "come," "down," and "heel." They also master walking politely on a leash without pulling or rushing ahead.

Additionally, they learn to retrieve objects and return them to their handler, as well as to jump over various obstacles.

In advanced obedience, dogs master more complex commands and exercises, including "go out," "scent discrimination," and "directed jumping." They learn to walk precisely at their handler's side, maintaining the proper position and pace during various movements.

Additionally, they learn to stay in a sit or down position, even amidst distractions. The benefits of obedience training are numerous - improved focus, heightened attention, and a stronger connection between dog and handler.

Obedience training helps a dog focus on their handler while tuning out distractions. It fosters clearer communication between dog and handler, reinforcing their bond. Additionally, it exposes dogs to a variety of situations and people, helping them grow into well-mannered and adaptable companions.

Obedience training also provides essential mental and physical stimulation, which helps curb boredom and prevent behavioral problems. A crucial task in obedience competitions is the "stand for examination," where the handler places the dog in a stand-stay position. A judge then approaches and must be able to touch the dog in three specific areas without the dog moving or showing signs of stress.

This scenario illustrates how to teach your dog to cope with the stress of being touched by a stranger in an unfamiliar setting. Since the handler is present, a well-trained dog understands they can rely on you to advocate for them, which boosts their confidence and ability to succeed in this challenge.

Luce has earned numerous AKC obedience titles and participated in various training sessions with different instructors. Despite her success, it often felt like she was going through the motions—doing it for my sake rather than her own enjoyment of formal obedience.

Nevertheless, she excelled in the ring and continued to bring home ribbons. That's when I discovered Rally obedience, which uses the same commands and skills but allows for verbal interaction with your dog during the course. Luce responded much better to this format, so we decided to sign up for classes and dive into the world of rally obedience.

Rally obedience is a team sport and a fantastic way to improve a dog's obedience skills while also enhancing their focus and attention. It strengthens the bond between the dog and handler, promoting teamwork through clear communication, making it both fun and engaging. Through rally obedience, dogs reinforce essential commands like sit, stay, heel, and recall, which helps them respond better to commands in everyday situations. This sport requires dogs to remain keenly attentive and responsive to their handlers throughout the course, helping them develop greater focus and attention, even in varying environments. This is a really fun and interactive way of training, encouraging positive interactions, deepening the connection between the handler and their dog.

Luce and I in a Rally Obedience Trial

Luce earned her second AKC title (her first was AKC Canine Good Citizen) by mastering tricks! Trick training is invaluable because it helps dogs develop a wide range of skills, from enhancing their ability to learn to improving communication, boosting confidence, and sharpening focus. It provides both mental and physical stimulation while deepening the bond between dog and owner. Through trick training, dogs learn to perform various behaviors, respond to lures, and understand cues like clicks or the word "yes," which trainers often use. This process helps them apply their learning to new situations and concepts, enhancing their adaptability.

Moreover, the shared journey of teaching tricks deepens the bond between dog and owner. Mastering these tricks lays the foundation for dogs to learn more intricate behaviors and compete in various activities, allowing them to build and apply new skills. Tricks like spinning or rolling not only enhance body awareness but also improve a dog's coordination and control. Trick training also provides an opportunity for trainers to experiment with techniques like shaping, luring, and targeting, all while creating effective training plans. Ultimately, trick training is an enjoyable way to keep dogs mentally stimulated, helping to prevent boredom and curb destructive behaviors.

The beauty of teaching tricks lies in breaking down specific movements into fun, manageable steps. For example, I taught Luce how to put on her brace by turning it into a trick, much like showing her how to wear a hat or a costume. I divided the process into small, simple steps and guided her through each one, gradually leading to the trick of putting the brace on and taking it off. By incorporating tricks into our routine, I was also able to teach her various body positions, such as lying on her side on command, moving just her back feet, and even stretching in different positions.

One trick changed the way Luce and I experienced the outdoors - riding in a buggy. As I mentioned earlier, I often took her outdoors in an all-terrain buggy while I jogged behind. This trick training encouraged her to stay calm and stable in the buggy, preventing her from jumping out and allowing her to remain relaxed as we passed by other people and dogs.

Luce's ability to ride safely in the buggy allowed me to be able to take her everywhere

Additionally, I used the K9 Sport Sack to carry her on trails. Getting her into the backpack required a bit of finesse; I had to gently guide the backpack over her front legs through designated openings and then maneuver her rear legs, including her injured leg, into the base of the pack. Once she was settled, I zipped it up, adjusted the straps, and then lifted her vertically to place the K9 Sport Sack on my back. This process required her to remain still while I handled her in a way that felt awkward. With some patience, she learned to stay calm during the whole routine.

Luce didn't get into K9 Nose Work until she was around six years old. Before that, I had never been exposed to this sport and didn't know much about it. A friend from the agility community suggested that we give it a try, and after our very first class, we were both hooked. Being a hound, Luce had a natural talent for using her nose! This training aligned perfectly with her instincts and added a new dimension to her overall development.

In all the other sports we practiced together, I was the one leading the way. But in K9 Nose Work, the roles shifted for the first time. Luce enters the search area first, where she's encouraged to find what we're looking for using her keen sense of smell, signaling her discoveries through changes in behavior. My role is simple: show her the search area, ask her to start looking, and then observe her behavior closely to call out a find when she alerts me.

K9 Nose Work is a low-impact activity that also allows Luce to be active and engage in a sport throughout her senior years. I realized what an excellent investment this would be for her future. In Nose Work, dogs search for specific scents, which not only teaches them to focus and solve problems but also enhances their communication skills.

The sport taps into their natural scenting abilities, boosts confidence, and deepens the bond between dog and handler. It's a mentally stimulating activity that requires concentration, engagement, and critical thinking. This kind of mental exercise tires dogs out, helping to prevent boredom and promote a sense of calm. Through this training, dogs learn to ignore distractions and zero in on the target scent.

Finding and signaling a scent successfully boosts a dog's confidence and independence. K9 Nose Work can be especially helpful for dogs that are shy, reactive, or lacking in confidence. As they learn to work independently and accurately identify scents, their self-assurance grows. This training taps into and strengthens their natural olfactory abilities. Dogs learn to differentiate between various odors and signal the presence of the target scent. Over time, this practice can enhance their overall scent detection skills and their ability to work in a variety of environments.

K9 Nose Work strengthens the bond between dogs and their handlers as they collaborate to search containers, interior rooms, exterior property, and vehicles. Handlers become attuned to their dogs' behaviors and cues, enhancing communication and teamwork. You'll observe your dog like never before. This shared activity fosters camaraderie and mutual enjoyment. Dogs also learn to signal their handlers when they've discovered a scent through specific behaviors, building trust and cooperation between the duo.

Luce and I doing an NACSW vehicle search

Additionally, Nose Work teaches dogs to respond to commands and stay focused, even in the face of distractions. They develop the ability to adapt to various search conditions, using problem-solving skills to locate scents - even in challenging situations. This knack for flexibility not only helps during searches but also carries over into other areas of their lives, making them more resilient and confident when faced with new challenges.

K9 Nose Work turned out to be one of the most incredible activities for Luce during her healing process. She's the kind of dog who thrives when given a job to do. As I mentioned in a previous chapter, a positive mindset is key to healing the body more quickly. Throughout Luce's recovery, we focused on Nose Work, which allowed her to stay on a leash, engage in minimal physical activity, wear her brace, and use her mental skills. This not only kept her mind active but also helped ease feelings of frustration, isolation, and a lack of stimulation.

Each of these sports taught her to respond to signals, develop body awareness, collaborate with me as a team, and navigate stressful and uncomfortable situations - all while knowing I'd be by her side. This process unintentionally built a strong foundation of trust between us. I drew on that trust when she faced her injury and went through therapy. By introducing new cues and adapting the ones she already knew, we were able to broaden her range of experiences together.

Be the Bark-itect of New Tricks

While dog sports like agility and K9 Nose Work teach specific skills, they also build life skills. These include improved focus, communication, and the ability to handle excitement and distractions - all valuable in everyday situations. Life skills training, in addition to basic obedience, further equips dogs for real-life scenarios. Now, let's take a moment to talk about the value of table, touch, and talk.

As I mentioned before, getting your dog comfortable on a table can be incredibly beneficial. It not only helps during vet visits and grooming sessions but also plays a key role in building their trust and confidence. When dogs are at ease on a table, it makes exams much easier for veterinarians, whether it's a routine checkup or something more involved. Many dogs are anxious about grooming, but when they're familiar with being on a table, the process tends to go more smoothly - with less stress for both dog and groomer.

Dogs of all sizes should be taught to feel comfortable on an examination/grooming table.

Gradually introducing your dog to the idea of being on a table, combined with positive reinforcement like treats and praise, can help foster their trust and confidence in you and other handlers. For some dogs, visits to the vet and being handled can trigger anxiety. By training your dog to feel comfortable on a table, you can reduce their fear and discomfort. Even a dog that's used to being examined on a vet's table might struggle with the experience when they have to go every few days for an entire year!

A calm, confident dog tends to be a happier dog. By addressing any anxiety or discomfort they may feel during handling, you significantly contribute to their overall well-being. Teaching them to stand, sit, or lie on their side on a table can be beneficial in various situations, such as conformation shows or simply keeping them still during daily routines.

Encouraging a dog to tackle challenging tasks starts with ensuring they are mentally prepared and focused. Positive reinforcement is key to shaping their behavior effectively. It's important to break complex tasks into smaller, manageable steps, reward their progress, and maintain consistency and patience throughout the training process. Ideally, you should begin this approach while your dog is healthy, but it's never too late to think creatively about their skills and how to link those to what you need from them now.

Here's a solid approach to get started:

Ensure Readiness and Focus

- **Mental Readiness:** Before beginning any training session, make sure your dog is mentally prepared. They should be alert, attentive, and eager to work with you.

- **"Ready" Routine:** Create a routine that signals it's time to train. This could be a specific cue—like a hand signal or verbal command—that your dog recognizes as the official start.

- **Attention-Grabbing Techniques:** Use techniques like "Watch me" to capture your dog's focus and ensure they're fully engaged before introducing commands.

Shaping Behavior with Positive Reinforcement

- **Lure and Reward:** Start by using a lure, such as a treat, to guide your dog into the desired position. Reward them immediately when they offer the behavior you're looking for.

- **Gradual Progression:** Break complex tasks into smaller, manageable steps. Once your dog masters a step, gradually increase the difficulty.

- **Consistency and Patience:** Stick with consistent training methods and be patient. Training takes time and repetition. Avoid punishment for mistakes - instead, celebrate progress and build confidence.

Introducing dogs to a variety of touch experiences - such as different vibrations, temperature changes, gentle handling, and firm pats - can build trust and improve body awareness, ultimately enhancing their well-being. This kind of practice also helps dogs feel more at ease with routine handling, grooming, and veterinary visits.

Using positive touch, whether through firm pats on the back or gentle strokes, can mimic grooming or a soothing massage, creating a sense of comfort and security while strengthening the bond between dog and owner. It's important to be aware of how your touch affects your dog - whether it brings calmness or sparks excitement.

Gradual exposure to handling different parts of a dog's body, combined with positive reinforcement, helps them become more comfortable being touched in various areas. This approach can greatly reduce fear or aggression down the road. When dogs are used to being handled, tasks like nail clipping, brushing, or administering medication become far less stressful for both dog and owner. Positive touch releases endorphins, which have a calming effect and help regulate the nervous system - ultimately lowering stress responses.

Touch can also be a powerful training tool. For example, you can teach a "touch" command, where the dog learns to target their nose to your hand, or use touch to redirect their attention when needed. Techniques like TTouch (Tellington TTouch) and other forms of canine massage offer therapeutic benefits, including pain relief, stress reduction, and improved mobility. Introducing puppies to human touch early on helps them develop healthy relationships and learn essential social cues.

When it comes to handling your dog, there are a few key factors to keep in mind. Every dog has their own preferences for touch - some may enjoy a firm pat, while others prefer a gentle stroke. It's important to pay close attention to your dog's body language to understand what they like and what makes them uncomfortable. Always aim to associate touch with positive experiences, like treats, praise, or playtime, to help your dog build a positive association with being handled.

Respecting your dog's boundaries is crucial—never force them into situations that make them uncomfortable. If your dog shows signs of unease, take a step back and try again later with a gentler approach. For dogs with a history of fear or sensitivity to touch, introduce it slowly and patiently, using positive reinforcement to build their confidence.

For dogs struggling with severe fear or aggression, it's wise to consult a certified dog trainer or behaviorist. They can provide expert guidance on how to safely desensitize and counter-condition your dog's negative associations.

Lastly, talking to your dog - even if they don't understand every word - can greatly enhance their well-being and strengthen your bond. Dogs are highly attuned to your tone and inflection, so regular communication builds trust, eases anxiety, and supports their cognitive development.

Here's a closer look at how your voice impacts your dog:

1. Emotional Impact

- **Tone of Voice:** Dogs are incredibly sensitive to the emotional tone of your voice. They can pick up on how you're feeling - even when you don't say a word.

- **Reassurance and Comfort:** A calm, soothing voice go a long way in reassuring your dog, especially during stressful moments.

- **Increased Oxytocin**: Research shows that gazing into your dog's eyes while speaking can trigger a boost of oxytocin - the hormone linked to bonding and relaxation - for both of you.

2. Cognitive Benefits

- **Cognitive Growth:** Regularly talking to your dog helps them get used to the rhythm and patterns of human speech, supporting their cognitive development.

- **Predictive Learning:** Consistently using certain words for specific events teaches your dog to associate words with experiences – helping them anticipate what's coming next.

3. Strengthening the Bond

- **Building Trust and Affection:** Talking to your dog shows your care and desire to connect, helping cultivate trust and affection.

- **Enhancing Social Connection:** Verbal communication deepens your emotional bond, making your dog feel more secure and cherished.

4. Possible Negative Effects:

- **Confusion or Frustration:** A harsh tone or yelling can confuse or upset your dog – and may even reinforce unwanted behaviors.

- **Misunderstandings:** Dogs don't understand words like humans do. Instead, they rely on your tone and body language. Still, even casual conversation with your dog can ease their anxiety, strengthen your bond, and boost their overall well-being.

Have A Crate Attitude

Luce has been crate-trained since she was a puppy, and that positive experience has paid off in big ways throughout her training. Crate training offers numerous benefits for both dogs and their humans: it supports housetraining, provides a safe space, helps prevent destructive behaviors, and makes travel or vet less stressful. It can also help ease separation anxiety and create a sense of calm in tense situations. When Luce was injured, her familiarity with the crate meant it didn't add to the stress she was already experiencing.

If you don't introduce your dog to the crate in a positive way, you risk doubling their stress—first from the situation that requires crating (like an emergency or vet visit) and second from the crate itself. That's just not fair to your dog.

Crate training offers a wide range of benefits. Because dogs naturally avoid soiling their sleeping area, a crate can be an effective tool for establishing a consistent potty routine. It also serves as a cozy, familiar den where your dog can retreat when feeling stressed or overwhelmed. When left unsupervised, a crate helps prevent chewing, digging, and other mischief. Crate-trained dogs are typically more comfortable in confined spaces, making travel and vet visits far less stressful for everyone involved.

By gradually increasing the time your dog spends in the crate, you can help them adjust to being alone and reduce separation anxiety. Crate training also gives you peace of mind, knowing your dog is safe and secure when you're not able to supervise them.

Crates can be incredibly useful for managing multiple dogs in a household - whether during training sessions, mealtimes, or when the dogs need a little space from each other. If your dog has suffered a torn CCL, it's especially important to limit dog-to-dog interactions. Dogs that are comfortable in crates tend to be less anxious during vet visits, making examinations and treatments go much more smoothly. In emergencies, a crate allows for quick, safe evacuation. It also gives your dog a quiet, secure retreat during stressful events like thunderstorms or fireworks.

Take Luce, for example. When she was younger, she attended daycare and comfortably went into a crate for her lunch and cool-down breaks. Because of her comfort with crating, I can now take her to dog sporting events, where she relaxes in her crate beside me. Although she wasn't crated during her recovery, she could have handled it easily. Her crate training also makes her respectful of X-pens, which I find especially helpful when needed.

As we wrap up our training discussion, here are a few key points to keep in mind. I mentioned that I've used KT tape on Luce's legs. If your dog isn't used to having anything attached to their body, this can be a great opportunity to teach a solid "leave it" command. I've found "leave it" to be useful in all sorts of situations - and it can even help you skip the dreaded cone or those stylish-but-sad no-lick pajamas.

Exposing dogs to new experiences - often called socialization - offers a range of benefits. It builds their confidence, reduces reactivity, and encourages adaptability. By introducing dogs to diverse situations, they learn appropriate social behaviors and develop the skills needed to navigate their world smoothly, leading to happier, more well-adjusted lives.

Well-socialized dogs are typically less fearful or reactive when faced with new situations. Having encountered a variety of experiences, they develop a more confident and curious outlook on the world. Socialization teaches dogs how to interact appropriately with other dogs, people, and different environments, reducing the likelihood of aggressive behavior.

Moreover, socialization helps dogs manage their emotions and impulses during stressful situations. Socialized dogs generally adapt more easily to new places, situations, and changes in their daily routines.

Well-socialized dogs are also more resilient and adaptable when faced with uncertainty. Engaging in social interactions helps them develop appropriate behaviors and learn how to interact positively and respectfully with others. Through these experiences, they become better communicators with both dogs and humans.

Early and consistent socialization is key to preventing a range of behavioral issues, such as excessive barking, separation anxiety, and destructive habits. It lays the foundation for a well-adjusted, well-behaved companion. A properly socialized dog is more likely to form strong bonds with its owners and family members, showing increased obedience and responsiveness to commands.

Moreover, socialization instills a sense of security and confidence in dogs, paving the way for a happier, more fulfilling life. They're also more likely to enjoy activities with other dogs and people. Don't wait until your dog is injured to forge a meaningful relationship with them. Train, communicate, observe, build trust, and expose your dog to new experiences. Striking a balance between physical and mental activities is essential. You never know when a challenging situation will arise, and having a wealth of experiences to draw upon can significantly aid in their recovery. Remember, no one understands your dog better than you do!

Chapter 7: From Torn to Triumphant

"It always seems impossible until it's done."- Nelson Mandela

When Luce first emerged from the hill that August day, holding her right rear leg aloft, I had no idea how far this moment would take us. It wasn't just the torn ligament or the sudden lameness that shocked me—it was the way my world shifted in a breath. One second, I was a guardian of a healthy, joyful dog; the next, I was a caregiver navigating pain, options, and uncertainty. That single moment asked everything of me: my emotion, my science, my patience, and my belief in something better.

What began as a suspected knee injury evolved into a complete diagnosis: cranial cruciate ligament rupture, meniscal tear, and iliopsoas strain.

As I confronted the overwhelming amount of information surrounding canine orthopedic injuries, I realized I wasn't just seeking treatment—I was building a path forward. I weighed every option, from surgical procedures like TPLO and TTA to less invasive alternatives. Ultimately, I chose conservative management—not because it was easier, but because it was right for Luce.

That choice defined our year.

Conservative management meant embracing a layered, patient, and proactive strategy. It meant physical rehabilitation, nutritional precision, and emotional support. I partnered with an extraordinary team—Dr. Froeling for chiropractic and acupuncture, Dr. Johnson and Dr. Belden for rehabilitation—and crafted a weekly schedule of therapies tailored to Luce's evolving needs.

There was no quick fix. Instead, there were hours logged in underwater treadmills, stretches, therapeutic lasers, and gentle massage. There were setbacks, but there was also resilience.

This veterinary trio worked in concert, ensuring continuity of care, precise treatment planning, and ongoing evaluation as Luce progressed through underwater treadmill sessions, various modalities, and targeted therapeutic exercises.

These experts didn't just treat the injury—they guided me through setbacks, adaptations, and the natural emotional toll of long-term recovery. They brought structure, science, and insight to a plan grounded in empathy and intuition.

The collaboration between the caregiver and the veterinary team became a model of shared leadership, reminding everyone involved that successful outcomes are rarely the result of a single voice—they're built on **teamwork, transparency, and trust**.

Nutrition played a central role. I embraced adaptive feeding—customizing Luce's diet for recovery, reducing inflammation, and providing mobility support.

I used whole foods, supplemented intentionally, and prioritized absorption over trends.

I monitored every shift in her behavior and digestion, paying close attention to what her body and spirit were telling me. This wasn't just rehabilitation—it was recalibration.

Full Circle

Unintended positive outcomes can emerge during rehabilitation, often surpassing the initial goals. These include unexpected improvements in mental health, overall physical well-being, the development of new skills, and the discovery of new passions or a renewed sense of purpose.

Before the injury, Luce consistently struggled to maintain normal Vitamin D levels. Every six months at her routine wellness check, we ran the same test—and every time, the results came back low.

I tried everything: adjusting her diet, and adding Vitamin D-rich foods. But nothing seemed to make a difference.

Then came the injury.

In the face of her recovery, I knew I had to do more than just manage her symptoms—I had to help her heal, truly heal. I transitioned her to a carefully curated frozen raw diet, rotating between three trusted brands. My goal was twofold: reduce inflammation by eliminating unnecessary carbohydrates and provide her body with the proteins and nutrients that support deep, cellular healing.

Months later, at her latest wellness visit, I asked the veterinarian to recheck her Vitamin D levels—just to see.

When the results came back, I was stunned: **for the first time in seven years, her Vitamin D levels were perfect.** No supplements. Just real, nourishing food and a body focused on healing.

It was a turning point. Luce wasn't just recovering from an injury—she was rebuilding her health from the inside out.

Around the time of Luce's injury, I made another startling discovery—one that had nothing to do with her leg but everything to do with her overall health.

Before she was injured, Luce was eating a commercially produced dehydrated base mix combined with raw meat. Curious about her long-term wellness, I had her urine tested for glyphosate, the widely used herbicide. The results floored me: **her levels were ten times higher than what's considered acceptable for a 150-pound human.**

At the time, her diet included grains and non-organic vegetables—ingredients I now believe were the primary source of the exposure. Knowing the risks of chronic glyphosate intake—gut disruption, inflammation, nervous system effects—I realized this wasn't just a number on a lab report. It was a red flag.

I changed everything.

I transitioned Luce to a frozen raw diet made only with organic vegetables and no grains. I changed nothing else—not her treats, not her environment—just the food.

After a few months on the new diet, I retested her glyphosate levels. This time, the results showed **a dramatic drop to nearly undetectable levels.**

Encouraged, I expanded her rotation to include two more frozen raw options—all free from grains and made exclusively with organic vegetables—and introduced supplements tailored to her recovery. When I tested her urine again later, her glyphosate levels remained negligible.

That confirmation was more than scientific validation—it was peace of mind.

Not only was Luce healing from her injury, but her entire system was being freed from a toxic burden I hadn't even realized she was carrying.

This journey has shown me that true healing doesn't just treat symptoms—it removes the obstacles that prevent the body from thriving.

There's something truly remarkable I want to circle back to—something that still gives me chills when I think about it: Luce's eyes.

In Chapter 5, I introduced *Iridology*—the practice of analyzing the patterns, colors, and textures in the iris to gain insight into the body's health. While unconventional, it's a tool I've found surprisingly insightful over the years.

Thankfully, I had clear photographs of both of Luce's irises taken *before* her injury. After her accident, I took a new set and began a careful side-by-side comparison. What I saw next stopped me in my tracks.

A new dark mark had appeared in her right iris—right in the zone traditionally associated with the right leg. This mark hadn't been there before. It was distinct, unmistakable. And here's what made it even more striking: the corresponding area in her *left* iris was completely unchanged.

It was as if her injury had etched itself not only into her physical body but into the very landscape of her eyes.

This tiny shift—barely visible to the untrained eye—was a quiet, powerful reminder that the body tells its story in unexpected ways. And if we're willing to look closely, to listen differently, we might see healing from a whole new perspective.

The following months were filled with acupuncture, chiropractic adjustments, underwater treadmill sessions, laser therapy, proprioceptive training, and functional exercises. Nutritional strategies were reexamined and adapted to promote healing, reduce inflammation, and preserve muscle mass. The "adaptive nutrition" approach I championed emphasized not just food, but also absorption, gut health, and individualized support.

Training and communication created emotional safety; nutrition and environment supported the physical. But the **veterinary team** helped transform intention into action. Together, these elements created the scaffolding that allowed Luce to truly recover.

Emotionally, Luce's journey paralleled her physical one. Together, we were grieving the loss of my other dog, Harley, while also navigating personal challenges. I learned to translate hardship into insight. The loss, the delays, the decisions—all reshaped my perspective, reinforcing the truth that recovery isn't linear - and neither is growth.

Progress came in increments—measured in centimeters of muscle regained, seconds of weight-bearing tolerated, and increasingly bold steps taken outdoors. The reintroduction of trail walks, controlled yard runs, and even swimming marked milestones in both physical recovery and emotional renewal. Every gain felt like a gift. Every pause taught me something new. Through it all, I came to understand: this journey wasn't just Luce's—it was ours.

Training proved to be more than just a skill set - it was the backbone of trust. Years of foundation work allowed Luce to accept hands-on treatment, communicate discomfort without fear, and be part of the process rather than just a subject to it. Our relationship, built on choice, respect, and mutual understanding, gave her the confidence to heal—and me the courage to keep leading her through it.

Tail up and Tongue out! Let the Twin Flags Fly!

Looking back now, I see more than the diagnosis, the rehab notes, or the supplements - I see the transformation that happened within me. I moved from fear to focus, from confusion to clarity, from overwhelmed to empowered. I learned to lean into discomfort, to listen better, and to trust that healing is possible when knowledge meets compassion.

The decision to forgo surgery in favor of conservative management ultimately proved to be the right one—for Luce. She made a full return to mobility - not in record time, but in real time—through patience, adaptation, and unwavering support. Luce didn't just recover—she triumphed. She runs again. She swims. She explores. She trusts me more than ever. And I trust myself more deeply than I ever imagined.

This choice also brought long-term benefits: reduced surgical risk, preserved joint structures, and a deeper partnership rooted in trust. It taught me to trust my instincts, to question defaults, and to engage fully in collaborative care. It affirmed that conservative management - when executed intentionally and with expert support - can be a viable and effective path to recovery.

This book began with a torn ligament. It ends with a truth: the unplanned obstacle didn't break us—it built us.

As of now, Luce has officially completed her formal rehabilitation program and has been cleared to return to full activity. That means running, swimming, jumping, and interacting with other dogs - all without the need for a brace. Since her release, she's participated in several Canicross trail races and canine obstacle course events. She completed each one without re-injury, and together, we've been achieving new personal best times.

One World Obstacle Course - Anniston, Alabama, October 2024

One World Canine Obstacle Course Race - May 2025

Luce's body is strong, and we're able to compete again. At the same time, it remains essential to monitor her condition. Therapy sessions will now be scheduled as needed.

Although she's made significant progress, her right rear leg will likely never return to full pre-injury status. Because of that, she'll continue receiving supplements and occasional therapy as necessary.

I still notice a slight tendency for her to shift weight onto her left leg and some subtle protective behavior around the right in certain situations.

But her confidence in using the previously injured leg continues to improve, and her muscle development continues to improve. We've also maintained monthly Adequan injections to proactively manage arthritis.

If you're holding this book because you're facing a similar challenge, know this—you are not alone.

There *is* another side to this. Healing takes time, but it also takes intention.

Build your team. Trust your instincts. Advocate relentlessly. Let love guide your science.

The obstacle may have been unplanned, but the healing was anything but accidental.

Together, we crossed this unplanned obstacle. And I promise—you can too.

Luce's graduation photo from rehabilitation - 2025

ABOUT THE AUTHOR

Jennifer Carter has dedicated her life to understanding—and celebrating—the incredible bond between dogs and their people. With certifications in canine nutrition and K9 Nose Work, plus degrees in Biological and Animal Science, Jennifer brings both heart and hard science to her work. She holds two Master's degrees, one from the University of New Haven and another from Virginia Tech, where she is currently pursuing her Ph.D. in pursuit of advancing canine health and behavior research.

Her passion doesn't stop at the books. Jennifer works hands-on with dogs every day, training her spirited partner, Luce, in a variety of disciplines including agility, tricks, rally, obedience, nose work, and Canicross. The duo competes in canine obstacle course races across the globe, putting her academic knowledge to the test in real-world, paws-on ways. From muddy finish lines to moments of quiet connection, Jennifer's work is rooted in the joy of the human-animal bond.

Whether in the lab, the ring, or on the trail, Jennifer's commitment to canine wellness shines through. Her mission is to equip dog lovers with the tools, understanding, and confidence to help their companions thrive—body, mind, and tail-wag.

You can connect with Jennifer on her website, www.harnesscanicular.dog and email at: harnesscanicular@gmail.com

References

Chapter 2

American College of Veterinary Surgeons (ACVS). (n.d.). Cranial cruciate ligament disease. https://www.acvs.org/small-animal/cranial-cruciate-ligament-disease

Arizona Canine Orthopedics and Sports Medicine (ACOSM). (n.d.). TPLO. https://www.arizonacanineorthopedics.com/tplo.html

Bergh, M. S., &Peirone, B. (2012). Complications of tibial plateau leveling osteotomy in dogs. *Veterinary and Comparative Orthopaedics and Traumatology*, *25*, 349–358. https://doi.org/10.3415/VCOT-11-09-0122

BoneVet. (n.d.). Ccl treatment options. https://www.bonevet.com.au/review-articles/ccl-treatment-options/#:~:text=TPLO%20is%20currently%20considered%20the,commonly%20favoured%20by%20orthopaedic%20surgeons

Boudreau, R. J.(2009). Tibial plateau leveling osteotomy or tibial tuberosity advancement? *Veterinary Surgery, 38(1),* 1–22. https://doi.org/10.11 11/j.1532-950X.2008.00439.x

Colorado State University Veterinary Teaching Hospital. (n.d.). *Canine cruciate ligament injury.* https://vetmedbiosci.colostate.edu/vth/service s/orthopedic-medicine/canine-cruciate-ligament-injury/

DePuy Synthes Vet.(n.d.). About [YouTube channel]. https://www.you tube.com/@DePuySynthesVet/about

Embrace Pet Insurance. (n.d.). Cruciate ligament injury. https://www.e mbracepetinsurance.com/health/cruciate-ligament-injury

Hans, E. C., Barnart, M. D., Kennedy, S. C., et al. (2017). Comparison of complications following tibial tuberosity advancement and tibial plateau leveling osteotomyin large and giant dogs 50 kg or more in body weight. *Veterinary and Comparative Orthopaedics and Traumatology, 30*(4),299–305. https://doi.org/10.3415/VCOT-16-07-0106

Harasen, G. (2004).Tibial plateau leveling osteotomy – part I. *Canadian Veterinary Journal, 45,* 527–528. https://pmc.ncbi.nlm.nih.gov/articles /PMC2751691/

INO Pets Parents Network. (n.d.).Cranial cruciate ligament. INO Pets
Parents Network. http://inopets.com/cranial-cruciate-ligamen

Kwananocha, I., Akaraphutiporn, E., Upariputti, R., et al. (2024).
Short-term outcomes of cranial cruciate ligament rupture treated surgically with tibial plateau leveling osteotomy or non surgically in small-breed
dogs weighing less than 10kg. *Journal of Veterinary Medical Science, 86*(4),
428–435. https://doi.org/10.1292/jvms.23-0512

Matres-Lorenzo, L., McAlinden, A., Bernarde, A., et al. (2018). Control
of hemorrhage through the osteotomy gap during tibial plateau leveling
osteotomy: 9 cases. *Veterinary Surgery, 47*(1), 60–65. https://doi.org/10
.1111/vsu.12749

McVey, C. L.(n.d.). Two orthopedic surgeries in two years return retriever to eight-mile hikes. Cornell University College of Veterinary Medicine. https://www.vet.cornell.edu/news/20180920/two-orthopedic-sur
geries-two-years-return-retriever-eight-mile-hikes

Montalbano, C., Deabold, K., & Miscioscia, E. (2021, October 6). An understanding of the potential complications
following TPLO surgery can help guide therapy and en-
able improved client counseling. *Today's Veterinary Practice*. https://todaysveterinarypractice.com/rehabilitation/evaluation-afte
r-tibial-plateau-leveling-osteotomy-a-guide-for-the-general-practitioner/

Nanda, A., & Hans, E. C. (2019). Tibial plateau leveling osteotomy for cranial cruciate ligament rupture in canines: Patient selection and reported outcomes. *Veterinary Medicine: Research and Reports,10*, 249–255. http s://doi.org/10.2147/VMRR.S204321

O'Brien, C. S.,& Martinez, S. A. (2009). Potential iatrogenic medi-al meniscal damage during tibial plateau leveling osteotomy. *Veterinary Surgery, 38*(7), 868–873. https://doi.org/10.1111/j.1532-950X.2009.00 578.x

Riemann, B. L.,& Lephart, S. M. (2002). The sensorimotor system, Part I: The physiologic basis of functional joint stability. *Journal of Athletic Training, 37*(1), 71–79. https://pmc.ncbi.nlm.nih.gov/articles/PMC16 4311/

Selmic, L. E.,Ryan, S. D., Ruple, A., et al. (2018). Association of tibial plateau leveling osteotomy with proximal tibial osteosarcoma in dogs. *Journal of the American Veterinary Medical Association, 253*,752–756. https://doi.org/10.2460/javma.253.6.752

Spinalla, G., Arcamone, G., & Valentini, S. (2021). Cranial cruciate liga-ment rupture in dogs: Review on biomechanics, etiopathogenetic factors, and rehabilitation. *Veterinary Sciences, 8*(9), 186. https://doi.org/10.339 0/vetsci8090186

Sprecher, C. M., Milz, S., Suter, T., et al. (2018). Retrospective analysis of corrosion and ion release from retrieved cast stainless steel tibial plateau leveling osteotomy plates in dogs with and without peri-implant osteosarcoma. *American Journal of Veterinary Research, 79*(9). https://doi.org/1 0.2460/ajvr.79.9.970

The City Vet Clinic. (n.d.). TPLO technique: The gold standard for cranial cruciate ligament rupture repair. Retrieved June 14, 2023, from https://thecityvetclinic.com/tplo-technique-the-gold-standard-for -cranial-cruciate-ligament-rupture-repair/

Wemmers, A. C., Charalambous, M., Harms, O., et al. (2022). Surgical treatment of cranial cruciate ligament disease in dogs using tibial plateau leveling osteotomy or tibial tuberosity advancement – A systematic review with a meta-analytic approach. *Frontiers in Veterinary Science, 9*, 1004637. https://doi.org/10.3389/fvets.2022.1004637

Wemmers, A. C., Pawlak, S., Medl, N., et al. (2023). Economic considerations on costs and pricing of two surgical techniques for treating cranial cruciate disease in dogs. *Animals, 13*(1505). https://doi.org/10.3390/an i13091505

Wucherer, K. L., Conzemius, M. G., Evans, R., et al. (2013). Short-term and long-term out comes for overweight dogs with cranial cruciate ligament rupture treated surgically or non surgically. *Journal of the American*

Veterinary Medical Association, 242(10), 1364–1372. https://doi.org/10 .2460/javma.242.10.1364

Zuckerman, J. S., Dyce, J., Arruda, A. G., et al. (2018). Fibular osteotomy to facilitate proximal tibial rotation during tibial plateau leveling osteotomy. *Veterinary Surgery*, 1–9. https://doi.org/10.1111/vsu.12945

Chapter 3

Chauvet, A., Laclair, J., Elliott, D. A., et al. (2011). Incorporation of exercise, using an underwater treadmill, and active client education into a weight management program for obese dogs. *Canadian Veterinary Journal, 52*(5), 491–496. https://pmc.ncbi.nlm.nih.gov/articles/PMC30779 98/

Cracking the Health Code. (n.d.a). *Hope for cruciate tears* [Video]. YouTube. https://www.youtube.com/watch?v=L_Rx6XZAd9A

Cracking the Health Code. (n.d.b). *Lameness, cruciate tears, hip dysplasia & osteoarthritis* [Video]. YouTube. https://youtu.be/L_Rx6XZAd9A

Drummond, M. J.,& Rasmussen, B. B. (2008). Leucine-enriched nutrients and the regulation of mammalian target of rapamycin signaling and human skeletal muscle protein synthesis. *Current Opinion in Clinical Nu-*

trition and Metabolic Care, 11(2), 222–226. https://doi.org/10.1097/M
CO.0b013e3282fa17fb

Fritsch, D., Allen, T. A., Dodd, C. E., et al. (2010a). A multicenter study of the effect of dietary supplementation with fish oil omega-3 fatty acids on carprofen dosage in dogs with osteoarthritis. *Journal of the American Veterinary Medical Association, 236*(5), 535–539. https://doi.org/10.24 60/javma.236.5.535

Fritsch, D., Allen, T. A., Dodd, C. E., et al. (2010b). Dose-titration effects of fish oil in osteoarthritic dogs. *Journal of Veterinary Internal Medicine, 24*(5), 1020–1026. https://doi.org/10.1111/j.1939-1676.2010.0572.x

Hamada, K., Matsumoto, K., Okamura, K., et al. (1999). Effect of amino acids and glucose on dogs' exercise-induced gut and skeletal muscle prote-olysis. *Metabolism, 48*(2), 161–166. https://doi.org/10.1016/s0026-049 5(99)90027-6

Hannah, S. S.,& Laflamme, D. P. (1998). Increased dietary protein spares lean body mass during weight loss in dogs. *Journal of Veterinary Internal Medicine, 12*(3), 224. https://pmc.ncbi.nlm.nih.gov/articles/PMC1028 4039/

Jona Team. *How the gut microbiome affects athletic performance.* Jona Health. https://jona.health/blogs/journal/how-the-gut-microbiome-aff ects-athletic-performance

Maehrlein, J. *Chronic raised cortisol and connective tissue breakdown: Understanding the link.* Jo Martin Osteopathy. https://www.jomartinosteopathy.com.au/resources/2025/3/8/chronic-r aised-cortisol-and-connective-tissue-breakdown-understanding-the-link

McCarthy, G., O'Donovan, J., Jones, B., et al. (2007). Randomized double-blind, positive-controlled trial to assess the efficacy of glu-cosamine/chondroitin sulfate for the treatment of dogs with osteoarthritis. *Veterinary Journal, 174*(1), 54–61. https://doi.org/10.1016/j.tvjl.2006.0 2.015

National Institute of Arthritis and Musculoskeletal and Skin Diseases. (2022, November). *What is arthritis & what causes it?* U.S. Department of Health and Human Services, National Institutes of Health. https://w ww.niams.nih.gov/health-topics/arthritis

Roush, J. K., Cross, A. R., Renberg, W. C., et al. (2010). Evaluation of the effects of dietary supplementation with fish oil omega-3 fatty acids on weight bearing in dogs with osteoarthritis. *Journal of the American Veterinary Medical Association, 236*(1), 67–73. https://doi.org/10.2460 /javma.236.1.67

Scott, K. C., Shmalberg, J., Williams, J. M., et al. (2013). Energy intake of pet dogs compared to energy expenditure at rest, sitting, and standing. In *The WALTHAM International Nutritional Sciences Symposium.*

Shmalberg, J., Scott, K. C., Williams, J. M., et al. (2013). Energy expenditure of dogs exercising on an underwater treadmill compared to that on a dry treadmill. Presented at the *13th Annual AAVN Clinical Nutrition and Research Symposium.*

Vandeweerd, J. M., Coisnon, C., Clegg, P., et al. (2012). Systematic review of efficacy of nutraceuticals to alleviate clinical signs of osteoarthritis. *Journal of Veterinary Internal Medicine, 26*(3),448–456. https://doi.org/10.1111/j.1939-1676.2012.00901.x

Chapter 4

Abshirini, M., Coad, J., Wolber, F. M., von Hurst, P., Miller, M. R., Tian, H. S., &Kruger, M. C. (2021). Green-lipped (greenshell™) mussel (Perna canaliculus) extract supplementation in treatment of osteoarthritis: A systematic review. *Inflammopharmacology, 29*(4), 925–938. https://doi.org/10.1007/s10787-021-00801-2

Arthritis Australia. (n.d.). Hyaluronic acid. https://arthritisaustralia.com.au/medication-search/hyaluronic-acid/

Bertoncini-Silva, C., Vlad, A., Ricciarelli, R., Giacomo Fassini, P., Suen, V. M. M., & Zingg, J.-M. (2024). Enhancing the bioavailability and bioactivity of curcumin for disease prevention and treatment. *Antioxidants, 13*(3), 331. https://doi.org/10.3390/antiox13030331

Bhadani, J. S., Agashe, V. M., Shyam, A., & Mukhopadhaya, J. (2025). The gut feeling: The role of gut microbiome in orthopedics. *Journal of Orthopaedic Case Reports, 15*(3), 308–311. https://doi.org/10.13107/jocr.2025.v15.i03.5418

Bito, T., Okumura, E., Fujishima, M., & Watanabe, F. (2020). Potential of Chlorella as a dietary supplement to promote human health. *Nutrients, 12*(9), 2524. https://doi.org/10.3390/nu12092524

Bornhöft, G., Wolf, U., von Ammon, K., Righetti, M., Maxion-Bergemann, S., Baumgartner, S., Thurneysen, A., & Matthiessen, P. F. (2006). Effectiveness, safety and cost-effectiveness of homeopathy in general practice: Summarized health technology assessment. *Forschende Komplementärmedizin, 13*(Suppl 2), 19–29. https://doi.org/10.1159/000093586

Chen, J., Huang, L., & Liao, X. (2023). Protective effects of ginseng and ginsenosides in the development of osteoarthritis (Review). *Experimental and Therapeutic Medicine, 26*(4), 465. https://doi.org/10.3892/etm.2023.12164

Cordingley, D. M., Cornish, S. M., & Candow, D. G. (2022). Anti-inflammatory and anti-catabolic effects of creatine supplementation: A brief review. *Nutrients, 14*(3), 544. https://doi.org/10.3390/nu14030544

El Ghouizi, A., Bakour, M., Laaroussi, H., Ousaaid, D., El Menyiy, N., Hano, C., & Lyoussi, B. (2023). Bee pollen as functional food: Insights into its composition and therapeutic properties. *Antioxidants, 12*(3),557. https://doi.org/10.3390/antiox12030557

Golden Flower Chinese Herbs. (n.d.). Cinnamon twig formula monograph. https://www.gfcherbs.com/Images/Cinnamon%20Twig%20Mo nograph.pdf

Gruenwald, J., Graubaum, H. J., & Harde, A. (2002). Effect of cod liver oil on symptoms of rheumatoid arthritis. *Advances in Therapy, 19*(2), 101–107. https://doi.org/10.1007/BF02850059

Gupta, R. C., Canerdy, T.D., Lindley, J., Konemann, M., Minniear, J., Carroll, B. A., Hendrick, C., Goad, J. T., Rohde, K., Doss, R., Bagchi, M., & Bagchi, D. (2012). Comparative therapeutic efficacy and safety of type-II collagen (UC-II),glucosamine and chondroitin in arthritic dogs: Pain evaluation by ground force plate. Journal of Animal Physiology and Animal Nutrition, 96(5), 770–777. https://doi.org/10.1111/j.1439-039 6.2011.01166.x

Harvard Health Publishing. (2016, October 17). The latest on glucosamine/chondroitin supplements. *Harvard Health Blog*. https://www.health.harvard.edu/blog/the-latest-on-glucosaminec hondroitin-supplements-2016101710391

Hauser, R., Matias, D., & Hauser, M. (n.d.). Curcumin and osteoarthritis. Caring Medical. https://caringmedical.com/prolotherapy-news/curcumi n-osteoarthritis/

Jo, H.-G., Baek, C.-Y., Song, H. S., & Lee, D. (2024). Network pharmacology and experimental verifications to discover *Scutellaria baicalensis* Georgi's effects on joint inflammation, destruction, and pain in osteoarthritis. *International Journal of Molecular Sciences, 25*(4), 2127. https://doi.org /10.3390/ijms25042127

Knuesel, O., Weber, M., & Suter, A. (2002). Arnica montana gel in osteoarthritis of the knee: An open, multicenter clinical trial. *Advances in Therapy, 19*(5), 209–218. https://doi.org/10.1007/BF02850361

Lee, J., Hong, Y.S., Jeong, J. H., Yang, E. J., Jhun, J. Y., Park, M. K., Jung, Y. O., Min, J.K., Kim, H. Y., Park, S. H., & Cho, M. L. (2013). Coenzyme Q10 amelioratespain and cartilage degradation in a rat model of osteoarthritis by regulating nitricoxide and inflammatory cytokines. *PLoSONE, 8*(7), e69362. https://doi.org/10.1371/journal.pone.0069362

Liao, T., Mei, W., Zhang, L., Ding, L., Yang, N., Wang, P., & Zhang, L. (2023). L-carnitine alleviates synovitis in knee osteoarthritis by regulating lipid accumulation and mitochondrial function through the AMPK-ACC-CPT1 signaling pathway. *Journal of Orthopaedic Surgery and Research,18*(1), 386. https://doi.org/10.1186/s13018-023-03872-9

Lubeck, B. (2024,September 16). Boswellia: A supplement to relieve inflammation? Verywell Health. https://www.verywellhealth.com/the-health-benefits-of-boswellia-89549

Ma, X., Cai, D., Zhu, Y., Zhao, Y., Shang, X., Wang, C., Zhang, H., Bian, A., Yu, H., &Cheng, W. (2022). L-glutamine alleviates osteoarthritis by regulating lncRNA-NKILA expression through the TGF-β1/SMAD2/3 signaling pathway. *Clinical Science, 136*(13), 1053–1069. https://doi.org/10.1042/CS20220082

National Center for Complementary and Integrative Health. (n.d.). *Homeopathy*. U.S. Department of Health and Human Services, National Institutes of Health. Retrieved June 1, 2025, from https://www.nccih.nih.gov/health/homeopathy

Nguyen, C., Savouret, J. F., Widerak, M., Corvol, M. T., & Rannou, F. (2017). Resveratrol, potential therapeutic interest in joint disorders: A critical narrative review. *Nutrients, 9*(1),45. https://doi.org/10.3390/nu9010045

Oberbaum, M., Schreiber, R., Rosenthal, C., & Itzchaki, M. (2003). Homeopathic treatment in emergency medicine: A case series. *Homeopathy,92*(1), 44–47. https://doi.org/10.1054/homp.2002.0071

Oh, D. K., Na, H.S., Jhun, J. Y., Lee, J. S., Um, I. G., Lee, S. Y., Park, M. S., Cho, M. L.,& Park, S. H. (2023). *Bifidobacteriumlongum* BORI inhibits pain behavior and chondrocyte death, and attenuates osteoarthritis progression. *PLoS ONE, 18*(6),e0286456. https://doi.org/10.1371/journal.pone.0286456

Oke, S. L. (2009).Indications and contraindications for the use of orally administered joint health products in dogs and cats. *Journal of the American Veterinary Medical Association, 234*(11), 1393–1397. https://doi.org/10.2460/javma.234.11.1393

O-Sullivan, I., Natarajan Anbazhagan, A., Singh, G., Ma, K., Green, S. J., Singhal, M., Wang, J., Kumar, A., Dudeja, P. K., Unterman, T. G., Votta-Velis, G., Bruce, B., van Wijnen, A. J., & Im, H. J. (2022). *Lactobacillusacidophilus* mitigates osteoarthritis-associated pain, cartilage disintegration and gut microbiota dysbiosis in an experimental murine OA model. *Biomedicines, 10*(6), 1298. https://doi.org/10.3390/biomedicines10061298

Peliushkevich, A.(n.d.). Joint support from anchovies. Klarity Health Library. https://my.klarity.health/joint-support-from-anchovies/

Pollard, B., Guilford, W. G., Ankenbauer-Perkins, K. L., et al. (2006). Clinical efficacy and tolerance of an extract of green-lipped mussel (Perna canaliculus) in dogs presumptively diagnosed with degenerative joint disease. *New Zealand Veterinary Journal, 54*(3), 114–118. https://doi.org/10.1080/00480169.2006.36622

Quigley, J. D., Campbell, J. M., Polo, J., & Russell, L. E. (2004). Effects of spray-dried animal plasma on intake and apparent digestibility in dogs. *Journal of Animal Science, 82*(6), 1685–1692. https://doi.org/10.2527/2004.8261685X

Reichling, J., Schmokel, H., Fitzi, J., & others. (2004). Dietary support with Boswelliaresin in canine inflammatory joint and spinal disease. *Schweizer Archiv für Tierheilkunde, 146*(2), 71–79. https://doi.org/10.1024/0036-7281.146.2.71

Rojas, C. A., Entrolezo, Z., Jarett, J. K., Jospin, G., Martin, A., & Ganz, H. H. (2024). Microbiome responses to oral fecal microbiota transplantation in a cohort of domestic dogs. *Veterinary Sciences, 11*(1),42. https://doi.org/10.3390/vetsci11010042

RxList. (n.d.). *Bupleurum: Uses, side effects, and more.* RxList. https://www.rxlist.com/supplements/bupleurum.htm

Srinivasan, K., Adhya, P., Sharma, S.S. (2019). Nutraceutical Potential of Ginger. In: Gupta, R., Srivastava, A., Lall, R. (eds) Nutraceuticals in Veterinary Medicine. Springer, Cham. https://doi.org/10.1007/978-3-0 30-04624-8_4

Stabile, M., Samarelli, R., Trerotoli, P., Fracassi, L., Lacitignola, L., Crovace, A., & Staffieri, F. (2019). Evaluation of the effects of undena-tured type II collagen(UC-II) as compared to robenacoxib on the mobility impairment induced by osteoarthritis in dogs. *Veterinary Sciences*, *6*(3), 72. https://doi.org/10.3390/vetsci6030072

Szymczak, J., Grygiel-Górniak, B., & Cielecka-Piontek, J. (2024). *Zingiber officinale* Roscoe: The antiarthritic potential of a popular spice—Preclin-ical and clinical evidence. *Nutrients, 16*(5), 741. https://doi.org/10.3390 /nu16050741

TNN. (2011, August12). *The nano effect of homeopathy. The Times of India.* https://timesofindia.indiatimes.com/life-style/health-fitness/hea lth-news/the-nano-effect-of-homeopathy/articleshow/9580370.cms

Yu, M. (n.d.). The role of collagen in enhancing joint health. Dr. Maggie Yu. https://drmaggieyu.com/blog/the-role-of-collagen-in-joint-health/

Versus Arthritis.(n.d.). MSM: Types of complementary treatments systematic review. Journal of Veterinary Medicine, Series A, 59(1), 1-9.

https://versusarthritis.org/about-arthritis/complementary-and-alternativ
e-treatments/types-of-complementary-treatments/msm/#:~:text=MSM
%20is%20rich%20in%20organic,MSM%20was%20combined%20with%2
0glucosamine

Zhu, D., Jiang, N., Wang, N., Zhao, Y., & Liu, X. (2024). A literature
review of the pharmacological effects of jujube. *Foods,13*(2), 193. https:
//doi.org/10.3390/foods13020193

Chapter 5

Acupuncture for Rehabilitation (Rehab Vet Blog). https://www.rehab.v
et/blog/acupuncture-for-rehabilitation

Beyond Dog Massage (Masterson Method). https://mastersonmethod.c
om/beyond-dog-massage/

Boström, A., Asplund, K., Bergh, A., & Hyytiäinen, H. (2022). Systematic review of complementary and alternative veterinary medicine in sport
and companion animals: Therapeutic ultrasound. *Animals,12*(22), 3144.
https://doi.org/10.3390/ani12223144

Boström, A., Bergh, A., Hyytiäinen, H., & Asplund, K. (2022). Systematic
review of complementary and alternative veterinary medicine in sport and

companion animals: Extracorporeal shockwave therapy. *Animals, 12*(22), 3124. https://doi.org/10.3390/ani12223124

Corbin Winslow, L., & Shapiro, H. (2002). Physicians want education about complementary and alternative medicine to enhance communication with their patients. *Archives of Internal Medicine, 162*(10),1176–1181. https://doi.org/10.1001/archinte.162.10.1176

Corti, L. (2014).Massage therapy for dogs and cats. *Top Companion Animal Medicine, 29*(2), 54–57. https://doi.org/10.1053/j.tcam.2014.02.001

Di Bartolomeo, M., Cavani, F., Pellacani, A., Grande, A., Salvatori, R., Chiarini, L., Nocini, R., & Anesi, A. (2022). Pulsed electro-magnetic field (PEMF) effect on bone healing in animal models: A review of its efficacy related to different types of damage. Biology, 11(3), 402. https://doi.org/10.3390/biology11030402

Guadagni, F. (2024,January 2). Why water? The theory behind the underwater treadmill. Veterinary Rehabilitation Services of Virginia. https://www.rehab.vet/blog/why-water

Guadagni, F.(2024, December 15). *Therapeutic laser therapy at VRSVA.* Veterinary Rehabilitation Services of Virginia.

Haussler, K. K., Hesbach, A. L., Romano, L., Goff, L., & Bergh, A. (2021). A systematic review of musculoskeletal mobilization and manipulation techniques used in veterinary medicine. *Animals, 11*(10),2787. https://doi.org/10.3390/ani11102787

Hodgson, H., Blake, S., & de Godoy, R. F. (2023). A study using a canine hydrotherapy treadmill at five different conditions to kinematically assess range of motion of the thoracolumbar spine in dogs. Veterinary medicine and science, 9(1), 119–125. https://doi.org/10.1002/vms3.1067

Kinesio Canine Tape. https://kinesiotaping.com/kinesio-canine-tape/

Levine, D., Johnston, K. D., Price, M. N., Schneider, N. H., & Millis, D. (2002). The effect of TENS on osteoarthritic pain in the stifle of dogs. Proceedings of the *2nd International Symposium on Rehabilitation and Physical Therapy in Veterinary Medicine*.

Ozuna, M. (n.d.). *Dog Body Care – Canine Kinaesthetics™*. https://www.dogbodycare.com

Platelet-Rich Plasma (PRP) Therapy (Rehab Vet Blog). https://www.rehab.vet/blog/platelet-rich-plasma

PRP Therapy in Equine and Canine (Rehab Vet Blog). https://www.reh
ab.vet/blog/prp-therapy-in-the-equine-and-canine

Stem Cell Therapy for Musculoskeletal Conditions (Rehab Vet
Blog). https://www.rehab.vet/blog/stem-cell-therapy-for-musculoskelet
al-conditions

Veterinary Manual (AJVR). https://avmajournals.avma.org/view/journa
ls/ajvr/79/8/ajvr.79.8.893.xml

Chapter 6

Blackburn, J. M. (1938). Animals and Men. By Prof. David Katz. London:
Longmans, Green & Co., 1937.Pp. xi + 263. Price 12s. 6d. Journal of Mental Science, 84(349), 408–409. https://doi.org/10.1192/bjp.84.349.408-a

Dog Body Care. (n.d.). About us. https://www.dogbodycare.com/about
-us.html

Hayduk, L. A. (1978). Personal space: An evaluative and orienting
overview. *Psychological Bulletin, 85*(1), 117–134. https://doi.org/10.103
7/0033-2909.85.1.117

Hediger, H. (1955). *Studies of the psychology and behavior of animals in zoos and circuses*. Criterion. https://archive.org/details/psychologybehav i00hedi/page/n3/mode/2up

Jung, E., Takahashi, K., Watanabe, K., de la Rosa, S., Butz, M. V., Bülthoff, H. H., & Meilinger, T.(2016). The influence of human body orientation on distance judgments. *Frontiers in Psychology, 7*, Article 217. https://do i.org/10.3389/fpsyg.2016.00217

McBride, G. (1971). Theories of animal spacing: The role of flight, fight and social distance. In *Behavior and environment* (pp. 53–68).Springer US. https://doi.org/10.1007/978-1-4684-1893-4_6

McBride, G., & James, J. W. (1963). Social forces determining spacing and head orientation in a flock of domestic hens. *Nature, 197*,1272–1273. https://doi.org/10.1038/1971272a0

Ozuna, M. (2023,March 6). *Movement Markers™: What in the world is a Movement Marker?* Tales from the Sonora. https://talesfromthesonora.com/2023/03/06/movement-markers-w hat-in-the-world-is-a-movement-marker/

Additional Reading

(Sources consulted but not cited directly)

Adebowale, A., Du, J., Liang, Z., et al. (2002). The bioavailability and pharmacokinetics of glucosamine hydrochloride and low molecular weight chondroitin sulfate after single and multiple doses to beagle dogs. *Biopharmaceutics& Drug Disposition, 23*(5), 217–225. https://doi.org/1 0.1002/bdd.315

Baker, S. J., &Baker, G. J. (2013). Surgical versus nonsurgical management for overweight dogs with cranial cruciate ligament rupture. *Journal of the American Veterinary Medical Association, 243*(4), 479.

Basko, I. (2009). Food therapy to reduce the stress of summer climate changes. *American Journal of Traditional Chinese Veterinary Medicine, 4*(1), 77–83. https://doi.org/10.59565/001c.83752

Bassit, R. A., Curi, R., & Costa Rosa, L. F. (2008). Creatine supplementation reduces plasma levels of pro-inflammatory cytokines and PGE2 after a half-ironman competition. *Amino Acids, 35*(3),425–431. https://doi.o rg/10.1007/s00726-007-0582-4

Bell, I. R., Caspi, O., Schwartz, G. E., Grant, K. L., Gaudet, T. W., Rychener, D., Maizes, V.,& Weil, A. (2002). Integrative medicine and systemic outcomes research: Issues in the emergence of a new model for primary health care. *Archives of Internal Medicine, 162*(2),133–140. https://doi.org/10.1001/archinte.162.2.133

Best, T. M. (1995). Muscle-tendon injuries in young athletes. *Clinics in Sports Medicine, 14*(4), 669–686. https://doi.org/10.1016/S0278-5919(20)30212-X

Boileau, C., Martel-Pelletier, J., Caron, J., et al. (2009). Protective effects of total fraction of avocado/soybean unsaponifiables on the structural changes in experimental dog osteoarthritis: Inhibition of nitric oxide synthase and matrixmetalloproteinase-13. *Arthritis Research& Therapy, 11*(3), R41. https://doi.org/10.1186/ar2649

Boileau, C., Martel-Pelletier, J., Caron, J., et al. (2009). Protective effects of total fraction of avocado/soybean unsaponifiables on the structural changes in experimental dog osteoarthritis: Inhibition of nitric oxide synthase and matrixmetalloproteinase-13. *Arthritis Research& Therapy, 11*(3), R41. https://doi.org/10.1186/ar2649

Bublitz, C., Medalha, C., Oliveira, P., et al. (2014). Low-level laser therapy prevents degenerative morphological changes in an experimental model of anterior cruciate ligament transection in rats. *Lasers in Medical Science, 29*(5), 1669–1678. https://doi.org/10.1007/s10103-014-1546-z

Buchholz, A. C., & Pencharz, P. B. (2004). Energy expenditure in chronic spinal cord injury. *Current Opinion in Clinical Nutrition and Metabolic Care, 7*(6), 635–639. https://doi.org/10.1097/00075197-200411000-00008

Chandran, B., & Goel, A. (2012). A randomized, pilot study to assess the efficacy and safety of curcumin in patients with active rheumatoid arthritis. *Phytotherapy Research, 26*(12), 1719–1725. https://doi.org/10.1002/ptr.4639

Creamer, D. G., & Muir, P. (2023). Arthroscopic treatment of chronic cruciate ligament rupture in the dog without stifle stabilization: 13 cases (2001–2020). *Case Reports in Veterinary Medicine, 2023*, Article 6811238. https://doi.org/10.1155/2023/6811238

CuraCore. Stop unnecessary surgery: Medical acupuncture rehab instead of TPLO. from https://curacore.org/vet/2024/07/06/stop-unnecessary-surgery-medical-acupuncture-rehab-instead-of-tplo/

DePuy Synthes Vet.(n.d.). TPLO Chapter 5: Benefits of TPLO [Video]. YouTube. https://www.youtube.com/watch?v=7nZK4GcQXO8

Eisenberg, D. M., Davis, R. B., Ettner, S. L., Appel, S., Wilkey, S., Van Rompay, M., &Kessler, R. C. (1998). Trends in alternative medicine use in the United States, 1990–1997: Results of a follow-up national survey. *JAMA, 280*(18), 1569–1575. https://doi.org/10.1001/jama.280.18.1569

Filbay, S. R., Roemer, F. W., Lohmander, L. S., et al. (2023). Evidence of ACL healing on MRI following ACL rupture treated with rehabilitation alone may be associated with better patient-reported outcomes: A secondary analysis from the KANON trial. *British Journal of Sports Medicine, 57*,91–99. https://doi.org/10.1136/bjsports-2022-105473

Hamidpour, R., Hamidpour, S., Hamidpour, M., et al. (2013). Frankincense (Ru Xiang; species): From the selection of traditional applications to the novel phytotherapy for the prevention and treatment of serious diseases. *Journal of Traditional and Complementary Medicine, 3*(4), 221–226. https://doi.org/10.4103/2225-4110.119723

Hart, J. L., May, K. D., Kieves, N. R., et al. (2016). Comparison of owner satisfaction between stifle joint orthoses and tibial plateau leveling osteotomy for the management of cranial cruciate ligament disease in dogs. *Journal of the American Veterinary Medical Association, 249*(4),391–398. https://doi.org/10.2460/javma.249.4.391

Huisheng Xie, & Aituan Ma. (2015). TCVM for the treatment of pruritus and atopy in dogs. *American Journal of Traditional Chinese Veterinary Medicine, 10*(2), 75–80. https://doi.org/10.59565/JPSQ9532

Kaneps, A. J.(2023). A one-health perspective: Use of hemoderivative regenerative therapies in canine and equine patients. *Journal of the American Veterinary Medical Association, 261*(3), 301–308. https://doi.org/10.24 60/javma.22.12.0556

Leach, E. S., Krotscheck, U., Goode, K. J., et al. (2018). Long-term effects of tibial plateau leveling osteotomy and tibial tuberosity advancement on tibial plateau subchondral bone density in dogs. *Veterinary Surgery, 47*(4), 566–571. https://doi.org/10.1111/vsu.12790

Malone, U. (2024,April 28). Study debunks longstanding medical myth that a torn ACL can't heal. ABC News. https://www.abc.net.au/news/2024-04-28/study-debunks-myths-around-acl-injury-healing-and-surgery/103773576

Molsa, S. H., Hielm-Björkman, A. K., & Laitinen-Vapaavuori, O. M. (2013). Use of an owner questionnaire to evaluate long-term surgical outcome and chronic pain after cranial cruciate ligament repair in dogs: 253 cases (2004–2006). *Journal of the American Veterinary Medical Association, 243*(5), 689–695. https://doi.org/10.2460/javma.243.5.689

Moreau, M., Dupuis, J., Bonneau, N. H., et al. (2003). Clinical evaluation of a nutraceutical, carprofen, and meloxicam for the treatment of dogs with osteoarthritis. *Veterinary Record, 152*, 323. https://doi.org/10.1136/vr.152.11.323

Olson, D. M.(2022). There are no gold standards and nothing gold about a standard. *Journal of Neuroscience Nursing, 54*(2),53. https://doi.org/10 .1097/JNN.0000000000000641

Reichling, J., Schmokel, H., Fitzi, J., et al. (2004). Dietary support with Boswellia resin in canine inflammatory joint and spinal disease. *Schweizer Archiv für Tierheilkunde, 146*(2), 71–79. https://doi.org/10.1024/0036 -7281.146.2.71

Rialland, P., Bichot, S., Lussier, B., et al. (2013). Effect of a diet enriched with green-lipped mussel on pain behavior and functioning in dogs with clinical osteoarthritis. *Canadian Journal of Veterinary Research, 77*(1), 66–74. https://pmc.ncbi.nlm.nih.gov/articles/PMC3525174/

Robinson, N. G.(n.d.). MOVE Integrative Rehabilitation and Physical Medicine (IRPM) handout. CuraCore. https://curacore.org/vet/wp-co ntent/uploads/070324-IRPM-Handout-03102022-Narda-Review-2.pdf

Robinson, N. G.(2020, May 13). Ten troubling truths about the TPLO (Tibial Plateau-Leveling Osteotomy) [Video]. CuraCore.org/VE T. YouTube. https://www.youtube.com/watch?v=knOUZCZAB4E

Setnikar, I., Giacchetti, C., & Zanolo, G. (1986). Pharmacokinetics of glu-cosamine in the dog and in man. *Arzneimittelforschung, 36*(6),729–735. https://pubmed.ncbi.nlm.nih.gov/3718596/

Tsokos, G. C., & Nepom, G. T. (2000). Gene therapy in the treatment of autoimmune diseases. *Journal of Clinical Investigation, 106*(2), 181–183. https://pmc.ncbi.nlm.nih.gov/articles/PMC314315/

Xu, J., Zhou, X., Guo, X., et al. (2018). Effects of unilateral electroacupuncture on bilateral proprioception in a unilateral anterior cruciate ligament injury model. *Medical Science Monitor, 24*, 5473–5479. https://doi.org/10.12659/MSM.909508

Zalta, J. (2008). Massage therapy protocol for post-anterior cruciate ligament reconstruction patellofemoral pain syndrome: A case report. *International Journal of Therapeutic Massage & Bodywork, 1*(2),11–21. https://doi.org/10.3822/ijtmb.v1i2.22

www.ingramcontent.com/pod-product-compliance
Lightning Source LLC
LaVergne TN
LVHW051223080426
835513LV00016B/1382